1976

Also by Christopher Sandford:

HISTORY
Houdini and Conan Doyle
The Final Over
Harold and Jack
The Man Who Would be Sherlock
Kennedy and Great Britain (originally *Union Jack*)
The Zeebrugge Raid
The Final Innings
The Man Who Conned the World
Midnight in Tehran
1964

MUSIC BIOGRAPHIES
Mick Jagger
Eric Clapton
Kurt Cobain
David Bowie
Sting
Bruce Springsteen
Keith Richards
Paul McCartney
The Rolling Stones

FILM BIOGRAPHIES
Steve McQueen
Roman Polanski

SPORT
The Cornhill Centenary Test
Godfrey Evans
Tom Graveney
Imran Khan
John Murray
Laker and Lock
The Cricketers of 1945

FICTION
Feasting with Panthers
Arcadian
We Don't Do Dogs

PLAYS
Comrades

1976

THE YEAR THAT SCORCHED

CHRISTOPHER SANDFORD

The History Press

For the Parish family

First published 2025

The History Press
97 St George's Place, Cheltenham,
Gloucestershire, GL50 3QB
www.thehistorypress.co.uk

British Library Cataloguing in Publication Data.
A catalogue record for this book is available from the British Library.

ISBN 978 1 80399 957 9

Typesetting and origination by The History Press
Printed and bound in Great Britain by TJ Books, Padstow, Cornwall

The History Press proudly supports

Trees for LYfe

www.treesforlife.org.uk

EU Authorised Representative: Easy Access System Europe
Mustamäe tee 50, 10621 Tallinn, Estonia
gpst.request@easproject.com

Contents

'I do not give you to posterity as a pattern to imitate, but as an example to deter.'

The Letters of Junius, 'Dedication to the English Nation' (1769)

'The question is not yet settled whether madness is or is not the loftiest intelligence – whether all that is profound does not spring from disease of thought.'

Edgar Allan Poe, *Eleonora* (1842)

'Anarchy in the UK'

The Sex Pistols (1976)

Acknowledgements

A harsh critic, reviewing my recent *1964: The Year the Swinging Sixties Began*, complained that I appeared to have only 'slightly changed' the book's structure (as opposed to its contents) from an earlier biography I wrote of the international conman Victor Lustig. I risk the same critic's ire here by freely admitting that this new book's structure hasn't been changed even as much as slightly from the one on 1964. In fact, it's identical. Dividing the story of a year into four main chapters that broadly follow the annual seasons still seems to me a reasonable enough way to go about the job, although I've made no superhuman effort to keep the compartments watertight. The subheadings that appear in each chapter hopefully give some idea of where that particular part of the tale is heading.

More to the point, I'd like to thank the following individuals or institutions for their help with the whole business, while again making clear that none of those listed can be blamed for the shortcomings of the text. As always, they're mine alone.

For archive material, input or advice, I should note, professionally: AbeBooks; *America*; the *Brazen Head*; the British Library; the British Newspaper Library; Cambridge University Library; Companies House; *Cricketer International*; the Cricket Society; the *Daily Express*; the FBI, Freedom of Information Division; the General Register Office; Peter Hain; *Hansard*; *Hedgehog Review*; The History Press; Imperial War Museum; the late Louis Kirby; Barbara Levy; the Library of Congress; the MCC Library; Christine McMorris; the Mitchell Library, Glasgow; the Mitre House Hotel, London; *Modern Age*; the UK National Archives; *The Oldie*; Bill Payne; *Plough*; Public

Record Office; Tim Reidy; Renton Public Library; Seattle Central College; *The Seattle Times*; *The Spectator*; Sussex County Cricket Club; Derek Turner; Vital Records; *Wisden Cricket Monthly*; and the late Tom Wolfe.

And personally: Leann Alspaugh; Reverend Maynard Atik; Pam and Dudley Ayres; Pete Barnes; Henry Blofeld; Rob Boddie; Robert and Hilary Bruce; Don Carson; the late Charles Cross; Mark Demos; Monty Dennison; the Dowdall family; Barbara and the late John Dungee; Steve Fossen; Malcolm Galfe; Dr Raul Garcia; James Graham; Karolyn Grimes; Steve and Jo Hackett; Duncan Hamilton; Nigel Hancock; Christine Hewitson; Alastair Hignell; Charles Hillman; Alex Holmes; Jo Jacobius; the late Julian James; Robin B. James; Tommy James; Bill and Morgan Johnson; Jo Johnson; the late Wilko Johnson; Lincoln Kamell; Bob Knowles; Terry Lambert; Alex Larman; Belinda Lawson; Gene Lemcio; the late Alexei Leonov; the Lorimer family; Robert Dean Lurie; Somar Macek; Les McBride; Dan McCarthy; Myra McEwan; the Macris; Lee Mattson; Jim Meyersahm; the late Jerry Miller; the Morgans; Harry Mount; the Murray family; Greg Nowak; Phillip Oppenheim; Valya Page; Robin and Lucinda Parish; Owen Paterson; Peter Perchard; Roman Polanski; the Prins family; Bill Reader; Neil Robinson; the Rushbrooke family; Debbie Saks; the late Sefton Sandford; Peter Scaramanga; Fred and Cindy Smith; the Smith family; the Stanley family; Jack Surendranath; Matt Thacker; Nick Tudball; Derek Turner; the late Diana Villar; Lisbeth Vogl; Rogena and the late Alan White; Richard Wigmore; Debbie Wild; the Willis Fleming family; the late Aaron Wolf; and Bill Wyman.

My deepest thanks, as always, to Karen and Nicholas Sandford.

C.S.
2025

Introduction

Blood on the Tracks

The young Metropolitan Police Inspector John Purnell remembered he and his fellow officers feeling disgruntled with life, and as time went by, 'freezing our arses off' during the bitterly cold Saturday night of 6 December 1975. They were part of Operation Combo, in which the Met had flooded central London with both uniformed and plainclothes officers in the hope of catching an IRA active service unit (ASU) that had been terrorising the capital. Just a week earlier, the *Guinness Book of Records* co-founder Ross McWhirter had been shot dead outside his home in suburban Enfield after offering a £50,000 reward for information leading to the ASU men's arrest.

The unit had targeted popular pubs, clubs and restaurants with bombings and shootings throughout 1975, and had murdered a 21-year-old unarmed police constable when he gave chase to several men down a road near Barons Court Tube Station in west London following what he took to be a common house burglary. On 23 October, the IRA cell had even managed to significantly put back the campaign against cancer when they detonated a bomb that killed Gordon Hamilton-Fairley, a pioneering Professor of Oncology at St Barts Hospital, after he had brushed against the booby-trapped car belonging to his next-door neighbour, the Conservative MP Hugh Fraser. The horrible circumstances of his neighbour's death had moved Fraser with every particle of his being with the resolve to 'treat the IRA as the street thugs they really are'.

These were far from isolated cases of organised violence around the English capital that autumn. After the regrettable error with the cancer doctor, the IRA unit had turned its attention to what it called 'ruling-class' restaurants, such as the popular Trattoria Fiore in Mount Street, where on 29 October their bomb ripped the scalp off an American tourist and another woman lost her foot, while several other diners were blinded or maimed by razor shards of flying glass.

On the night of 18 November, it was the turn of Walton's restaurant in Chelsea, where a 5lb bomb containing an assortment of nails and ball-bearings was flung through the front window, killing a man and a woman and injuring twenty-three other people, the oldest of them in his mid-seventies. In the period from July to December 1975, the gang averaged more than a shooting or a bombing a week in the capital, a level of violence against civilian targets that had been unmatched since the IRA's own 'S' (or Sabotage) campaign on the British mainland of the late 1930s.

So the various stakeout teams involving Inspector Purnell and his colleagues that cold December night were bored but watchful, sitting in their unmarked cars in residential streets as far afield as Clapham and Chiswick, or loitering among the crowds milling around Leicester Square or Oxford Circus, hoping to catch sight of anything out of the ordinary. It was a routine broken only by the welcome arrival of a female colleague bearing mugs of hot soup to Purnell and his partner, Sergeant Phil McVeigh, as they stood stamping their feet in an attempt to keep themselves warm in a shop doorway, or walked in tight circles around the corner of Park Street and North Row close to Marble Arch. Having been sustained only by an endlessly replenished supply of Players cigarettes, the two officers thought the soup a 'sensational result', profusely thanking the WPC, who said cheerfully as she returned to a waiting car, 'It's all yours now, lads'. Years later, Purnell admitted that three hours in to their nine-hour shift, he and McVeigh were 'bored out of our boxes', with only a couple of passing pedestrians and a dog noisily fouling the next doorway for company.

Shortly after 9 p.m. that boredom was rather dramatically relieved. Over Purnell's radio came the news that the IRA gang had apparently just fired shots through the window of Scott's restaurant in nearby Mount Street, a location they, the ASU, had visited earlier in the autumn by throwing a bomb through the open front door, killing an elderly diner and injuring fifteen others in the process. Moments later, a dark Ford Cortina drove slowly but erratically past the two policemen, crossed Oxford Street against the red traffic light and headed north along Cumberland Place. Anyone familiar with the then popular Thames Television show *The Sweeney* need only think of a scene from that same programme, but with the responding officers on foot rather than in the back of a screeching Rover P6, to get some of the flavour.

Rapidly abandoning the soup and stubbing out their cigarettes, the men ran to the corner of North Row and commandeered a passing black taxi. 'I literally said to the cabbie, "Follow that car!"', Purnell recalled. 'He said, "Blimey, I've always wanted this to happen!" Of course, we didn't tell him that it was full of armed terrorists.'

Within five minutes, the chase led them to the dead-end Alpha Close, near Regent's Park, where the Cortina's four passengers abruptly abandoned it. The street was nearly empty of other traffic – much of Britain was, after dark, fifty years ago – leaving Purnell and McVeigh to again continue their pursuit on foot.

Noticing they were not alone, one or more of the fleeing ASU men turned and opened fire, the bullets ricocheting against the side of a parked car. In short order, other officers arrived on the scene to join the chase, which continued down the darkened Rossmore Road, an elevated street that crosses the railway lines from Marylebone Station. One of the newly arrived reinforcements was a 21-year-old trainee constable named Ian Blair, who, thirty years later, went on to become Commissioner of the Metropolitan Police, and later still to write of his involvement:

We turned the corner, and there [was] the car ... It was a very defining moment. I think I spent the next half an hour pretending to be a bush. They got out of the car and started firing at us. It is an interesting experience being shot at when you have absolutely nothing to shoot back with. I loved everything about that whole job.

Here some discrepancy exists with the account of the first man on the scene, John Purnell, who in 2007 recalled of the events that night:

I've never for one second associated Ian Blair with [the incident] in any shape or form, and his story of seeing the gang get out of the car and then being shot at is totally impossible. They didn't fire at him. When the men got out of the car there were three people present: a cab driver, Phil McVeigh and myself. At that stage there wasn't another police officer in sight. I wish there had been.

All parties agree on the salient point that the four IRA men, having hurriedly abandoned their vehicle, then ran down a flight of steps from Rossmore Road and pushed their way through the unlocked front door of a block of council flats at 22 Balcombe Street, adjacent to the station. In a flat on the first floor, an elderly couple, John and Sheila Matthews, were just settling down in front of their black-and-white Baird television set next to the two-bar electric fire in their sitting room to enjoy an episode of the American police drama *Kojak*. They both initially assumed that the loud gunshots that they could hear nearby were part of the show's soundtrack. The couple were soon disabused on this point.

A moment later, four wild-eyed young men carrying handguns barged through the front door and announced that they were taking them hostage. Mr Matthews, a retired postman, had his legs tied together with his wife's tights, while Mrs Matthews was dragged into the hall with a gun at her head by one of the gang, later identified as a London-born carpenter-turned-Irish Republican named Harry Duggan. Duggan shouted at the police gathered at the front door of the building below them, 'Fuck off, you bastards!' There were some further remarks of this sort, both to and fro, over the next few minutes, with the police using megaphones for amplification. The lengthy exchange rattled the flat's front windows.

A six-day standoff ensued. The police surrounded the building and, with a telephone dropped onto the balcony of the flat from the roof, continually talked to the four Irishmen, who identified themselves only as 'Paddy' or 'Mick' for the officers' benefit. Over the course of the week the latter's tactics ranged from what might be called the *Sweeney* school ('You come down here or we'll kick your arses up to your shoulder blades') to the more reasoned approach of remarking how the men were betraying the principles of Wolfe Tone – the eighteenth-century father of Irish Republicanism – at which, eschewing the conversational high road, Duggan angrily threw the negotiating phone out the window with another colourful epithet. The ASU men weren't without a mordant sense of humour, however, because from time to time the strains of Engelbert Humperdinck's 1967 hit 'Release Me' could be heard issuing loudly from the flat's front room.

In the late morning of the sixth day, with the hostage-takers' request for a plane to take them back to Ireland having been refused by negotiators, and having long since exhausted the Matthews' supply of tinned goods and instant coffee, some cardboard boxes containing sausages, Brussels sprouts, potatoes and peaches were lowered to the flat from the balcony above. In what may have been a psych-ops exercise on the part of the authorities, a BBC radio broadcast stated that armed members of the Special Air Service were about to be deployed to resolve the crisis. This seemed to focus the Irishmen's minds, and shortly after their midday meal, all four ASU men came out with their hands up to be swiftly driven away to the nearby Paddington Green Police Station. Their two hostages were in turn taken to University College Hospital, where a spokesman said they were 'shaken and weak' but otherwise unharmed.

In an apparent revenge attack five days later, a powerful homemade bomb exploded at Biddy Mulligan's pub in Kilburn, north London, sending eight customers to hospital with injuries. Under questioning – which the UK National Archives describe, perhaps euphemistically, both as 'intense' and applying 'deep psychology' – the four ASU members gave up the address of a nearby London flat they and their colleagues had used as their base for the previous several months. When they visited the premises, the police recovered a list of other potential objectives, such as the British Museum, Madame Tussauds and the National Gallery, as well as 10 Downing Street and Buckingham Palace.

The authorities found evidence that the unit was also considering less obvious targets, including power plants, water-pumping stations and sewage works. A typed note attached to an eighty-six-page 'Action List' included the dates and venues of specific functions, among them events held by the British Law Society, the Coldstream Guards and the passing-out parade of the Junior Sea Cadets, a national organisation of 9–12-year-old boys sponsored by the Royal Navy.

In February 1977, the four Balcombe Street hostage-takers were found guilty at the Old Bailey of twenty-five terrorism-related charges, including seven murders. Each of the men was given twelve life sentences, with the rec-ommendation that they serve not less than thirty years. One of the defendants saluted the bench with a V-sign and another shouted 'Up the Provos!' as they were taken down to the cells.

After twenty-two years, all four were released under the terms of the amnesty negotiated under the 1998 Good Friday Agreement. On 10 May of that year, the men made a dramatic appearance on stage at a special Sinn Fein conference in Dublin, where they enjoyed a ten-minute standing ova-tion as Gerry Adams, the absentee MP for Belfast West, hailed them as 'our Nelson Mandelas'. The remark was prominently featured in the daily US papers serving cities such as New York and Boston with large Irish immigrant communities.

It's worth lingering on the Balcombe Street siege and its aftermath for a moment, if only because the whole affair seems to highlight certain fundamental characteristics of British life on the eve of the year this book seeks to revisit. Whether in the long campaign of violence itself, or such details as the haphazard manner of the police stakeout, or the press photographs of the interior of the Balcombe Street flat, with its fashionless mahogany and chintz furnishings, Formica-topped kitchen, coffin-sized radiogram and tobacco-stained floral wallpaper, it's an illustrative story.

The US city of Boston happened to be celebrating its 'Billion-Light Christmas Bonanza' over the weekend of 12–14 December 1975, with a gaudily lit downtown 'starlight garden' and ranks of sparkling, Disney-themed dancing holograms, so that the grim black-and-white pictures of the Matthews' Dickensian front room must have seemed to belong to some primitive, faraway world. There may have been no village in the rural Carpathians where living conditions were quite as archaic as in parts of Britain in the hang-over years following the Swinging Sixties.

***

Apart from the matter of basic home furnishings or personal style, it some-times seemed as if the UK wasn't really a properly formed country at all, as much as a series of geographically connected tribes linked by physical prox-imity and their exposure to certain words that defined the era: inflation, shortages, strikes, redundancies, violence, hooliganism, divorce, Europe. It was a time of unease and despair, punctuated by disaster. A three-day working week, and homes plunged into darkness by recurrent industrial action. Desert emirates cutting off the nation's oil supply. The pound in freefall. Terrible crimes against the person reported in the daily press, of which the sprees of the so-called Black Panther and Yorkshire Ripper were only the most heinous.

And in the background loomed still greater calamities and afflictions across the world. The ice age was returning. The governments of large parts of the world – Uganda first came to mind – lay in the hands of homicidal maniacs. Nobody was quite sure if the UK was really in or out of Europe. Kohoutek's Comet was hurtling towards the planet. Lord Lucan had apparently gone ber-serk and murdered his children's nanny. The Bay City Rollers had the biggest selling single of the year in the pop chart. For some unfathomable reason, people wore extravagantly flared trousers and ties, and jackets with lapels the width of hang-glider sails. And overlaying it all was the pervasive economic gloom that led the leader writer of the *Wall Street Journal* to compare aspects of the contemporary UK to the Weimar Republic of the 1920s.

To Britons of a certain age, it must seem that their whole lives have been spent contemplating the prospect of some form of imminent financial Armageddon. The annual inflation rate in the UK in December 1975 was 25.15 per cent, which was bad, certainly, but down from a high of 27.25 per cent the previous August, the worst such figures anywhere in the industrialised world. A future Conservative prime minister would characterise the era as one of 'darkened streets, unlit offices, sports matches cancelled, frozen, broken-backed Britain ruled under a permanent state of emergency'. It would be going too far, but not, perhaps, going entirely in the wrong direction to say that the prime minister, Labour's Harold Wilson, was at times in despair at the reigning state of affairs and at his apparent inability to rectify the situation. Barbara Castle, Wilson's Social Services Minister, would write of a particularly fraught Cabinet meeting that spring:

> Harold was sitting in his chair, obviously in a shattered state. Mike [Foot] sat at one end of the table opposite him; Jim Callaghan at the other, head in hands. 'Have a drink,' said Harold morosely and as I helped myself he added, 'I was very insulting to Barbara just now and I apologise.' I went over and kissed him affectionately on the forehead. 'Don't I get a kiss?' said Jim, gloomily. 'God knows I need it.' So I kissed him too and sat down next to him … Harold had obviously calmed down a bit, but he was still in a pretty neurotic state, so for an hour we had to listen to him.

As we'll see, the married Wilson, who, it turned out, was salving his melancholy in the arms of his Deputy Press Secretary, also married and twenty-two years his junior, would abruptly resign from office in March 1976, giving rise to a whole raft of conspiracy theories yet to be fully scotched. Was he the victim of a plot by the security services, who thought he had communist sympathies and was in fact a KGB asset, or had the onset of Alzheimer's disease already dulled his faculties? In some ways, Wilson stands as the human embodiment of his nation in the mid-1970s: a once-brilliant success story increasingly mired in a state of paranoia and quite possibly what we would now characterise as clinical depression, operating in a disturbed political climate at a time of exceptional turmoil.

Of course, it's always a mistake to try and assemble random historical facts into a neatly unified pattern that few people would have recognised at the time. Whether in their claim that Britain overnight became a socialist Mecca with the advent of the welfare state in 1945, or that the country as one succumbed to a priapic fit characterised by the sight of bare-thighed young women swaggering around Carnaby Street in their Mary Quant miniskirts to a backdrop of herbally tinged joss sticks and the wafted strains of *Sgt Pepper* in the Summer of Love, twenty-two years later – with a sort of communal nervous breakdown triggered by the Suez Crisis at the midpoint between the two poles – social historians are always keen to identify what seem to them to be the transformative shifts in our national life. Such judgements are generally only possible with the aid of hindsight. Few of those confronted by the individual pieces of the jigsaw can picture the completed puzzle.

It should be said that there were several points of light, too, if not distinct optimism, amid the doldrums, even if it sometimes took a friendly outsider to locate them. Bernard Nossiter, a prize-winning reporter who served as the *Washington Post*'s London correspondent in 1976, began his book *Britain: A Future That Works* by mocking all 'the scribes and prophets of doom', who had for so long queued up to predict the nation's wholesale collapse. On the contrary, Nossiter argued, despite 'undeniable material challenges', Britain under Harold Wilson and his immediate successor in office was 'healthy, democratic [and] as stable a society as any of its size in Europe'. Making the choice of leisure over goods and moving towards an economy based as much on services and the arts as on manufacturing, the UK 'might be a model for the future of all successful post-industrial Western nations', he added.

Nossiter found grounds for cheer in a wide variety of British walks of life, large and small: increased longevity, ever-improving and largely cost-free healthcare, better universities, greater variety in the shops, more books sold, cleaner air, the return of fish to the Thames. Speaking about leisure, Nossiter informed his readers that there were 265 state-run sports centres in Britain in 1976, up from twenty-three in 1971, with plans for another 500 by 1980. People were flocking to huge new indoor retail malls, such as the Birmingham Bull Ring or Brent Cross in north London, while forsaking such traditional resorts as Skegness or Clacton for more exotic destinations like Miami or Los Angeles for their holidays. The average attendance at an English First Division football match stood at a fraction under 30,000, modest by modern standards, but often enlivened by the crowd's creative adaptation of the lyrics of popular Top 40 hits and willingness to put the boot in to the opposition fans.

Even England's more pastoral summer sport of cricket had staunched its long post-war haemorrhage of paying customers by introducing a series of comparatively breakneck limited-overs competitions and, just the previous year, an inaugural World Cup. The West Indies beat Australia in the final, which saw the normally cathedral-like calm of Lord's transformed into a reasonable facsimile of Wembley, complete with rattles and horns and a blaze of flags, along with singing, cheers and 'even a few jeers from the shirtsleeved patrons of the Tavern', the *Daily Telegraph* tutted.

The frivolous side of life dominated the press on Friday, 2 January 1976, the day marking the beginning of the end of the extended festive season. 'ARISE, SOOTY OBE!' was the banner headline in the *Daily Mirror*, referring to the New Year's Honour conferred on Harry Corbett, the middle-aged operator of the nation's beloved yellow bear glove puppet. The *Daily Mail* also reported on the award but was chiefly exercised by the matter of 'GOVERNMENT DEPARTMENT'S SECRETS FOUND DUMPED IN WHITEHALL SKIP'. *The Times* led with the ever-popular 'SALE FEVER JAMS ROADS', noting that after a disappointing Christmas, retailers had got off 'to a bright start' to 1976, while the *Wolverhampton Express and Star* combined three media staples into the surely unbeatable 'SALE FRENZY BLOCKS TRAFFIC: ROYALS DELAYED', splashed under its masthead.

Turning to the classifieds, readers were urged to take advantage of seasonal bargains on 'Real Imitation Leather Chesterfield sofas' for 'that gentleman's club look' retailing at £135 (£1,080 in today's money) apiece, or treat themselves to a winter break at 'newly built deluxe hotel, with fully carpeted guests' lounge and large TV' on the Isle of Wight, with single rooms starting at just £7 a night. Meanwhile, a 'spacious, three-bedroom luxury flat' in London's desirable St John's Wood was offered for just £24,500 on a ninety-nine-year lease, while a four-bed manor house in Sevenoaks with 'two acres of woodland, rhododendrons, shrubs and lawns, with a carpet of bluebells in season' was yours for £30,000, or £200,000 and £240,000 respectively.

There was a good deal more in the press promoting the virtues of three-piece suites, fitted carpets, cars, cameras, cold remedies, castor oil, miracle ointments, denture repairs, toupees, trusses and medical aids in general. Much of Britain's employment landscape still existed in a sort of extended Edwardian limbo, with 'Wanted' columns full of openings for domestic servants, private chauffeurs ('only Rolls-proficient men need apply') and 'well-spoken English girls' for immediate employment as nannies – including one vacancy for a 'privately-educated young woman to oversee Lady Charlotte, aged three, and twins Georgina and Edward, aged two months, in tandem with other resident staff at home in Kensington'. Many of the displays for goods and services retained their essential 1950s air of apology for the tastelessness of having to promote their wares in the first place, with taglines such as 'If we have a rival in our field, we should be glad to know of it', or 'Any Interested Parties are invited to correspond or call by appointment at our Premises'.

On 3 January, a Saturday, the press all led with variants of the *Mirror*'s 'WHIPLASHED!' to describe the gales that had buffeted much of the British Isles, with winds recorded at 109mph at RAF Wittering in Cambridgeshire. Coastal streets were flooded, rail and air traffic came to a standstill and roads everywhere were blocked by fallen trees. The roof of one of the stands at the Stoke football ground blew off and the Old Vic Theatre in London was evacuated when scaffolding collapsed, smashing a plate-glass window and causing a heavy chandelier to crash to the ground in the foyer. Eleven people died in a variety of accidents. In retrospect, perhaps it was only an apt way in which to start what would prove to be a consistently turbulent year.

***

Nor could it be concluded from events elsewhere in early 1976 that this was likely to be an era of undisturbed peace and prosperity for humanity as a whole. The Atlantic Alliance had recently been tested, first by Britain's refusal to commit troops to the cause of the long US campaign in Vietnam, and then by the appointment of 57-year-old Anthony Crosland as Foreign Secretary. As the US Secretary of State and globetrotting superstar Henry Kissinger wrote of his opposite number, 'Crosland's articulate petulance – combined with a languid, offhand manner – served to turn him into the *enfant terrible* of diplomacy. He also turned out to have a bizarre sense of humor, inventing a game in which each side scored points whenever the other committed some absurdity.' Kissinger once ruefully told me that he had been debited 'many marks by Crosland' when at a state dinner attended by the royal family in July 1976, a senior US diplomat had in all seriousness enquired of Prince Philip if he had fought for the Axis side in the Second World War.

Strategic Arms Limitation Talks (SALT) between the United States and the Soviet Union similarly reached a nadir in 1976, with Kissinger reporting, 'We went to [the Kremlin] in February, proposing a workable way forward. They turned us down flat.' There were no further substantive arms control talks that year.

Leaving aside the bloody aftermath of the decade-long US adventure in South East Asia, civil wars or coups erupted in Morocco, Nigeria, Argentina, the Congo, Angola, Lebanon, Uruguay, Algeria, Syria and Thailand. There were repeated terrorist outrages of varying degrees throughout Western

Europe, not to mention the continuing IRA campaign in Britain itself. A series of riots broke out among the residents of the racially ostracised Soweto township in Johannesburg against the centrally imposed apartheid regime of the National Party in Pretoria, while the 50-year-old schoolteacher-turned-Marxist fanatic known as Pol Pot blithely continued his psychotic reign of terror that, over time, by the most widely accepted estimates, led to the deaths of fully a quarter of Cambodia's 7 million citizens, through execution, torture, starvation and disease.

A frantic edge also crept in to the behaviour of the leaders of China, where the death in January 1976 of the long-serving Prime Minister Zhou Enlai saw large crowds gather in Beijing's Tiananmen Square to mark his passing. The late premier's elderly boss, Chairman Mao Zedong (himself to die later in the year) interpreted the demonstrations as being directed against state orthodoxy, if not to create a rival icon to himself, and ordered his Red Guard to disperse the mourners. In response, a crowd of over 100,000 forced their way into nearby government buildings to protest their affection for the values enshrined by Zhou, and as many as 600 men, women and children died in the subsequent purge of 'counterrevolutionary wreckers' said to have disturbed the peace.

Taken as a whole, this all fell some way short of fulfilling the 'year of universal harmony and goodwill' heralded in international affairs by the United Nations Secretary General Kurt Waldheim (who, unlike the Duke of Edinburgh, actually was a former Wehrmacht officer) in his annual address to the General Assembly in January 1976.

★★★

Louis Kirby was at this time a 47-year-old pipe-smoking former political correspondent, who had recently been handed the unenviable job of editing London's *Evening News*. Born in Liverpool, Kirby had started his journalistic career as a reporter covering weddings and funerals for the *Wolverhampton Express and Star*, then spent two years in Bermuda before joining the *Daily Mail*'s Manchester office in 1953. He remained with Associated Newspapers for the next half-century – a remarkable record of loyalty, even in an era when journalists were less inclined to flit promiscuously from title to title and group to group – serving in turn as the paper's lobby correspondent and chief reporter with the *Mail*'s sister paper, the *Daily Sketch*, before taking over the reins at the *News* in 1974.

Kirby's brief was to turn the ailing broadsheet into a tabloid without lowering its editorial standards or compromising its mid-market appeal. The tone of the *News* was a curious paradox as a result. Although dedicated to 'the fundamental interests of the common man' and fiercely opposed to the ideas that 'material gain should inevitably be the prerogative of the upper crust' or that management 'need rest in the hands of a public-school elite', to quote two of Kirby's editorials, the paper was plagued by a series of shop-floor disputes throughout the 1970s.

By the middle of the decade, the *News* was selling some 600,000 copies a day, roughly half the total it had enjoyed in its prime, although sometimes the figure sloshed around like water in a bathtub, gaining or losing 100,000 or so in response to a particularly arresting headline or a photograph of a swimsuit-clad Princess Margaret on the front page. The paper's distinctive red, black and yellow delivery vans remained a familiar sight around Greater London each weekday afternoon, darting between shops and pitches like so many shoals of tropical fish, but changing consumer habits eventually brought about a merger with its long-time rival, the *Evening Standard*. As critics observed, even by 1976 the *News* seemed to have abandoned the ideals of its glory days as the respectable working Londoner's outlet of choice in its bid to match its more disreputable competitors. But despite being dumbed-down (or perhaps for that reason), the paper remained defiantly old-school, with its curiously dated spot-the-ball competitions on the back page and its tendency to take every opportunity it could to display images of scantily clad women. Above all, it was a recognisably British confection, with all that implied in the mid-1970s.

'I just didn't have the heart for it,' Kirby told me shortly before his death at the age of 77 in 2006:

> It wasn't the London newspaper I really wanted. The things that most interested me were politics and the whole way the state grew out of all recognition from how our fathers and grandfathers would have known it. You didn't even need a passport to travel around in those days, and look at the way we're treated now. I certainly didn't want the [*News*] to become a paper for the chattering classes ... And yet every time you went to a [board meeting] and said anything about serious journalistic standards, the people in the room would begin to shift their feet and start coughing and you knew you'd lost them. But then the moment you said something about beefing up the paper's gossip columns, or having lots of photos of toffs arsing around and

women with their chests hanging out – anything with shock value – everybody would be sitting there *beaming*.

Looking back on it, Kirby thought that 1976 was really the year the world went a bit barmy. It seemed to him like looking at an old-fashioned lantern show, full of flickering images of *Sweeney*-like car chases, bombings, strikes, the Sex Pistols, a scorching summer and fashions that ran the gamut from flares and spandex to young people with safety pins through their noses. 'Of course,' Kirby concluded, 'that's hindsight. But even at the time, it did feel like the curtain was finally falling on the peace-and-love scene of the 1960s. One had an uneasy feeling about what was coming next.'

I

Winter

THE PARANOID STYLE

Just after 6 o'clock on the wet Monday evening of 5 January 1976, a dark red Ford Transit van came over a hill to be confronted by a man in army uniform flashing a powerful torch at it on an otherwise deserted road near the town of Kingsmill, about 40 miles south of Belfast in County Armagh. The van was carrying a driver and eleven other men, who were on their way home after working a shift at a textile factory in the nearby village of Glenanne, and they seem to have initially assumed that the man with the torch was nothing more ominous than a member of the British Army out on patrol, a common enough sight in an area known as 'bandit country' for its frequent clashes between the security forces and members of local paramilitary units. As the vehicle came to a stop, however, several other figures dressed in combat fatigues and with blackened faces emerged from behind the hedges flanking the road. A man 'with a clipped English accent' and with an Armalite assault rifle in his hands, briskly ordered all twelve men to get out of the van and to line up facing it with their hands on the roof. A moment later, he asked, 'Who is the practising Roman Catholic here?'

The only such person was 56-year-old Richard Hughes, who remembered that, at that point, two of his co-workers had reached out and squeezed his hands, apparently in the belief that he was about to be shot. For a moment, the three men had stood staring up at a distant red glow in the cold night sky, which seemed like another terrible omen. 'I thought I was a dead man,' Hughes recalled.

Instead, the man with the English accent advised Hughes to turn around and to run with the utmost speed away from the van. Still terrified, he paused to ask in which direction he should go, and at that the man with the rifle, dropping the formality of his tone, told Hughes to 'just piss off down the fucking road'. As he did so, he was followed by two of the other men in combat uniform, who unceremoniously bundled him over a wire fence to the side of the road and ordered him to lie face down in the wet bracken. At that point, Hughes recalled, a burst of automatic gunfire had rung out, followed by a 'terrible silence' and then the sound of the man with the English accent shouting, 'Finish the bastards off!'

In the ensuing bloodbath, ten workmen, aged from 19 to 58, lost their lives, while an eleventh, 32-year-old Alan Black, shot eighteen times, survived only by lying motionless beneath the body of one of his colleagues and pretending to be dead. He later remembered how the youngest of the victims was crying out for his mother at the moment a gunman shot him point blank in the face. Other men were moaning in their death throes, and parts of the van itself had disintegrated in the chaos, half its front dashboard blown into the road, the shattered instrument gauges adding a surrealistic touch to the horror.

'The noise of the gunfire was deafening,' Black recalled:

And what they'd done, they'd deliberately shot us all at waist-level, I suppose to stop anyone running away. And that lasted maybe ten seconds. And the next thing ... I was hit multiple times and so was, I take it, everyone else. It was made even more awful because of these screams of pain ... The [teenaged victim] fell across my legs. It was absolutely horrific. He was crying out, "Mother! Mother!" And the next thing, the gunfire stopped and the same guy that had done all the talking told them to finish it off.

One of the first police officers on the scene, Constable Billy McCaughey (himself later imprisoned for committing a sectarian murder) recalled, 'When we arrived, it was utter carnage. Men were lying two or three together. Blood was flowing, mixed with water from the rain.' Another emergency responder remarked that the victims were 'just lying there like dogs, blood and body parts everywhere. It was like a scene from a butcher's shop.'

More than thirty years later, thus speaking in the tones of the twenty-first century, the European Court of Human Rights in Strasbourg ruled that there had indeed been a breach of Article 2 (Right to Life) of their charter that week in County Armagh. But this referred to 'the lack of proper zeal and integrity' of police investigating the deaths of six Roman Catholic civilians who had perished in two separate gun attacks by Loyalist paramilitaries on Sunday, 4 January, roughly twenty-four hours before the Kingsmill massacre. In the nuanced view of the court, which awarded each of the bereaved families €10,000, 'the [Catholic] victims' human rights were demonstrably infringed by the United Kingdom government, [and] in particular by the subsequent 1999 enquiry into the six deaths, which had lacked the requisite independence, transparency and accountability'. Events such as those on 4 January were regrettable in themselves, the court held, but were exacerbated precisely because they were 'insufficiently prosecuted [to] any reasonable standards a civilised society might expect'.

These were of course eminently fair points on the court's part, even if relatively few outside the legal profession could hope to possess the judges' academic objectivity on the issue. To laymen, there had been first a terrible mass murder, followed by the next night's even greater atrocity on the road outside Kingsmill. Taken together, the events of early January 1976 were a stark reminder that the Irish sectarian struggle of the time was by no means confined to the streets of the British mainland. To this day, no one has ever been held to account for the Kingsmill slaughter. A 2011 report by the Historical Enquiries Team of the Northern Ireland Police concluded only that members of the Provisional IRA had in all probability committed the crime and, perhaps unsurprisingly, that the victims were 'specifically targeted because of their religion'.

Other than the central tragedy of the lives lost, perhaps the most important aspect of both the ASU attacks around the British mainland and the twin tragedies of 4–5 January 1976 is the insight they provide into the impenetrable logic of Ireland's troubles as a whole. On one level, there was a large and, to varying degrees, disaffected Irish population in London, more than 500,000-strong by 1976, with roughly 1,000 new arrivals swelling their numbers each week from the Republic, which constituted what the UK Cabinet delicately termed a 'broadly receptive pool of potential or active support for the IRA, and which assert[ed] itself in repeated attacks on life in the city', with no fewer than a dozen bombs exploding around the West End on the single day of 29 January 1976.

There were unlicensed Irish pubs and clubs, as well as popular establishments like the evocatively named Biddy Mulligan's, clustered around the Kilburn area, where it might have been thought unwise to openly express excessive sympathy for the British crown. At that time, the Provisional IRA even operated a branch office from an otherwise nondescript four-storey family home flying a green flag with the silhouette of a man holding a rifle on it, overlooking the banks of the Grand Union Canal near Kensal Green Cemetery, and there were frequent marches protesting the British presence in Ulster.

The ground was fertile for a degree of direct action on the streets of the English capital and other cities, therefore, in opposition to the Westminster government's policy, and when no such activity existed, the tabloids of the day often seemed to compete to fabricate it. The *Daily Mirror*, for instance, reported in February 1976 that the IRA had 'hired assassins from behind the Iron Curtain to gun down British troops', while the *Daily Express* alleged that 'billions of pounds of social security benefits [had been] illicitly diverted to fund the IRA campaign'.

On another level, the Northern Ireland question also played a starring if necessarily submerged role in the secret-intelligence controversies that so beset the final weeks of the Harold Wilson government. Colin Wallace, who had served as Senior Information Officer of army operations in Belfast, later wrote about an MI5 campaign to present – or smear – Wilson as under both KGB and IRA control by insisting that his ultimate aim before leaving office was to see a 'Red Shamrock Irish Workers' Republic' established in the UK. To that end, Wilson was alleged to have used his meeting with the IRA in early March 1976 to encourage them to end their latest ceasefire – if true, either an unorthodox request by a sitting prime minister or an intriguing glimpse into the looking-glass world of what was coming to be called the 'secret state'.

We'll return to the vexed matter of Wilson and the UK's security establishment, but for now it's enough to note that the whole question of British direct rule of Ulster, which was first introduced in March 1972, was sufficient to unite the feuding creative duo of John Lennon and Paul McCartney, the first of whom took part in a march holding a banner reading 'For The IRA – Against British Imperialism', while the latter released a single with the striking title 'Give Ireland Back to the Irish', which, despite a BBC ban – or for that same reason – became a Top 20 hit. It was an anomaly by a songwriter whose next release was a close adaptation of the beloved nursery rhyme 'Mary Had a Little Lamb', which hit No. 5 on the chart.

***

Speaking to a Cabinet subcommittee in the week after the Kingsmill tragedy, Harold Wilson, somewhat belying his reputation as a Republican sympathiser, gloomily predicted a 'long and involved' standoff over Ireland, with a 'likely unsatisfactory outcome'. As the bombs and shootings continued, both in Ulster and on the mainland, the British public 'might well come to demand a strike at the [IRA's] heart'. As in Vietnam, Wilson continued, the struggle was rapidly coming to encourage the view that 'a great power cannot beat determined fanatics, [but] they cannot ignore them, either'. The prime minister had no immediate suggestion to break the impasse, remarking merely with the note of world-weary ennui that characterised his final weeks in office, 'It is a fact of human life that there will be outrages perpetrated by a fanatical or mentally disturbed minority against the peaceful majority'.

The bitter truth of Wilson's aphorism, at least as it applied to individual acts of violence, struck home again shortly after 7 o'clock on the dismally wet evening of Tuesday, 20 January 1976, in a darkened side street just north of Leeds city centre. A 42-year-old mother of three named Emily Jackson, who worked as a bookkeeper for her husband's building firm, had taken up position outside the town's Gaiety pub earlier that evening to pursue her supplementary job as a prostitute. In due course, she was approached by a small, soft-spoken man of about 30 at the wheel of a lime-green Ford Capri. The man's courtship technique was direct: he briefly looked Jackson up and down and then asked her how much.

'A fiver,' she replied. The woman got into the car, and the two of them drove off together in the direction of the town centre, before parking on a patch of derelict land behind a dimly lit block of flats in Enfield Terrace, near today's Leeds City College. Once there, the man, who somewhat unimaginatively gave his name as John, apparently had a change of heart based on his sudden revulsion at his companion's sickly sweet brand of perfume.

Pretending that the Capri had stalled, the man then got out to look under the bonnet, while Jackson fatally volunteered to help him by holding her lighter while he examined the engine. As she did so, he took a step backwards and hit her twice with a hammer he removed from under his jacket. The man then dragged his victim's inert body into an adjacent yard, pushed up her sweater and bra, and pulled down her skirt and underwear. Taking a cross-ply Phillips screwdriver from the car, and by now 'seething with hate for her', as he later put it, he proceeded to stab her a total of fifty-two times in the neck, breasts, lower abdomen, groin and back. Following this frenzy, he then searched the yard until he found a rough-hewn plank of wood some 3ft long and thrust it violently between the woman's legs.

'I left her lying on her back, and never took anything from her,' the man later remarked. 'Just as I was about to get back in the Capri, a car came round with its lights on and stopped a few yards from us. I didn't know what make of car it was, but it scared me. I put the hammer and the screwdriver on the car floor and drove away. I went straight back to my mother-in-law's house for a cup of tea,' he added.

Two passing workmen found Emily Jackson's lifeless body at around eight the following morning. A news photograph was taken of the scene as plainclothes officers with long sideburns, all of them smoking and dressed uniformly in heavy winter coats with upturned collars, peered into the recesses of a puddle-stained yard surrounded by crumbling brick walls – the whole tableau reminiscent of some ghastly Jack the Ripper outrage of nearly a century earlier.

Apart from the human suffering, the terrible story of the serial killer later named as Peter Sutcliffe also serves to illustrate some of the joyless detail of life as it still existed for many residents of a large industrial area in 1976: streets of undifferentiated red-brick houses packed together as tight as dominoes, where indoor plumbing was far from universal, family members took a bath with bowls and pitchers in front of the kitchen stove, and where many young women, destined for a life of cultural and material poverty that could leave them looking haggard and washed-up before their 30th birthdays, went 'on the game', as the jargon of the day had it, simply in order to make ends meet. Social revolution might be in the air in the form of the rollout of Concorde and the advent of punk rock, but looking out over many British city streets on the darker days of 1976 was still to be immersed in a scene of Dickensian antiquity, although even that great chronicler of Victorian slum life might have been shocked by the sheer profusion of sexual liaisons of one form or another by no means bound by any consideration of mutual affection.

It has to be said that the initial investigation into the brutal death of Emily Jackson was neither distinguished by forensic brilliance nor by excessive tact on the part of the West Yorkshire Police. As constituted in 1976, that force was a chronically cash-strapped, somehow recognisably northern-provincial agency, suffused with certain old-school if not Wild West attitudes. Women such as Emily Jackson and her fellow victim, 28-year-old Wilma McCann, found fatally stabbed and dumped in a park in the Chapeltown area of Leeds ten weeks earlier, were officially described as of 'doubtful morals' when it came time to brief the press, although some of the in-house terminology was considerably less elevated. Such individuals were 'whores', 'slags', 'bints', 'prozzies', 'slappers' and 'tarts' – not exactly asking to be bludgeoned and left to die like a dog in a municipal wasteland, perhaps, but not to be mourned in quite the same way as the mayor's lady wife, either.

Before taking his leave of Emily Jackson, Peter Sutcliffe had paused to repeatedly stamp on her upper thigh, leaving behind an impression of his shoe which was in time identified as a Dunlop Warwick boot, size 7. It later emerged that Sutcliffe had actually been questioned by the authorities as far back as 1969, after he had seen fit to hit a local prostitute across the back of her head with a stone rolled into a sock, an assault that brought a visit to his home from two officers but no subsequent criminal charges, and that a work colleague had been sufficiently alarmed by his behaviour to write a letter about him to the police.

In all, Sutcliffe would be brought in for questioning on roughly an annual basis throughout the 1970s, and on at least one occasion his interviewers had missed the fact that at the time he was wearing an identical pair of Dunlop boots as in the photograph they were showing him of the marks on Emily Jackson's body. It also transpired that his car had been spotted in the Leeds red light area no fewer than sixty times in the months immediately before and after the January 1976 attack. Even Sutcliffe was surprised by the police lassitude in the matter, later telling a court, 'It was just a miracle they did not apprehend me earlier – they had all the facts.'

Sutcliffe, a name now synonymous with evil, was born in 1946 in Bingley, an otherwise irreproachable market town located just north of Bradford. Somehow, it fails to come as a surprise to learn that he had a violently troubled upbringing: his mother, Kathleen, was regularly abused by his father John, who was also an alcoholic. Taunted as a mummy's boy at school, his home life was equally chaotic. In one pivotal scene, his father posed on the phone as his wife's lover, luring her to a local hotel to expose her infidelity to him, and bringing both the adolescent Peter and his younger brother with him to witness the ensuing confrontation. This seems to have been a formative if not a defining moment in all the family members' lives. Peter later remembered that his father had 'had a wild look on his face, like an animal. I think it may have turned his mind.'

Peter Sutcliffe left school shortly after his 15th birthday and began a series of menial jobs, including working as a gravedigger, a profession his colleagues reported he had enjoyed rather too much, even volunteering to wash corpses on overtime, before drifting into the long-distance driving business in 1975, when he was 29. He was dismissed by one employer for the theft of used tyres but found another haulage job at around the time he assaulted Emily Jackson.

Having known her since they were teenagers, Sutcliffe had married 24-year-old Sonia Szurma, the daughter of Ukrainian and Polish-born refugees, in August 1974. She, in turn, was diagnosed with paranoid schizophrenia, thus adding another layer of complexity to Sutcliffe's already troubled view of women and what constituted an acceptable adult relationship with them. One way or another, their marriage would soon fall short of the mutually respectful, monogamous ideal. Sonia began an affair with their local ice-cream salesman, and Peter spent much of his off-duty life spying on sex workers or soliciting their services. Sutcliffe's marriage turned into his parents' marriage with the volume up.

He started attacking women in earnest in July 1975, when he viciously beat and stabbed a 36-year-old victim, who survived only after extensive brain surgery. A second woman he assaulted a month later escaped to tell police that her attacker was about 30, small, gap-toothed and with a distinctive Bradford accent. West Yorkshire detectives eventually called on Sutcliffe a total of eleven times to enquire about his possible involvement in the series of violent crimes in their area. They cleared him on each occasion.

***

Early in January 1976, the BBC screened three successive programmes on the theme of 'Why is Britain becoming harder to govern?', exploring the theory that the post-war national consensus epitomised by jolly workmen and their paternalistic bosses who went around in bowler hats and carried a copy of *The Times* rolled up under their arms finally seemed to have run its course. In fact, it appeared to some of the programmes' contributors that a culture of rampant egoism had replaced the former note of self-effacing service to Queen and Country and was now the distinguishing characteristic of much of Britain's population under the age of 30. Many blue-chip panels of bishops, Cabinet ministers, charity organisers, chairs of local government committees, senior police officers and sundry academics and headmasters were paraded on screen to that end. The formidably highbrow Professor Anthony King, of the University of Essex, spoke of a rising tide of 'mass alienation from the dictates of authority', and the Labour MP John Mackintosh, known for his advocacy of devolution, worried that popular disenchantment with the established political parties might allow the rise of a 'dangerous Hitlerite alternative which will impose its right-wing programme', a reference to the National Front Party, which had fielded ninety candidates (all of whom lost their deposits) at the most recent general election, largely on a platform of trenchantly stated opposition to current levels of non-white immigration to the UK, frequently expressed in bluntly demotic terms. (The author vividly remembers a Union Jack-laden speaker van repeatedly circling the streets of central Cambridge at around this time, from which the peak-decibel slogan, 'Don't be a cunt, Vote the Front' issued at intervals.)

Apart from such abstract considerations of the UK's governance, the ruling Labour Party was itself divided over the question of possible public-sector spending cuts, which remained a live political issue throughout 1976, with the Cabinet split on both narrowly economic and more broadly ideological lines. Denis Healey, the generally pragmatic Chancellor, had demanded total annual savings of £3.77 billion, and was challenged by Dr Kissinger's friend (and until 8 April, Secretary of State for the Environment) Anthony Crosland, who argued for the more modest figure of £2.45 billion. Chairing a Cabinet meeting on 15 January, Harold Wilson noted 'the widespread impression that there are serious and acrimonious differences between colleagues in the present difficult situation', adding that there was a 'pervasive mood of unease' about the 'continuing questions both at home and abroad commanding HM Government's attention'.

One such challenge of the kind Wilson noted was the recurrent issue of Britain's hotly contested fishing rights with Iceland, or 'Cod Wars' as the press dubbed them. The dispute had begun as long ago as 1952, and had dragged on cyclically ever since, seeming to resolve itself only to flare up again with renewed vigour, much like one of the premier's own gastric attacks, he privately noted, at roughly biennial intervals.

The central problem concerned whether Iceland had the right to unilaterally extend its territorial waters to first 4, then 12, and ultimately to as many as 200 miles around its coast, an area traditionally fished by large British trawlers operating out of English east coast ports like Hull and Grimsby. To the press, here was a story that combined the principle of Britain's unrivalled sovereignty over her home seas with a comic whiff of nineteenth-century jingoism in one irresistible package. Images of British fishing boats clashing with their adversary's somewhat ramshackle coastguard vessels were a staple of the nightly news in the early weeks of 1976. In one incident on 7 January, the Royal Navy frigate HMS *Andromeda* was rammed by a harpoon-firing Icelandic patrol boat. Back in Westminster, Anthony Crosland, who represented Grimsby in

Parliament, took time away from debating the nuances of public spending cuts to announce that the whole affair was both 'faintly ludicrous [and] yet a more pressing threat to the Western alliance' than any other issue currently on the world stage.

For all its tendency to follow the plot of some bygone Peter Sellers comedy in which a global superpower is invaded by a ragtag force clad in chainmail and carrying longbows and suitcases, Crosland was surely right to note the serious implications of the latest spasm of the Cod Wars, as configured in early 1976. As even 'Sunny Jim' Callaghan, the Foreign Secretary, put it in a Cabinet meeting on 15 January:

> The dispute over fishing limits with Iceland has been discussed by the Defence and Overseas Policy Unit, and it was agreed that the time factor is now working against us. It is true that under naval protection our trawlers are catching twice as much fish as the Icelanders have offered us, but the situation will change in the course of 1976 when additional countries come to claim a 200-mile fishing limit, as we might like to do ourselves. The Secretary-General of NATO has taken it upon himself to mediate in the dispute. We have publicly welcomed his initiative, but have privately warned him that it will not be enough for him to secure a reinstatement by the Icelandic government of their earlier offer of a 65,000 ton catch. We have said that we are prepared to reduce our figure to below 100,000 tons to achieve a settlement, but the Icelanders must also move on their figure. [Failing] that, we need to consider what other direct measures we might adopt.

Loosely translated: The members of Her Majesty's Government were men of peace, but if someone wanted a war they could have it, at least up to the point of the nation's ability to wage one. By early 1976, observers at a major British set-piece event such as the State Opening of Parliament could only ruefully note that all the Edwardian gold braid and sashes on display looked distinctly Ruritanian when one came to consider how few British soldiers, sailors and airmen remained on active duty.

After a series of meetings held over the early winter weeks, the Cabinet's response to the fishing-rights standoff was split down ideological lines, with a small majority of ministers, including Roy Jenkins, Judith Hart, Denis Howell and Roy Mason, all supporting various shades of direct intervention and the likes of Barbara Castle, Michael Foot, Shirley Williams and Tony

Benn lobbying for the negotiated option. Denis Healey, for all his relative prudence with the nation's finances, was the most consistently bellicose member of the pro-war group, automatically downcast the moment that prospects for peace brightened and striking one reporter covering a constituency meeting in Leeds as 'flushing red in the face' on the subject of Iceland, leading to genuine fears that the Chancellor 'might literally explode' when describing the perfidy of Geir Hallgrímsson's right-leaning Independent administration in Reykjavik.

'If we go to war, it will be because we have had it imposed upon us. Each of us is at his post, ready to defend a state where respect for the rule of law and common decency among men finds one of its last refuges,' Healey announced, sounding more like a crusading statesman asserting the primacy of man's inalienable rights in the face of an encroaching fascist tyranny than a modern-day politician addressing a quarrel between two rainy islands in northern Europe about the ownership of some fish swimming around in the inhospitable waters between them.

Harold Wilson himself played little direct part in the great cod debate, or for that matter in any of the other pressing issues awaiting his attention on the weekly Cabinet agenda. One way or another, Britain's only prime minister to date to have formed administrations following four general elections was a sadly reduced figure from the firebrand who had electrified his audience with his 1963 'white heat of technology' speech and his scorn for the old-boy network that at a stroke had seemed to make him the voice of the future, not just for his party but for the nation at large. Perhaps by now there was little to personally admire in Wilson, a strange mixture of progressiveness and pipe-smoking, mac-wearing 1950s northern tradition, his critics sniffed, but at one time, his undoubted political skills had commanded the respect of subordinates and enemies alike. Many of the reforms of his first two terms in office had been pushed through with only a wafer-thin working majority in the Commons. But by January 1976, Wilson was no longer the obsessive micro-manager or peerless tactician of old. According to his otherwise admiring biographer Ben Pimlott:

News began to leak out of No. 10 of recurrent stomach upsets, and lengthy consultations with his doctor Sir Joseph Stone. 'Harold talked a lot about his health,' says a close official. 'He was very worried about it, and so was his wife. He had Joe Stone with him a lot of the time, especially if he went abroad.'

Colleagues noticed a slackening of pace ... Officials were starting to find out that the famous Wilson appetite for red boxes was no longer as it had been. He began to resist taking boxes to Chequers, and sometimes they came back unopened ... The PM's puffy and jaundiced appearance encouraged gossip about alcohol. One paper that described him as 'something of a late-night brandy addict' received a writ. Close aides, however, were well aware of his increasing resort to the spirit bottle, especially before Question Time in the House.

There was another sign that Wilson's mind might be drifting towards the early stages of Alzheimer's that would ultimately destroy him. This was his ever-deeper sense of paranoia, his conviction that he was always being plotted against, that every setback was proof of some shadowy cabal determined, if not to assassinate him, at least to silence him politically. Even ten years earlier, he had persuaded himself that his administration was the target of a vast establishment conspiracy.

In time, Wilson's persecution complex grew so acute that he came to believe that his enemies were following him even when he went on his summer holidays to the Scilly Isles, not a part of Britain generally known for its air of racy intrigue. When the prime minister got back to Downing Street after one such visit, he promptly had his Minister of Defence make enquiries about whether there had been any 'unusual activity' by Soviet vessels in the vicinity of the Scillies while he and his family had been in residence, or if any 'foreign spy ships disguise[d] as trawlers' had perhaps been sent to keep watch. And what about the profusion of seagulls he had seen circling above the family's modest three-bedroom bungalow in St Mary's, Wilson wondered? Might the birds have been fitted out with miniature cameras or directional mikes, the better to record his comings and goings?

Ben Pimlott expressed the general mood when he said that Wilson had seemingly lost his bearings by early 1976, although, like many a paranoid individual, 'there was no disputing that there were people who truly were out to get him'. Foreign interference with the workings of the British government was one thing, but there was also 'plenty of funny stuff to be reckoned with closer to home'.

By 1976, MI5, at least in the form of the agency's Principal Scientific Officer and self-styled 'spycatcher' Peter Wright, had concluded that 'the prime minister kept some rum company'. There was, for example, the Anglo-Austrian industrialist Rudi Sternberg, whom Wilson had knighted despite Sternberg's close business ties with the East German regime, and Joseph Kagan, a Lithuanian-born textile manufacturer whose firm produced Wilson's signature Gannex raincoats, similarly knighted and in turn elevated to the peerage before being convicted on charges of theft and false accounting and spending ten months in prison as a result. When asked by a TV interviewer why the British security services had taken such a close interest in their own prime minister, Peter Wright replied, 'Because, for ten years, he collected a large group of advisers and friends around him who were not to be trusted, and we knew that.'

'But that doesn't make him a traitor, or even a security suspect, surely?' the interviewer persisted.

'It certainly does,' said Wright.

Finally, there was the matter of Wilson's continued if necessarily furtive exploration of the limits of his wedding vows to his wife Mary, a published poet and formidable political brain in her own right, whose home life *Private Eye* had turned into the long-running comic fantasia 'Mrs Wilson's Diary'. In the *Eye*'s hands, the Wilsons' 10 Downing Street was a place of mundane domesticity, of Spam garnished with brown sauce accompanied by Wincarnis sweet wine.

It was a harmless enough bit of fun, part of the acknowledged British gift for not taking the nation's elected officials too seriously, but by early 1976 the Wilsons' family arrangements weren't necessarily a laughing matter to the parties involved. Over the years, the prime minister had consistently refuted allegations that he was playing away with his Political Secretary, Marcia Williams, the future Baroness Falkender, particularly after the press had discovered that she had had two young sons born out of wedlock. (The boys' father was later outed as the political editor of the *Daily Mail*.) Wilson's actual affair with his press adviser Janet Hewlett-Davies, then aged 37 to his 59, went unrevealed until 2024.

The whole episode was tragic, but not without its farcical aspects. In January 1976, Mary Wilson, still in the dark about her husband's infidelity, would innocently approach Hewlett-Davies to ask if they could go flat-hunting together. 'You live in Ashley Gardens' – a red-brick Victorian mansion block close to London's Victoria Station – she remarked one morning. 'We're thinking of moving there. Could you help me look?' Hewlett-Davies complied, and later in 1976 the Wilsons duly took possession of a flat adjacent to her own, where Mary remained until her death at the age of 102 in June 2018, twenty-three years after Wilson himself had succumbed to a combination of Alzheimer's disease and cancer.

***

The mid-1970s were as restive in the United States as they were across the Atlantic. The Watergate scandal had brought about the first, and to date only, resignation of the nation's president when Richard Nixon was summarily replaced by Gerald Ford. The US economy continued to stagnate as inflation hit 12 per cent in the first quarter of 1976 – a figure, admittedly, the Wilson government could only dream of – oil prices soared, and the stock market lost half its value.

Perhaps no single headline captured the US malaise of the era quite like the special, 72-point banner splashed across the masthead of the New York *Daily News* on 30 October 1975. It read 'FORD TO CITY: DROP DEAD', a reference to the president's reluctance to grant further federal funds to the nearly bankrupt city.

Meanwhile, an assortment of post-Vietnam countercultural groups persisted in their determination to subvert the status quo by detonating bombs across the country, each fresh incident drawing attention to now dimly remembered but then pervasive radical cells such as the Weather Underground, the New World Liberation Front and the Puerto Rican independence group, Army Boricua. A disproportionate number of the attacks seemed to occur in and around the San Francisco area, where such events became so common that an FBI spokesman (always male, in those days), briefing the press about the latest bomb outrage in February 1976, referred to the city as 'the Belfast of North America'.

In the midst of this destabilised atmosphere came one of the decade's most electrifying criminal flashpoints, as notorious in its way as the trial of the psychotic London gangland Kray twins before it, or the US football star-turned-alleged-double-murderer O.J. Simpson that followed. It began early on the morning of 4 February 1974, when four members of a previously little-known guerrilla group called the Symbionese Liberation Army (SLA) abducted a 19-year-old university student named Patricia Hearst from her San Francisco apartment, pushing her into the boot of a stolen car as her fiancé ran out into the street behind them, vainly pleading with them to let her go.

In the febrile mood of the city in the mid-1970s, the few bystanders present apparently concluded that they were witnessing merely a minor domestic dispute involving a negligee-clad young woman and her rival suitors. They would soon learn otherwise.

The victim bundled away that morning was the granddaughter of the press baron William Randolph Hearst (1863–1951). He was the founder of one of the world's largest media empires, with fifteen daily newspapers and as many weekly or monthly magazines, followed in time by dozens of TV and radio franchises, not to mention owner of a 77,000-acre estate, perched on a hilltop between San Francisco and Los Angeles. He also served as the inspiration for Orson Welles's *Citizen Kane*. As a young woman who stood to inherit a quarter share of the family trust fund, then estimated at $1.4 billion ($11 billion today), 'Patty', as the media, over her objection, chose to call her, seemed to represent the wealth and privilege that the SLA – a broad-based protest group that, among other causes, espoused gay liberation, animal rights, feminism, Black Power and economic Marxism, which they promoted with the logo of a suitably sinister seven-headed cobra – wanted to usurp.

Three days later, the SLA sent a letter to a San Francisco radio station announcing that they had taken Hearst and were now holding her hostage as a 'prisoner of war'. The group demanded that in exchange for her release, Patricia's father, Randolph Apperson Hearst, feed the entire 4 million-strong population of the Bay Area three times a week, free of charge, for the foreseeable future, a daunting task even for one of his capacious resources.

Several thousand bagged lunches were duly distributed, often to the bemusement of the beneficiaries themselves, although in the end, the project seemed to simply peter out. Two months later, a further communiqué arrived that proved far more shocking to the Hearst family. It was from Patricia herself, announcing that she was joining her kidnappers in their campaign to foment civil unrest in the Bay Area. Henceforth, she would only answer to the *nom de guerre* Tania, a choice inspired by Che Guevara's romantic partner, Tamara 'Tania' Bunke, who was killed in August 1967 by government troops in Bolivia, where she had gone to help him incite revolution. In due course, Hearst went on to take part in the armed robbery of a San Francisco bank, in which the surveillance footage of the young heiress dressed in a black maxicoat and wielding an M1 carbine while yelling at the bank's customers to 'Get up against the wall, motherfuckers!' quickly became one of the defining images of the era.

In September 1975, Tania and her colleagues were captured by authorities, hiding only a few miles away from where she had been abducted nineteen months earlier. Hearst stated her occupation as 'Urban Guerrilla' and asked her lawyer to inform the world, 'I am smiling, I feel free and strong, and I send my greetings to all the oppressed sisters and brothers around the world'. 'The revolution is going to start quite soon,' she added to reporters. 'I am going to start it.' At the time of her arrest, Hearst's weight had dropped to just 87lb, she had apparently stopped menstruating, and a court-appointed psychologist described her as 'a low-IQ, low-affect Zombie'.

Hearst's trial on bank robbery charges began on 15 January 1976 and unsurprisingly polarised opinion, with several news outlets portraying her as a wayward brat who had willingly chosen a life of violent crime, while by contrast, the Hearst media preferred to see the whole matter as a tragic case of an innocent young woman who had succumbed to the newly coined Stockholm Syndrome, in which a kidnap victim begins to identify with his or her captors. Speaking of this process of indoctrination, Patricia – as she now again referred to herself – told the court that at the time of the bank job, 'I didn't even think. I just did it, and if I had not done it and if [the SLA] had been able to get away they would have killed me.'

On 20 March 1976, Hearst was found guilty of bank robbery and using a firearm during the commission of a crime, and given the maximum sentence of thirty-five years. One of her attorneys took the opportunity to remark that if in fact there was a double standard for the wealthy, 'in this case it went to the opposite extreme', and his client had received harsher punishment than would have been thought proper had her name been Smith or Jones. An appeals court subsequently reduced Hearst's sentence to seven years, of which she ultimately served twenty-two months.

Perhaps Patricia Hearst truly was a tragic victim of serial brainwashing and sexual abuse on the part of the SLA, as she always claimed. Set against this, Hearst's detractors would point to the moment during her captivity when she and two of her kidnappers had decided to go clothes shopping together in downtown San Francisco. The SLA members had walked into a store, leaving her alone in a parked van, with the key in the ignition. She was free to leave, but elected to wait for her abductor-colleagues, who, having shoplifted some goods, were chased out of the front door onto the street by a young sales clerk. At that, Hearst had proceeded to pick up a machine gun lying on her lap, point it out of the window and squeeze the trigger. The gun jammed, however, so she laid it down, reached back and picked up another automatic weapon from the back seat of the van and sprayed a volley of bullets across the street, miraculously not hitting anybody, but successfully allowing her two comrades to escape with her and return to the group's hideout. Later that night, one of her two shopping companions told Patty that he was proud of her and, following that, she had had sex with another of her abductors, though whether willingly or as part of the process of 'coercive persuasion' she claimed to have been subjected to at the hands of the SLA remains a point of some debate to this day.

IRON LADY

For those inclined to a more optimistic view of human nature, a sign that a policy of grudging co-existence, or détente, might be emerging in East–West relations came with the signing in August 1975 of the Helsinki Accords, which notionally protected human rights, reaffirmed the principle of sovereign international borders and promoted trade and cultural exchanges between thirty-five participating nations, most notably the United States and the Soviet Union. It was a significant step, at least as a symbol of the desire of the world's two acknowledged superpowers not to go to war, let alone to obliterate one another in a nuclear exchange. But it might be fair to say that détente still remained a work in progress in the mid-1970s, and much of the ensuing friction came to revolve around the parties' differing attitudes towards exporting their respective political systems, often accompanied by a supply of arms and other materiel, to what was then called the Third World.

When the US Secretary of State Henry Kissinger went to call on the Soviet presidium at the Kremlin in January 1976, the following public exchange occurred:

> Reporter: Will Angola be among the subjects discussed?
> Leonid Brezhnev [General Secretary of the Communist Party, chairman
>   of the presidium and head of state]: I have no questions about Angola.
>   Angola is not my country.
> Kissinger: It will certainly be discussed.
> Andrei Gromyko [Soviet Foreign Minister]: The agenda is always adopted
>   by mutual agreement.
> Kissinger: Then we will discuss it.
> Brezhnev: We will not.

Kissinger himself later told me that this 'strained' repartee was sadly typical when discussing world affairs with the Soviet leadership, 'Their side would inevitably succumb to the temptation to peddle the Marxist-Leninist line to a country like Angola, even if they had no compelling national interest there. It put the wider US–Soviet relationship at unnecessary risk as a result.'

Today, social historians may point to the Helsinki Accords as the beginning of the end of the Cold War, but if so, they fell some way short of ushering in any immediate era of 'mutual concord and goodwill between free peoples around the world' of the sort promised in the treaty's preamble. In January 1976 alone, there was domestic upheaval or armed conflict to one degree or another in Venezuela, where President Carlos Andrés Pérez – later forced from office on embezzlement charges – abruptly seized control of all foreign oil companies doing business in his country. Italy, in turn, suffered one of its recurrent political crises when its elected government fell for the thirty-seventh time in thirty-three years, amidst a bribery and corruption scandal of its own.

A few days later, it was the turn of Ecuador's President General Guillermo Lara to hurriedly resign, in his case mere minutes before a petition to that effect was due to be presented at his Quito office by a group of heavily armed troops. In Beirut, as many as 1,600 men, women and children died in sectarian clashes between opposing Christian and Muslim militias, followed by a reprisal attack that killed a further 580 civilians, two days later.

Later that week, rival religious groups similarly attacked each other around the normally sedate oasis town of Amgala, in the Western Sahara, with upwards of 200 casualties. Proving, if nothing else, the cyclical nature of much of the post-war geopolitical debate, the United States meanwhile vetoed a UN Security Council resolution that would have recognised the existence of an independent Palestinian homeland. And those were just the set-piece disputes around the world, which also saw an unrelenting continuation of various guerrilla bombing campaigns, as well as a series of earthquakes, tidal waves, shipwrecks, plane crashes, fires, strikes, art thefts and the ever-escalating Cambodian genocide, as well as the death, on 12 January, of the prolific British author Agatha Christie at the age of 85.

★★★

The Queen of Crime's bibliography, with seventy-four novels published and 2 billion worldwide sales, second in popularity only to the works of William Shakespeare and the Bible, may be the most impressive in modern English literature. However, for sheer Stakhanovite effort the polymathic writer and composer Anthony Burgess (1917–93) could have made a strong bid for second place. As a rule, the author of *A Clockwork Orange* and thirty-three other novels, assorted plays, short stories, children's fiction and scholarly linguistical and musical studies did not go gently into middle age. Burgess once said that he had expected his later fifties to 'bring calm, indifference, tolerance, a quiescence of the passions, a cooling sorbet before the final great Yeatsian rage of lust for girls in mini-skirts or the nylon-rendings of the tricyclical Betjeman beast, but I have not found it so at all' (I once had the pleasure of interviewing him, and he really did speak like that).

Among other things, Burgess was one of those who deplored both the decline in public manners and the petty intrusions of authority on the average citizen's life. 'The rot gets worse every year – the rotting away of simple courtesy I mean,' he remarked in 1976:

> Christmas shopping in London is hideous these days. Go up or down the escalator in Selfridges, and a recorded voice tells you peremptorily to keep to the right or left: no 'please' or 'thank you' – incredible when you consider that the wording of this directive had to be worked out beforehand. Outside in Oxford Street a policeman with a loud-hailer orders you about. On the tubes 'mind the doors' and 'all change' are unqualified by even minimal politeness.

Burgess told me that when entering a bookshop, he was appalled even then to see how so many of the newly released titles on display seemed to consist of 'rows of abject drivel, all of them draped with neon-pink covers and infantile lettering, featuring some leather-clad oaf or a rubber-bosomed young bit in torn stockings astride an Italian motor-scooter, with legs splayed and an insolent smirk on her lips'.

Burgess's own contribution to the state of English literature in 1976 was the novel *Beard's Roman Women* – a title not to be confused with the distinguished classicist Mary Beard, who was then still a 21-year-old postgraduate student at Cambridge, but a mordant reflection on the indignities of growing old. The book's recently widowed central character is plagued by midnight phone calls from his late wife, to whom he says he's sorry for having rejected her 'gross, sick body', but even so, he doesn't want her back, thank you.

In broadly that same spirit, 1976 also saw the publication of 53-year-old John Braine's novel *Waiting for Sheila*, another rumination on the male libido in later life and dismissed by one critic as:

... like a sad case-history from a sex manual ... a story told by a whiny, self-pitying old fool [whose] prose style gets ever more tortuous when going on about his 'wound' or 'that fishy female odour'. It's too bad, because Braine (*Room at the Top*) can still write scenes in sharp, clear detail – scenes that here are obscured by dubious psychology and drowned in maudlin, droning self-dramatisation.

Other reviews of the book were not quite as good as this one.

On a lighter note, the popular American wordsmith Neil Simon published his wisecrack-laden play *California Suite*, generous in its rapid-fire comic exchanges, if perhaps less so in its compelling insights into the human condition. Both Alfred Hitchcock and John Wayne completed their final films, respectively *Family Plot* and *The Shootist*, that winter.

Meanwhile, the pop charts were dominated by the seemingly unstoppable rise of the likes of Hall & Oates, Barry Manilow, Peter Frampton, the Eagles, ABBA and the question of whether or not David Bowie had succumbed to the blizzard of cocaine in which his latest album, *Station to Station*, seemed to have been recorded, or if he was merely entering another of those exploratory creative phases for which he was known.

Perhaps proving that the 1960s hadn't so much died musically as adapted to changing circumstances, three of the four ex-Beatles (John Lennon was on self-imposed hiatus) released new material, although there was both a symbolic and sadly literal closure to one chapter of the group's history involving their long-time road manager and plausible claimant to coveted 'fifth Beatle' status, Mal Evans. It was a shocking but somehow not wholly surprising story.

To all outward appearances, the thickset, bespectacled Evans had changed little since the day in August 1963 when, as a 28-year-old Liverpool telephone engineer, he had first signed on as an assistant to the Beatles' manager, Brian Epstein. However, like most of the band's entourage, he never quite recovered from their protracted and ugly breakup. Shortly after separating from his wife Lily, Evans had done what many a British rock music veteran does when London ignores his services. He drifted out to California, where he scratched a living as a gofer and would-be record producer while working with a ghostwriter named John Hoernle on his tell-all memoir *Living the Beatles Legend*.

On 5 January 1976, just a week before the book was due to be delivered to its publisher, Evans's girlfriend Fran Hughes asked Hoernle to come urgently to the couple's rented Los Angeles apartment, warning him that Mal had 'flipped out' from taking pills. A struggle ensued when Hoernle arrived, during which

Evans picked up a .30-calibre rifle he kept under his bed. At that point, Hughes called 911 to summon the authorities.

At the official inquest, it was said that Evans had ignored repeated police requests that he lay down his weapon, which he instead 'pointed deliberately' at the responding officers. Other eyewitness accounts seem to at least partially contradict this version of events. According to them, following the initial scuffle Evans had locked himself in his bedroom, where he could be heard sobbing uncontrollably and threatening to shoot himself. To avert this, the officers had broken down the door and fired six rounds at Mal's head and chest, killing him instantly. An autopsy showed a 'therapeutic level of Valium' and the equivalent of one pint of beer in his system. Mal Evans was aged 40 at the time of his death.

Paul McCartney was later to call Evans 'a big lovable bear' and to rue the events of that dark Monday night in Hollywood. 'Had I been there I would have been able to say, "Mal, don't be a twat." In fact, any of his friends could have talked him out of it; he wasn't a nutter.' Of the four Beatles, only George Harrison called Fran Hughes to offer his condolences.

Evans's body was cremated in Los Angeles three days after his death, which was ruled a justifiable homicide. Possibly because the richly gifted but alcoholic singer-songwriter Harry Nilsson made the arrangements, the urn carrying the deceased's ashes was somehow lost in the post on its way back to England. *Living the Beatles Legend* has never been published.

★★★

When Harold Wilson complained in a Cabinet subcommittee on 14 January 1976 that Great Britain was in some ways 'close to becoming ungovernable', he may have been doing no more than giving voice to his personal frustration at the reigning state of affairs as he experienced them after two years of what was now his fourth and final administration. Or his comments may have reflected some of the general trend ignited by the West's 1960s modernisation crisis and recently given fresh impetus by the Watergate scandal and its fallout, which rendered old-fashioned notions of deference and instinctive compliance with national authority less fashionable than ever before.

As one manifestation of this trend, the public outing of Western security services agents became something of a sport for the press in 1976. In Washington, a retired CIA officer, Philip Agee, founded a newsletter that began publishing the identities of his former colleagues in the field, leading to the murder of one of those listed, Robert Welch, the agency's station chief in Athens, that winter. The Paris newspaper *Libération* similarly displayed the names of fifty-six alleged 'spies [and] unwanted guests' living in France, while in London, the magazine *Time Out* identified sixty-one 'Americans here snoop[ing] on the lives of ordinary Britons', the spur for several of those named to hurriedly seek postings elsewhere.

One way or another, it seemed that Wilson might have had a point when, on 19 January, he observed to Denis Healey and a few others of his circle, 'The whole world is galloping down the road to its own destruction ... People want to kick over the old principles which made our country great.'

Moving from the metaphysical or abstract to more practical realms, Wilson was also confronted by the latest outbreak of the IRA bombing campaign, with a series of twelve simultaneous explosions in central London on the night of 29 January. However, an IRA man named Paddy Hackett spectacularly failed in his mission to wreak havoc on the city's Tube network when the homemade device he was carrying exploded prematurely in his arms as he walked with it towards the rush-hour South Kensington Station, causing him to lose one of his hands and part of a leg.

It was not an especially happy Cabinet that met later that week in Downing Street, therefore, even if there was a glimmer of relief at the news that Concorde had just successfully completed its first scheduled commercial journey with a three-and-a-half-hour flight from London to Bahrain. The airliner's development cost, shared with the French, had originally been estimated at £70 million (or £550 million in our terms), but the final price was about ten times this figure. In another example of that peculiarly British marriage of the sublime and the slightly absurd, the passengers on the aircraft's return journey to Heathrow the following day were first advised that they had flown at speeds in excess of 1300mph, and were then obliged to wait a further forty minutes on landing while two men in brown overalls repeatedly attempted and failed to locate a wheeled staircase that would fit the plane's cabin door.

***

In December 1967, a middle-aged professional couple paid £28,000 for a four-bedroomed, terraced house in Flood Street, just off the Kings Road in west London. Nothing particularly remarkable in that, one might think, except that the new owners were Denis and Margaret Thatcher. After the latter's election as Conservative Party leader in February 1975, the house would serve both as a meeting place for her future ministerial colleagues and as a symbol of the upward social mobility she so urged on her fellow citizens.

Margaret Thatcher was aged 49 at the time she consigned her predecessor Ted Heath to the back benches, an act of regicide that led to a twenty-five-year period of mutual coolness, during which she went on to become an icon of almost religious veneration to some believers – a figure steeped in Protestant values, dedicated to the ideal of family and driven by a sense of her movement's unfailing rectitude. By 1976, her political qualities already commanded a wide literature, but the author Kingsley Amis captured another potent aspect of her appeal when he wrote in his diary following an invitation to dinner at Flood Street:

> The house is one of those neat little joints between the Kings Road and the Chelsea Embankment, comfortable and decorated in boldly unadventurous style … I was rather overcome with the occasion and the close propinquity of Mrs. T … She wore one of those outfits that seem to have had more detail in them than is common, with, I particularly remember, finely embroidered gold-and-scarlet collar and cuffs on her blouse. She was one of the best-looking women I had ever met and for her age … remarkable.

Amis's unpublished assessment of his hostess's charms was even more fulsome, and hinted at Thatcher's heady mixture of matronly authority and raw sex appeal which he encapsulated in the admiring term 'Iron Knickers'.

As it happened, there was to be a more austere variant of the sobriquet, first heard following a speech at London's Kensington Town Hall on 19 January 1976, when Britain's Opposition leader remarked that the Soviet Union was 'bent on world domination' and, what was more, taking advantage of détente to exploit civil unrest in Angola and elsewhere in the Third World. Thatcher continued her global *tour d'horizon* by referring to Britain's ambivalent position in the European Community and calling for its member states to maintain their discrete national identities and resist any move towards closer federation, before observing that the UK was presently 'fighting a war of survival against the forces of darkness in Northern Ireland', and concluding, 'We need more combat troops in order to prevail, as we must'.

Reviewing the foreign-affairs component of Thatcher's speech in a leading article published five days later, the Soviet Army newspaper *Krasnaya Zvezda* (*Red Star*) mocked her as 'the Iron Lady'. The paper's attempt at satire could only be counted a mixed success. Thatcher's approval rating among undecided British voters jumped by seven points in a poll published on 2 February, with more than two-thirds of respondents reacting positively to her new title.

Even so, this was not yet the season of unbounded Thatcherism, as it came to be known. Striking an unusually emollient note, the Conservative leader told her party conference that autumn, 'My administration will look forward to discussion and consultation with our adversaries abroad, [and] to reaching agreement with the trade union movement here at home about the policies that are needed to save our country.' Strange as it may seem in light of future developments, there were those close to the Tory leader in 1976 who had actually begun to wonder whether she might seek to dilute certain parts of a 'messianic guiding policy based largely on 19th-century Puritanical evangelism', to quote her nemesis Ted Heath, or in short, sell out her principles in order to get elected.

The prospect of a new Conservative administration must at times have seemed tantalisingly close at hand to Thatcher and her inner circle in the early part of 1976. On 19 February, Harold Wilson's government published its cyclical White Paper on public expenditure for the accounting period beginning two years later, not generally the occasion for unduly raised levels of adrenaline either in Parliament or the nation at large, but in this case, a significant moment in the internecine struggle for the soul of the Labour Party that persisted throughout much of the 1970s. Battle was immediately joined between the party's left and right as to the paper's merits.

Departing from the dry arcana of the details of domestic growth projections and available governmental resources normally heard on these occasions, the chancellor Denis Healey remarked in the Commons:

> To be blunt, the United Kingdom is living beyond its means ... In the last three years, public expenditure has grown by nearly 20 per cent in volume, while output has risen by less than two percent. The ratio of spending to gross national product is equally unacceptable, as is the current tax burden. In 1975–76, a married man on average wages is paying about a quarter of his earnings in income tax, compared with a tenth in 1960–61 ... These figures are simply not sustainable.

As a consequence, he now proposed to slash some £2 billion from the spending the government had previously scheduled for the years 1977–78, and a further £3 billion for 1978–79.

Healey's announcement aroused furious opposition from the left wing of the Labour Party and from interest groups likely to be affected by the cuts. The head of the National Union of Teachers called the news 'catastrophic, the economics of bedlam', while the Royal Automobile Club, reacting to planned reductions in the rate of new road building, complained of 'another spoke driven in the wheel of bringing Britain grinding to a stone-age halt', in its colourful, if slightly mixed metaphor.

There were lively scenes in the Commons itself as the debate on the government's plans reached its climax, with the veteran left-wing Labour MP Eric Heffer repeatedly shouting, 'Stalinist! Stalinist!' as his party's chancellor passed him on the way to the division lobby, while another colleague, Russell Kerr, the Australian-born member for Feltham and Heston, hissed 'Bastard!' when he saw Healey return. The latter's own version of these events was that, on resuming his seat, 'one of the rebels used demotic language to cast aspersions on my paternity, so I praised his virility in similar terms.' This was a notable paraphrase on the chancellor's part. According to one eyewitness, Healey's precise riposte to his critics on the floor of the House was 'Go fuck yourselves.'

It's worth remembering that there were many ordinary Britons for whom life in 1976 wasn't one so much about ripe ideological exchange on the proper role of government in a free-market economy and more about basic survival. That same month, the Treasury revealed that the average weekly wage for a skilled male was £60, and for his female counterpart, £37, roughly the equivalent of £475 and £290 today. The average house price was then £17,000 (£135,000), and the cost of a new Ford Cortina £2,025 (£16,200), while a gallon of petrol would have set you back as much as 77p (£6), a packet of twenty cigarettes 45p (£3.60) and a pint of beer 33p (£2.60). The popular children's programme *Blue Peter* was sufficiently concerned about the cost of living that winter to devote most of its twenty-five-minute broadcast on 17 February to a blow-by-blow demonstration of how to stay warm in bed at night using sheets of torn-up newspaper as a supplement to blankets. 'Just one thing, though,' the presenter concluded cheerily. 'With all this paper about, I shouldn't go to bed with a candle too near if I were you.'

Meanwhile, terrorist bombings continued on a near-industrial scale, both in Northern Ireland and on the mainland, with a series of frightful 'friendly fire' incidents in which innocent bystanders were maimed or killed by devices intended for members of the British security forces. On the evening of 7 February, 18-year-old Rachel McLernon and her 16-year-old brother

Robert were killed when they went to investigate an apparent accident in which a Ford Escort appeared to have left the road and crashed into an adjacent field near their family home in Cookstown, County Tyrone. The car had in fact been booby-trapped with the aim of attracting the attention of a police or army patrol, and it exploded when the two teenagers touched the driver's side door. Rachel was engaged, while her brother had been due to take his O levels that summer. There was little room for technical sophistication in most such devices, merely the murderous intent to do harm to whomever was unlucky enough to be in the vicinity.

Callous as it is to use the word 'fortunate' in relation to human collateral, it might fairly be said that at least the McLernon siblings died instantly, ghastly as their fate was. Others of those trapped in the endless cycle of sectarian violence were less lucky. Less than a week after the McLernons lost their lives, a 34-year-old London bus conductor-turned-IRA bomber named Frank Stagg died on the sixty-second day of his hunger strike in Wakefield Prison. Stagg had previously endured the excruciatingly painful and dehumanising practice of being forcibly fed by means of a tube pushed through each nostril, or by the variant of one inserted direct into the stomach, a scene 'often accompanied by extreme violence, [with] an orderly required to hold down the patient, while a second manipulated the apparatus', in the measured words of the subsequent Home Office report.

Taken as a whole, events such as those seen at Cookstown or Wakefield did not conspicuously add to the reputation of the United Kingdom of 1976 for moral enlightenment, or in some cases, even the most basic standards of humanity.

***

On the same day as Frank Stagg's squalid death, a dark-haired, early middle-aged man was found lying, stabbed through the heart, in a darkened alleyway behind a west Los Angeles apartment building. At around 9 o'clock that Thursday evening, a nearby resident named Ron Evans heard a male voice loudly scream, 'Oh, my God! No!', following which he had run outside just in time to see a man he described as slim and long-haired, with an unusually pale complexion, fleeing the scene on foot, while a second figure lay motionless on his back, his white shirt front soaked in blood.

Evans attempted to give mouth-to-mouth resuscitation, while another bystander alerted by the noise ran to the payphone at the end of the street to call an ambulance. It arrived too late to save the victim's life. He was pro-nounced dead at the scene, which by a mild coincidence happened to be adjacent to the home rented by the actor Peter Falk while he was appearing as the title character in the popular TV series *Columbo*.

Unlike the murder cases routinely cracked by the raincoat-wearing fictional sleuth, however, the mystery surrounding the death of the man fatally stabbed on the night of 12 February defied straightforward resolution. Within days of the discovery of the victim's lifeless body, Los Angeles detectives were privately admitting they were completely in the dark as to the circumstances of his murder, or any motive for it, although it was speculated that a drug deal and/or a sexual encounter of some sort gone tragically wrong might be involved.

The whole sorry affair might have gone on to be dismissed as just another statistic among the roughly 22,000 homicide cases then reported each year in the United States, more than a third of them unsolved, but for the iden-tity of the deceased. He was the once widely popular stage and screen actor Sal Mineo, the third of four children of Sicilian-born parents who had gone into the coffin-making business in New York, a profession of limited appeal to their artistic son who had soon moved west in search of more congenial work. His big break had come with his casting in 1955's *Rebel Without a Cause*, in which he played the delicately wired and sexually ambiguous character 'Plato' Crawford, opposite the film's stars, James Dean and Natalie Wood.

Mineo, who was just 16 years old when *Rebel* opened, later called Plato 'the first gay teenager in Hollywood history'. Amplifying on the theme in a 1972 interview, in which he also joked about having 'a girl in every port, and a couple of guys, too', he added, 'You watch [*Rebel*] now, and you *know* the character had the hots for James Dean'. In an early rehearsal, Dean himself had offered the film's director Nicholas Ray a piece of technical advice, 'Tell the kid to look at me the same way Natalie does'.

It has to be said that Sal Mineo was not one of those precocious child stars who never quite seem to take the step up to a career as a gainfully employed adult actor. But nor was his a case of an entirely smooth transi-tion. After *Rebel*, Mineo returned to play opposite James Dean once more in *Giant*, already seemingly typecast in the role of the brooding teen sidekick. Set against this, he earned critical praise and a second Oscar nomination for his performance as a Jewish Holocaust survivor in 1960's *Exodus*. Despite these plaudits, Mineo never translated his early success into a mature screen career, and by 1963, when he was still only 24, he was left to remark, 'One minute it seemed I had more movie offers than I could handle, and the next no one wanted me'.

Mineo was convinced that he had been blackballed by Hollywood and the reason for this had little to do with his technical acting ability. Perhaps the rumours involving his sexual preference were a factor, if so a prejudice his direction of the unflinchingly gay-themed play *Fortune and Men's Eyes*, with its graphic prison-rape scene, did little to dispel. Mineo's last screen appearance was in a small part as a talking chimpanzee in 1971's *Escape from the Planet of the Apes*.

Five years later, Mineo was booked to open in the role of a house burglar in an intellectually undemanding stage farce by the name of *P.S. Your Cat is Dead*. He had been returning home from rehearsals for the play to the Hollywood studio apartment he shared with his male acting coach, Courtney Burr, when he met his death.

In January 1978, a 21-year-old part-time Los Angeles pizza-delivery man and convicted thief named Lionel Williams was belatedly charged with Mineo's murder, the result not so much of diligent police work as of Williams's tendency to openly brag to his fellow inmates of being the guilty party while serving time for an unrelated offence. There was the minor discrepancy of the suspect being a black man, whereas the only eyewitness to the 1976 crime had described Mineo's assailant as being white. However, the prosecution at the subsequent trial was able to persuade the jury to disregard such details, which it attributed to it having been dark outside at the time the assault had occurred. Williams was swiftly convicted of the murder, which was said to have been a commonplace mugging that had gone wrong, and sentenced to life imprisonment, ultimately serving twelve years.

The question of Sal Mineo's lonely and violent death was never entirely put to rest, though, and still exercises the Hollywood gossip mills today. There was the matter of the needle puncture marks found on the victim's body, for instance – proof, apparently, of his longtime drug habit, and all it entailed – as well as the large stash of erotic pictures featuring both male and female models found in the rented apartment he shared with Courtney Burr. The popular assumption at the time was that Mineo's life might indeed have been brutally ended by his chance encounter in the dark alley, but that the tragedy had antecedents that lay buried somewhere back among the sometimes chaotic events of his thirty-seven years alive.

Not long after Williams's conviction, a typed letter was delivered to the West Hollywood Police Department. It contained details of Mineo's murder, such as the shape and colour of distinguishing scars on his body and the exact amount of change found in his pocket, which had never been revealed in public, and ended with the words, 'I hereby confess that I did assault Sal Myneo [*sic*] who did me wrong. God forgive me.' The writer of the note was never positively identified, but it served to add one last twist to the plot of the real-life mystery of Mineo's brief but troubled life.

CARRY ON ENGLAND

Film audiences who might have long forgotten Sal Mineo's very existence but for the sad news of his death lined up that same week for the opening of Martin Scorsese's *Taxi Driver*, which broke attendance records on its release in both London and New York. By early 1976, it was an axiom bordering on the clichéd to suggest that it took more than a little madness to drive a cab amidst the menace and jammed chaos of Manhattan's streets. In Scorsese's remorseless new film, the eponymous character, not so much played as inhabited by Robert De Niro, for once wasn't so much a creature of gnarled resilience or the butt of stale night-club jokes. He was, though, an unmetered psychotic, and more particularly an alienated Vietnam veteran possessed by burning contempt for the squalor he sees all around him, yet who spends his off-duty hours with junk food and blue movies.

On one level a comparatively slow-burning thriller, on another *Taxi Driver* is really about a series of failed attempts to connect, each one of them more hopeless than before. Travis Bickle, the human time bomb played by De Niro, asks a girl out on a date and takes her to a porn cinema. He ingratiates himself to a charismatic, Kennedy-esque political candidate, only to attract the attention of his security detail. He wants to befriend a child prostitute, but that, too, ends poorly. In the end, he's so lonely that when he famously asks, 'Who you talkin' to?', he's in fact addressing himself in a mirror.

Perhaps one of the reasons *Taxi Driver* resonated with so many people is because of this human void that lies at its centre. At one time or another, we've all felt as alone as Travis Bickle. Fortunately, most of us are better at dealing with it than Bickle, whose haunting line, 'Someday a real rain will come and wash all the scum off the streets' signals a climactic orgy of violence that delivers both a visceral shock and a palpable sense of relief of the 'It had to happen, and it's happened' variety.

Taxi Driver wasn't the first indication that mainstream Western cinema might be taking a turn away from all-round family entertainment. That accolade arguably belongs to 1967's *Bonnie and Clyde*. However, by popular consensus, it did breathe new life into the whole business of what constituted a popular international box-office success: in this case, an unsettling, immersive sense of what being trapped in a steel cage on wheels with strangers for anything up to eighty hours a week might feel like, and, incidentally, an equally unsparing glimpse into the dark heart of New York City as it teetered on the brink of terminal bankruptcy in 1976 – an existential crisis to which we'll return.

Of course, Western cinema wasn't all suddenly a case of oppressive allegorical psychodrama and gun-spattered mayhem that winter. For those of more broadly comic sensibilities – or who believe that if you want to really understand what a culture thinks about itself, you should look at what it laughs at – there was an ebullient and wildly popular Hollywood satire by the name of *The First Nudie Musical*, advertised by a poster featuring a pair of unfeasibly large breasts, which combined an undemanding storyline and set-piece songs with titles like 'Lesbian Butch Dyke' and 'Dancing Dildos' in a confection that packed New York's 68th Street Playhouse six times a day for four months.

Across the Atlantic, *Carry On England* – the twenty-eighth outing of the beloved *Carry On* franchise and, it has to be said, not its most distinguished – played out like a budget-conscious mash-up episode of *Dad's Army* and *It Ain't Half Hot Mum*. But despite, or because of this fact, it proved a genuinely and unapologetically lowbrow success.

Shot in the sagebrush desert around Lake Fenton, New Mexico, for a relatively lavish $3 million, David Bowie's star-making vehicle *The Man Who Fell to Earth* opened to generally warm notices that same month. There were barbs that the film's lead was typecast as the titular character whose mission ends in alcoholic ruin, although Bowie himself was in thrall just then not so much to the Bacchic rites as to half the cash crop of Bolivia. He somehow remained a very British sort of extraterrestrial, always or usually able to function on a practical level.

In that context, John Lennon was still then in the final phase of his extended 'lost weekend' and often to be seen driving around Los Angeles with his crew, drinking copious amounts of brandy and savouring the city's after-hours clubs. Ringo Starr, Mick Jagger, Keith Moon, Harry Nilsson and Bowie himself were all then resident in the city and were variously part of the ex-Beatle's entourage.

At around five one morning that January, Lennon drove everyone back to Bowie's rented home set amongst a row of identical Spanish-style bungalows with neatly manicured lawns on North Doheny Drive in Beverly Hills, where they watched the Thin White Duke get out of the car and stagger up the path to the front door. 'We drove off, and it turned out it wasn't Dave's house after all,' Nilsson later told me. 'He was sitting there all morning with some merchant banker and his wife.'

Later in the winter, Bowie moved to a lakeside home in the Montreux suburb of Blonay, where, had he so wished, he could look out of his bedroom window on a vista of whitewashed houses with steeply angled roofs and lush vineyards sloping down to the water, which was covered with a dove-blue haze. He never forgot how he was treated in Switzerland, where after breakfast most afternoons he liked to walk up the road outside his villa, where the dust raised by the passing wooden ox carts of local fruit pickers coated the leaves of the apple trees, or casually stroll around the nearby lake with his family, where no one ever hassled them. The tax break didn't hurt, either.

In the charts themselves, it was the season of Barry Manilow's 'I Write the Songs' and, proving its durability as an artistic theme, a large number of successive No. 1 hits with the word 'love' or its close variants in the title, among them 'Love Rollercoaster', 'Let Your Love Flow', 'Silly Love Songs', 'Love to Love You, Baby', Paul Simon's '50 Ways to Leave Your Lover' and the Miracles' 'Love Machine', with its rousing, if also slightly trade-specific chorus: 'My voltage regulator cools/When I'm standing next to you/Electricity starts to flow/And my indicator starts to glow, woo ...'

In the visual arts, there was the arrangement at London's Tate Gallery of 120 red-fire bricks displayed in two layers in a six-by-ten rectangle by the American minimalist sculptor Carl Andre, with the title 'Equivalent VIII', which provoked a lively debate about the proper function of a state-subsidised public artwork. One visitor to the Tate was sufficiently moved by what he saw as a decadent waste of taxpayers' money to throw blue liquid – later revealed as vegetable dye – over the piece. But even the furore over the bricks paled in comparison to the storm that blew up over the more obviously subversive 'Prostitution', on show across town at the Institute of Contemporary Arts. This featured a collage of syringes, bloody tampons and soiled knickers alongside various girlie-mag centrefolds, apparently the better to represent the precariousness of the female struggle for respect in 1970s Britain. Somehow unsurprisingly, this was not altogether to the taste of Nicholas Fairbairn, the 42-year-old Tory MP, known for his right-wing views and flamboyant Scottish baronial dress sense, with a pair of silver antique duelling pistols tucked under his tartan jacket, who denounced both 'Prostitution' and the culture that spawned it as 'wreckers of life' and 'the detritus of a once-proud society intent on destroying itself'.

There may not be much to detain us in Fairbairn's varied and always forthright opinions on the death-wish afflicting Western civilisation, but he surely spoke for many of his fellow Britons in 1976, who were either, according to taste, defenders of the remaining legacy of the Dunkirk Spirit and the illusion of continuing post-war unity or else the hopelessly Jurassic losers in a generational clash that had permanently moved the guardrails defining the limits of what constituted acceptable behaviour.

The Tate bricks are now conservatively valued at £4 million, and still on display in London. Carl Andre himself later stood trial for the murder of his third wife, a fellow artist who plunged to her death from a window of the couple's thirty-fourth-floor New York apartment after neighbours had reported hearing them arguing violently. His acquittal provoked an uproar among many of those in the art world who had previously championed him, some of whom, in turn, proceeded to vandalise his work wherever it was shown. It must have seemed to Andre that over the years he had managed to alienate both the public and his own natural constituency before he died in January 2024 at the age of 88.

***

The February 1976 Winter Olympics held in Innsbruck had a troubled history. Five years earlier, the Olympic organising committee had awarded the games to Denver, Colorado, but in the event, the city's bid team didn't have long to savour its success. Within days, the *Denver Post* had begun to ask awkward questions about the prospect of the effectively bankrupt city spending millions to construct the necessary infrastructure, including a vast refrigerated bobsled trough that would be used for eight days and then abandoned, as well as the inconvenient fact that the city's nearby Mount Sniktau, the venue for most of the competition's downhill skiing events, was in fact a windswept series of rocky crags more suitable to dirt-biking than alpine sports and almost completely devoid of snow by the latter part of each February. In a statewide referendum in November 1972, Colorado voters decisively rejected funding for the whole project, meaning that for the first and only time, a host city that had been awarded the Winter Games refused them. Three other cities in turn declined the honour, leaving Innsbruck – still with most of the facilities from the 1964 games it had hosted intact – to step forward.

The Soviet Union, East Germany and the United States respectively led the eventual medals table, although Britain struck gold in the form of the wonderfully fluid 'Nureyev of the ice', as 26-year-old Birmingham-born John Curry became known. Already in the lead after the first two rounds of his event, Curry skated a final programme that was judged flawless in its cool beauty of movement. There were three immaculate triple jumps, and the whole routine was a compelling blend of athletic grace and tribal musical interpretation.

Curry earned not only the gold medal and an OBE in that summer's honours list, but also a backlash in some quarters for revealing his homosexuality just before the Innsbruck Games began. While most press coverage was sympathetic, the *Daily Mail* thought the announcement 'stunning', which was mild compared to the views expressed in the peak-volume chants on the subject from the terraces of various British football stadiums. John Curry died of an AIDS-related heart attack in April 1994, aged 44.

★★★

Shortly after 8 o'clock on the otherwise mild Saturday evening of 5 October 1974, the sky over the core retail and residential area around Commercial Road in central Guildford, Surrey, was lit up by the flames of an explosion. The blast peeled off the front wall of the busy Horse and Groom pub on the corner of North Street, known to be popular with British Army personnel based at the nearby Pirbright Barracks. Four soldiers, three of them teenagers, and one civilian standing together at the bar were either killed outright or died of their injuries shortly afterwards. A second device exploded forty minutes later at the Seven Stars Hotel in central Guildford. The bar there had been hurriedly evacuated after the first blast while the manager and his wife searched the premises, and they, too, were badly injured. Both locations were scenes of the utmost devastation.

'Gaping holes and fallen masonry were everywhere,' says Ken Hiller, a local reporter who was one of the first to arrive at the Horse and Groom:

> Craters were packed so tightly together that the debris from one was piled against the rim of the next in a heap of rubble, wood, glass and twisted radiators. There wasn't an undamaged foot of space. Mounds of smashed

furniture, bottles, crockery, old framed photographs and bits of food were thrown around a sagging wreck of a building.

Some of the ensuing damage was almost surreal: the pub's darts board had been flung through the air to be embedded in what remained of the building's back wall, while the large clock behind the saloon bar had had its glass shattered but survived, the hours on its face showing like a skeleton.

A 19-year-old Royal Household Cavalry soldier named Alexander Findlay had been standing immediately next to his four fellow servicemen who perished. 'I saw a flash and heard a roar,' he recalled. 'It blew my eardrums out. I came to, and there was a live electric cable wrapped around my leg, which kept giving me violent shocks every few seconds. I couldn't move, and you couldn't see for the dust, the dirt and the smoke.'

The first emergency crews arrived on the scene some twelve minutes after the blast. A fireman named Andrew Saunders would remember that he and his colleagues had been 'giggling to ourselves on our way to the pub – we were so used to getting hoax calls we didn't believe it'. Saunders would be quickly disabused of any levity when he arrived to see the front of the building blown out and a man sitting on the road with blood gushing from a scalp wound. Inside, he found a gaping hole in the floor of what remained of the pub's lounge bar opening on to the cellar. Peering down, Saunders saw 'bodies lying among the rubble, and men and women who were experiencing torrential blood loss'. Sixty-six people were injured in the attacks, while a subsequent device thrown through the window of the Kings Arms pub in Woolwich, south London, the following Monday night, claimed another two lives and sent thirty-five victims to hospital.

On 4 March 1976, at the end of a six-week trial, a 40-year-old Irish-born woman living in north London named Anne Maguire was found guilty of handling the explosives that had been used in the twin Guildford bombings. Five other members of her family and one of their friends were also convicted and all seven were given sentences of between four and fourteen years. Passing judgement, Justice John Donaldson said, 'There can be no greater offence than this, for it strikes at the very root of the way of life for which generations have fought and, indeed, died to preserve.'

Chief Constable Peter Matthews, of Surrey Police, who led the investigation into the Guildford bombings, pronounced himself well satisfied, remarking, 'We are delighted with the result – these were the people we were after.' Mrs Maguire herself was less reconciled to the verdict, shouting, 'I'm innocent, you bastards!', among other unappreciative remarks, as she was carried away kicking and screaming from the dock. Fourteen years later, the convictions were quashed amid criticisms of the scientific evidence presented at the original trial, and in time, the defendants received both compensation and a public apology from the prime minister. An IRA cell had meanwhile claimed responsibility for the two Guildford bombs, but no one has since been charged with the crime.

Speaking in the House of Commons on 5 March 1976, the day after the Maguires' original sentencing at the Old Bailey, the Northern Ireland Secretary Merlyn Rees remarked:

> I believe the House will share the government's deep regret that the opportunity provided by the recent Constitutional Convention has not succeeded in its task of devising a workable system of government for Northern Ireland. My strongly held view is that there is no instant solution to the challenges of the province. Indeed, it would be a grave mistake to pretend otherwise … It is clearly not possible at this time to make progress towards a devolved system of peaceful government for Northern Ireland. The problem is intractable. Our immediate aim must be for a period of relative stability so that we may at least tackle the issue of criminality and unemployment in the region.

This was to put only the best possible face on the paralysing mutual hostility that characterised the government of Northern Ireland as much as its sectarian relations of the day. By early 1976, some people were beginning to wonder if Merlyn Rees was quite the right man to bring a new spirit of enterprise to the troubled province. Undoubtedly conscientious, he seemed to increasingly lose hope of reimposing any power-sharing initiative following the collapse of the Sunningdale Agreement in 1974, or for that matter any initiative at all, and was frequently in a state of utter despair at the resulting impasse.

Rees's proposed title for his Northern Ireland memoirs was *No Solution*. The publishers didn't find that appealing, but he insisted that it summed the situation up. In 1976, the various attempts to rationalise the affairs of the province continued to be a case of false dawns, disappointments and a grim sense of resignation conveyed in one minister's infamous but coldly realistic phrase that progress consisted in achieving 'an acceptable level of violence' in the area.

Meanwhile, the armed struggle on the British mainland continued. On 4 March, the same day the Maguire Seven were convicted at the Old Bailey, nine passengers were injured when a device exploded on the forecourt of London's busy Cannon Street Station. Lest their intentions not already be clear to the public, the IRA released an overnight statement, warning, 'You have given us the label of terrorists ... Now we will act as terrorists.'

Two more victims were lost to the intractable Irish troubles on 15 March, when a bomb exploded prematurely on the Tube at West Ham Station in east London. The bomber himself, a 36-year-old Republican from County Donegal named Vincent Donnelly, was still on board at the time, and before fleeing the scene turned to shoot dead the train's driver, Julius Stephen, a recent West Indian immigrant to Britain with a young son, who had left his cab to investigate. Donnelly then fled into the street and was confronted by a 24-year-old Post Office engineer named Peter Chalk, who was working nearby. Chalk was also shot and killed, the victim of someone else's war.

Donnelly was eventually cornered by several unarmed police officers in an alleyway. Realising he had no means of escape, he shouted, 'You English bastards!' and then turned the gun on himself and fired a single shot into his chest. Unlike his two victims, Donnelly survived his wounds and was later convicted of murder and given a life sentence. Released under the terms of the Good Friday Agreement in 1998, he died in his bed at the age of 80.

Less than a fortnight after Donnelly's killing spree on the Underground, it was the turn of the 8,000-strong crowd at the Ideal Home Exhibition in west London's Olympia to be targeted when a bomb left in a litter bin exploded in the middle of the busy Saturday afternoon of 27 March. It was a scene from hell. As the initial smoke of the blast cleared, the amplified voice of an Olympia official, not bothering to hide his note of alarm, could be heard coming over the loudspeaker system, ordering everyone to evacuate the building immediately. A stampede ensued.

At the top of the hall's main staircase a man lay on his back next to the scene of the explosion, with what was left of his legs propped up on a twisted shard of chair in someone's attempt to slow the spurting blood, while hundreds of exhibition-goers were screaming and struggling past him on their way down the stairs to one of the building's two exits. A passer-by named Phil Macready, rushing in the opposite direction to try and help, 'heard uproar' as people 'literally trampled over one another' to get out.

'Then the firemen arrived,' says Macready:

I heard one of them say that they had a defective map, or had read the map wrong, and had taken a wrong turning to get there. They immediately started spraying down the lobby with foam. People were slipping over as this stuff got underfoot. No one had a proper evacuation plan ... I heard someone shout that a second bomb had gone off, and that brought more panic. There was a ghastly noise going on the whole time, swelling up inside the hall. It was like the sound of cattle in an abattoir. It got louder and louder, until all of a sudden it was silent again. After that people just lay around on the pavement outside moaning, with their heads in their hands, some of them with bits of glass still stuck in their bodies. The police and ambulance crews seemed as stunned as the public were when they finally arrived.

A 79-year-old woman died and eighty-five other victims were injured, four of whom lost limbs, in the Olympia bombing.

Shortly after this incident, the first notices advising passengers to 'beware of bombs' and to 'report anything suspicious', the harbinger of today's 'See it, say it, sorted', began to appear in Britain's rail stations and other high-volume locations. At least some of our modern public security apparatus can be traced back to mid-1976. Whether our obsession with safety could be said to have fostered a climate of anxiety that makes people feel more insecure, not less, or that our everyday language has been debased by the promiscuous use of terms like 'existential', 'catastrophic' and 'irreversible' to inflate potential threats, is a discussion for another day.

★★★

Contention surrounding another area of state policy periodically distracted the press from the continuing terrorism crisis that month. Speaking in the House of Commons on 4 March, the increasingly beleaguered Chancellor Denis Healey did his best to cling to vestiges of his characteristic optimism when speaking about the overall state of the economy.

'It is true,' Healey was forced to admit, over the surrounding uproar:

... that the retail price index rose by 23.5 per cent over the past twelve months ... Yet year-on-year rates of inflation have now fallen for five successive months. There is clear evidence that the deceleration in price inflation has firmly established itself, and we should see a continuing modest but sustained fall in the next few months, as well as associated prospects for tangible benefits delivered to all British households.

There were millions of such households, even so, for whom it was far from a golden new dawn of economic prosperity. Healey knew this, although, his Commons statement of 19 February aside, he rarely said as much in his public speeches.

At the institutional level, the most potent symbol of Britain's seemingly imminent headlong plunge into the abyss was the regular series of flights taken by senior Treasury officials in order to discuss the terms of the UK's latest International Monetary Fund (IMF) bailout in Washington DC. By the mid-1970s, such loans had become a familiar option for developing nations in Africa but were still considered unusual for a major Western democracy. One remark doing the rounds, which was thought not to be entirely in jest, was that the IMF's lavish new Washington headquarters building was paid for by the interest on British debt.

'By [1976] we really had to say enough ... The Keynesian era of borrow and spend was over, and the only way forward for the country was to stop living in a permanent state of economic siege,' Healey once told me. 'It was getting to the point where we had to trim our sails – or else,' he added, raising his famously luxuriant eyebrows in emphasis. By then, the word 'stagflation', an unholy brew of recession and runaway prices, had also entered Healey's thinking. 'We had private meetings about what national bankruptcy might actually look like,' he admitted. 'Could we even survive as a sovereign country, or become a sort of 51st state of the USA?' And always lurking like a pantomime villain in the wings was the IMF, with its swingeing interest rates and host of other demands on the beneficiaries of its loans. It was fast turning into a mutually dependent and deeply troubled relationship that would become headline news around the world six months later.

In the meantime, there was the much-quoted editorial of the *Wall Street Journal*:

> The British economy ... is sinking ... Britain's current contribution to the world is to reveal the ultimate result of economic and social policies [which] insist that the state must fulfill all needs, and all income must be redistributed ... The result can only be still slower growth and still lower living standards for all the British, rich and poor alike. Goodbye, Great Britain, it was nice knowing you.

One direct result of the UK's malaise was seen in the figures chalked up everywhere from the new state-of-the-art electronic display at the London Stock

Exchange down to the humble high street kiosk showing the latest sterling exchange rate. In early 1974, £1 was typically worth in the $2.80–$3 range. By September 1975, the figure had slipped to around $2.40. In mid-March 1976, the rate was $1.85 and falling sharply on a daily, if not hourly, basis until coming close to the basement of dollar-to-pound parity later in the year. To keep the currency afloat, Healey and his colleagues were borrowing, not just from the IMF but from the central banks of more prosperous industrialised nations, some of whom had been the UK's mortal enemies just thirty years earlier. (For that matter, Healey himself had served with the Royal Engineers in Italy and was landing officer for the British Assault Brigade at Anzio in 1944, where he was known as a cool head under fire. Twice mentioned in dispatches, he was subsequently awarded the MBE.)

The plight of sterling also had direct consequences for British holiday-makers, whose horizons had broadened significantly from the vogue for caravanning along the coast of Devon and Cornwall or the time-honoured charms of a fortnight in a seaside guest house. The UK was clearly becoming a more continental country by 1976. More and more people drove German cars, went on package holidays to Spain, drank Italian wine or copied French fashions. But set amidst this comparative boom changing the traditional face of the British travel industry were two specific challenges facing the would-be transatlantic tourist. The first was that the pound in his or her pocket now bought only half the amount of local currency it had done just three years earlier. And the second was the fact that a regular scheduled return journey from London to New York on the newly coined British Airways would have cost something like £210 (or £1,600 in today's money), at a time when that represented nearly a month's worth of a working man's salary and six weeks' of a woman's.

The intending flier in 1976 might have heard of a 54-year-old Canterbury-born businessman named Freddie Laker, but not yet been able to take him up on his proposal to carry them across the Atlantic for only £32.50 each way in the winter and £37.50 in the summer. Laker was still then mired in the fifth of what proved to be a six-year attritional battle to be granted a licence to operate a no-booking, walk-on service to compete with that provided by British Airways and the major US carriers.

The latter did everything in their power to thwart this threat to their price cartel, but Laker was nothing if not tenacious. A lifelong aviation enthusiast, his big break had come in 1948 when a friend lent him £38,000 towards the £42,000 cost of buying a dozen war-surplus civilian versions of the

Halifax bomber, plus all their spares. Within weeks, the Soviet Union had imposed a total blockade on all traffic into Berlin. Laker had rapidly deployed his newly acquired fleet as part of the Anglo-American airlift to supply the city, and in later years always fondly remembered how he had made his first money by carrying food and medicine on his planes' outward flights and filling the empty seats with strapped-in dead bodies on their return. Laker's first 'Skytrain' service between London's Gatwick and New York's JFK finally took off in September 1977 – and collapsed again in 1982.

Back on *terra firma*, the Britain of early 1976 often seemed to be one of an unrelenting struggle for existence. The mid-1970s were in some ways the nation's low tide. Not since the Great Depression had the country been so wracked with economic and social strife, most obviously characterised by soaring prices and the near-daily terrorist outrages, or 'spectaculars', as they were sometimes euphemistically known. To Kingsley Amis, it was a time of 'shabby trains and surly shopkeepers, and towns whose names were a byword for dullness and decorum'.

But the decade was also paradoxically, in some ways, the UK consumer's finest hour. Colour television sets outsold black-and-white ones for the first time in 1976. A state-of-the-art model like the popular Bush BC went for around £220, along with the annual £18 licence which allowed the subscriber to watch all of three terrestrial channels, with the exciting introduction of a rolling-news 'Teletext' service on both BBC and ITV starting that autumn.

There was a similar advance in the world of computers. Up until now, these had generally been vast, family refrigerator-shaped devices, full of flashing lights and rapidly spinning and reversing spools of magnetic tape, as opposed to something you could casually extract from your pocket every few moments. But there was a significant development that winter with the simultaneous introduction of no fewer than three competing models – the Apple II, the Commodore PET and Tandy Corporation's TRS-80 – any of which could easily fit on someone's home or office desk, if admittedly costing $1,200, or around £6,500 in today's terms, a price that, like the pound itself, would fall rapidly in the months ahead. Hitherto largely the preserve of university science labs or the more go-ahead commercial offices, the basic PC would now go on to become part of the fabric of everyday life, and as such, a milestone down the road to the essentially solitary work environment many of us know today.

In another major lifestyle shift, millions of people were increasingly concentrating their shopping excursions into one weekly trip to the nearest supermarket, as opposed to popping down to a local outlet that was, as often as not, staffed by two or three elderly, dyspeptic men in aprons, had sawdust on the floor and closed early each Thursday. In particular, north London's Brent Cross Centre, opened by Prince Charles on 2 March 1976, brought a touch of a distinctly American retail experience across the Atlantic. Set on a sprawling 55-acre site decorated in brutalist shades of sludge and grey, Brent Cross provided 'coatless shopping' in a climate-controlled maze of corridors lined by dozens of gaudily lit outlets that only rarely seemed to run out of stock and which stayed open until after five in the afternoon. Something about the basic proposition of the place must have commended itself to the British consumer as the way of the future, because it still attracts an annual 13 million visitors today.

'IS EVERYTHING ALL RIGHT, HAROLD?'

There were strange scenes in and around the House of Commons on the evening of Wednesday, 10 March 1976, following yet another debate on the matter of whether the Labour Party was in fact the vehicle of full-blooded socialism or merely of moderate social democracy, at whose conclusion the Chancellor of the Exchequer had invited his critics to go fuck themselves. It also happened to be the eve of Harold Wilson's 60th birthday and, leaving the jeers and catcalls of the Chamber behind him, the premier and his Foreign Secretary James Callaghan drove off to attend a party hosted by Wilson's publisher friend, George Weidenfeld.

Feeling the burden of conversation fell on him since the prime minister was in one of his Trappist moods, Callaghan, a keen sportsman, opened by remarking cheerily that the West Indian bowlers seemed to have done all right in their Test match that day with India. Wilson said nothing. After a further minute or two of heavy silence, the premier then suddenly turned to his ministerial colleague and, eschewing the matter of the cricket, briskly informed him that he had decided to resign from office as soon as Monday of the following week.

No one else in the Cabinet knew of the decision for the next five days, during which Wilson narrowly survived a no-confidence motion in his leadership, triggered by his handling of the public spending crisis, at which point the prime minister belatedly let Denis Healey in on the secret by summoning him into the small gents' lavatory outside the Cabinet Room in Downing Street. It was vital to restore confidence in the government, Wilson said, and this could not be done without a change of leadership. He told the Chancellor that his decision in the matter was final.

Healey was not best pleased to subsequently learn that Callaghan, his primary rival in the race to replace Wilson, had been given a five-day head start in the matter. By the night of 15 March, the whole elaborate court of senior political colleagues and, more narrowly, personal aides and advisers, as incalculable as that of any oriental sultanate, was rife with intrigue and gossip as to their chief's future. Joe Haines, the government's Principal Press Secretary, was 'broadly aware that an announcement of some sort might be in the works', while Haines's deputy, Janet Hewlett-Davies was on grounds well beyond this, having been told of the prime minister's plans as they lay in bed together at his official country residence, Chequers, on the Saturday night of 6 March, while Mary Wilson was away flat-hunting in London. Several of the senior permanent civil service also knew of the decision, or had heard the rumours, while to others it came as a bolt from the blue. Wilson had briefed his Home Secretary Roy Jenkins on the evening of the 15th, only after ushering their Cabinet colleague Tony Benn, the Tribunite who publicly opposed the government's spending cuts, out the front door of No. 10 following another heated exchange of views on the subject.

Benn therefore knew nothing definite about Wilson's plans, although he later admitted that he had heard 'a strong rumour that a crisis might be brewing, and that this had to do with the theft of some prime ministerial papers that might cause a scandal'. He was also too astute not to realise that he was being ushered out of the Downing Street door that evening for a reason.

After parting from his colleague in this way, Wilson had taken Roy Jenkins into a little-used den next to No. 10's downstairs reception room and briefed him, too, on his decision to quit. The prime minister then stepped back into the building's central corridor, shook Jenkins's hand and wished him luck, before turning to his left to enter his Private Secretary's adjacent office.

The first person to greet him there was Tony Benn, who, in a scene that could have been torn from the script of an episode of *Yes, Minister*, had swiftly walked around the corner and entered No. 10 by the back door while Wilson and Jenkins had been in conference. 'Is everything all right, Harold?' Benn enquired solicitously. 'You seemed to me not quite yourself when we parted just now.'

Benn later told me that his sudden reappearance on the scene had served only to add to Wilson's apparent distress, manifested in an unnerving calm. 'He grunted at me and turned on his heel, as though not wanting to lose his cool in public.' Perhaps it was just a case of the increasingly infirm Wilson being weary of the whole circuslike business of continuing to lead the country while simultaneously navigating the rocks of his own party's ideological civil war. As Benn observed, 'Harold seemed to just grow colder and colder and colder.'

***

On 11 November 1965, a 46-year-old former RAF pilot named Ian Smith, who had served for the previous twelve years as Prime Minister of Rhodesia, broadcast a rousing proclamation to the country's 8 million citizens that was modelled broadly on the American Declaration of Independence. In the course of his address, Smith remarked that it was an 'inalienable and historic truth' that his country had enjoyed de facto self-rule since 1923, claimed that 'Rhodesians of every stripe' now supported their government's request for unilateral independence (UDI) from Westminster and deplored the fact that an 'effete cabal' sitting 5,000 miles away should persist in 'maintaining an unwarranted jurisdiction ... to the detriment of the future peace, prosperity and wellbeing of Rhodesia'.

Smith further declared that in the opinion of his ruling Rhodesian Front Party, 'procrastination and delay will injure the very fabric of our nation', and it was essential that 'our people now immediately obtain their sovereign independence, the justice of which is beyond question'. Annexed to his proclamation was a new constitution that formally severed British responsibility for Rhodesia's affairs. Smith later told his nation in the rhapsodic terms of politicians immemorial, 'We have struck a blow for universal justice, civilisation and Christianity ... We will maintain our independence [as] a beacon light of liberty for all humanity.'

Shorn of some of its revivalist rhetoric, Smith's essential message to the Rhodesian people was that he and his ministerial colleagues were painfully aware of the 'wind of change' and the rapid decolonisation of Africa going on all around them, and had declared UDI as a means to delay the transition to majority rule by an indigenous black population that outnumbered the country's whites by a ratio of fourteen to one. As a result, two African nationalist parties immediately launched an armed insurgency against the Smith regime, resulting in a series of paramilitary clashes not wholly dissimilar in tone to the IRA struggle on the British mainland and characterised by acts of medieval barbarity on all sides. If the Rhodesian people were never the participants in an officially declared war, their sufferings were at least as great as those involved in the contemporaneous US 'police action' in Vietnam.

Tim Peech, a 31-year-old farmer from the Macheke District, east of the state capital Salisbury, was a third-generation Rhodesian who believed that white settlers like himself could stay, survive and prosper in what would inevitably become a black-ruled country. A vocal critic of Smith's policies, Peech went on to organise several meetings with Macheke's tribal chiefs to work out a *modus vivendi* with black nationalist guerrillas in the region. While travelling through the outlying bush on one of his peace missions in 1976, he was waylaid and clubbed to death by the irregular troops with whom he had sought dialogue. One of Peech's companions had remonstrated with the freedom fighters standing over his friend's fallen body, which they said was that of a 'white gangster'. The horrified witness said, 'Surely you know he was trying to make peace with you?'

They sneered, 'We did it just for fun.'

Tim Peech left behind an American-born wife, Michela, as well as a young son and a daughter.

By the spring of 1976, the Rhodesian standoff had devolved into a war of political and military attrition, and as such, an irresistible temptation for the rulers of the Soviet Union. In the post-war years, the USSR's commitment to the ideal of an international class struggle – or, if you prefer, its paranoia-fuelled territorial megalomania – had pulled it into parts of the world that, by any objective calculation of interests, could hardly have been considered vital. On 4 March, the UK's Ambassador in Washington, Peter Ramsbotham, conveyed his government's concerns in the matter to Henry Kissinger.

'The position [in Rhodesia] has marched on for the worse. As David Ennals [head of the foreign office's Rhodesia desk] said yesterday, there has been massive communist infiltration. We are anxious about a racial war, too. The situation is volatile in the extreme.'

In his reply, Kissinger characteristically took the opportunity to assess the bigger picture of Rhodesia, which he depicted as yet another pawn in a global Cold War orchestrated by the Moscow presidium and their surrogates in Havana:

I can tell you that, in spite of the possible outcry here, we will not accept any more Soviet or Cuban intervention in Africa. The consequences for the region, and, I might say, for the South Americans, for the Caribbeans – including Britain's black Caribbean possessions – of a victorious Marxist army having won will be extremely serious. We can't have a Marxist-Cuban army marching all over Africa.

A fortnight later, the UK government announced a new proposal to pre-empt the spectre of any 'malevolent' third-party interference in Rhodesia, calling instead for a precise timetable for majority rule in the colony within twenty-four months.

Speaking that same night at a conference of the World Affairs Council in Dallas, Kissinger praised the British initiative as 'most constructive' but coupled this with a warning to any 'Marxist-inspired adventuring' in the area. 'American cooperation is not available to those who rely on foreign troops,' Kissinger continued, perhaps discreetly ignoring certain of his nation's own recent armed excursions around the world. 'The United States cannot acquiesce indefinitely in the presence of expeditionary forces in distant lands for the purpose of pressure and to determine those countries' political evolution by force of arms.' Within twenty-four hours, Ian Smith turned down the British initiative.

The Rhodesian question also rekindled other issues involving superpower relations and their proxy battles around the world. By mid-1976, the 69-year-old Leonid Brezhnev had developed serious health problems which made it difficult for him to grasp the nuances of strategic arms control, let alone such matters as the fine detail of Soviet–American wheat quotas that even competent political brains struggled to master. Taking their lead from the SALT treaty signed in May 1972, the continuing multilateral disarmament talks in Vienna sought to ban new offensive missile construction programmes, while leaving each major Cold War combatant with a generous stockpile of existing rockets capable of destroying the planet in a nuclear Armageddon.

In the midst of the discussions, Brezhnev – or, if not him, the upper echelons of the Soviet military complex – saw fit to position a new and potentially devastating intermediate-range missile, the SS-20, aimed at London and other targets in Western Europe. The quest for this 'additional degree of national self-defence', as the ailing Soviet supremo put it, in a written statement that, again, possibly owed some of its deeper logic to others, was 'a legitimate reinforcement of the [USSR's] national security provisions', representing merely 'a first step in the direction of ensuring equilibrium on the continent', and in effect, no more than a 'prudent readjustment of the [existing] balance of power in that hemisphere to assure the continued and untroubled harmonious existence of the peoples of the Soviet Union and their fraternal comrades'.

Meanwhile, the arsenal of 440 of the highly mobile SS-20s, which could be transported on the back of a modified army lorry and fired with pinpoint accuracy at targets up to 4,000 miles away, was met in turn by the US deployment of the LGM-118 Peacekeeper or MX intercontinental missile system, which itself could be rapidly moved around on 'racetracks', or long oval roadways, in a sort of high-stakes shell game initiated against watching Soviet spy satellites. Each MX came equipped with twelve separate re-entry vehicles, and each of these was armed by a 300-kiloton warhead (twenty times greater than the destructive force of the device that had been dropped on Hiroshima). No wonder, perhaps, that the prevailing strategy at the heart of the precarious nuclear balance of power as it existed in 1976 went by the name of Mutual Assured Destruction, or MAD.

★★★

Two poignant stories took a grip on the US public's imagination in the winter of 1976. The first was the pitiable case of 21-year-old Karen Ann Quinlan, a New Jersey high-school graduate who had recently left her family home in Roxbury Township, about 40 miles outside New York, to move in with a group of roommates said to have been broadly disillusioned by the older generation. The young woman had lapsed into a coma after a night out with friends at a local bar, where she consumed an injudicious mix of alcohol and pills.

In a landmark lawsuit filed on 12 September 1975, Quinlan's grieving parents asked a judge to allow the hospital ventilator apparently keeping their daughter alive to be disconnected because there was no hope she would ever recover. The judge demurred, but in a 7–0 decision announced on 31 March 1976, the New Jersey Supreme Court ruled that Karen Quinlan's interest in having her life-support systems removed exceeded the state's interest in preserving her life as long as medical authorities saw 'no other reasonable alternative' to successfully treating her. Following the decision, Quinlan was transferred to a local nursing home, where she defied medical opinion by continuing to breathe unaided while receiving food through a tube inserted in her nose.

Unlike the 'sleeping beauty' image depicted in newspaper articles and impressionistic artists' sketches, however, Quinlan did not rest peacefully. As time went on, her body began to display distinct patterns. She would thrash wildly at times and turn her head violently away from visiting doctors and nurses seeking to feed or bathe her, all the while unable to otherwise communicate or respond. Once an athletic young woman, who liked to swim and dance, her weight dropped to a skeletal 65lb as she lay, largely in the foetal position, with no expression on her face other than a recurrent frown.

The plight of Karen Ann Quinlan triggered a debate about the ultimate definition of human existence which consumed the press and public in the United States and beyond. As a result, ordinary people found themselves wrestling with fundamental questions of life and death, as medical and legal issues merged with those of ethics and theology. To some, it was only logical that this was a case for the compassionate exercise of 'judicious neglect', in which doctors quietly accede to the private pleas of relatives of pain-ridden or terminally ill patients and discontinue extraordinary measures to keep them alive. There were equally robust arguments by others who were opposed to the death-with-dignity school, a position one or two of them illustrated by daubing the Quinlans' front door with red paint.

In time, the family's local Catholic priest became involved, reminding critics that Church teachings, including a declaration on the subject by Pope Pius XII in 1957, held that there was no moral obligation to continue every means to sustain life when there was no realistic hope of the patient's recovery, and indeed, to do so might be considered a form of the cruel and unusual punishment proscribed by the US Constitution's Bill of Rights.

The whole tragic episode spawned headlines, sermons, marches, books, scholarly articles, made-for-TV movies and singularly tasteless late-night talk show jokes, and if nothing else, forced millions of people around the world to consider the question of what should be considered a viable human life.

Karen Ann Quinlan died of respiratory failure, brought on by acute pneumonia, on 11 June 1985, at the age of 31, more than a decade after she had first slipped into a vegetative state. Her case remains a landmark in the continuing debate about whether any of us should be allowed to die with dignity or, instead, be called on to endure what might be the unendurable.

The other somehow quintessentially American tragedy in March 1976 involved a well-regarded 39-year-old Foreign Service Officer named Bradford Bishop. By all accounts, he was one of those individuals – again a peculiarly American phenomenon – who seem to have it all, in material terms, and yet go spectacularly wrong. A native of Pasadena, California, Bishop had graduated with honours from Yale University before serving in the US Army as a counterintelligence operative. He spoke six languages fluently, wrote unpublished but accomplished novels for his own amusement, travelled widely, enjoyed good food and fine wine, dressed well, kept himself trim and sported a full head of wavy brown hair along with piercing blue eyes, a cleft chin and an unfortunate habit, so natural he was apparently unaware of it, of tossing back his head so that he could seem to be looking down his nose at people.

Bishop was prodigiously clever and knew it, and may well have considered his latest role as an assistant in the Division of Special Activities and Commercial Treaties at the State Department's headquarters in Washington to have been beneath one of his learning and attainments in life. 'Worrying about the translation of contracts for manganese shipments from some tyrant king in Ghana', as he put it in a letter written to a former Yale classmate named Tom McKinnon.

Bishop's home life was also a matter of concern, his wife Annette and his widowed, live-in mother Lobelia both apparently complaining to him that he was treading water in his career. After he had been passed over for a promotion he was expecting that winter, Lobelia wrote to him, 'My own boy, I am making a mother's loving plea for you. It is that you stand up and finally let the world hear of you.' Surely few maternal prayers can have been as hideously answered as this one was.

On the warm Monday afternoon of 1 March 1976, Bishop calmly told his State Department secretary that he was feeling unwell and planned to go home early for the day. A colleague named Roy Harrell saw him walking towards his car a few minutes later and said that he had looked agitated – 'grim, pale, really striding out, tie flapping over his shoulder, looking like the model in a headache commercial'.

The authorities believe that Bishop then drove to his nearby bank, where he withdrew several hundred dollars, before stopping at a hardware store to buy a carpenter's hammer, a shovel, a pitchfork, some plastic sheeting and a large petrol can. Somehow, this particular combination of goods rarely bodes well, either for the purchaser or their immediate circle.

No one is quite sure what Bishop did for the next two hours, although one plausible theory is that he visited a prostitute of his acquaintance in her apartment on Nebraska Avenue in north-west Washington, about halfway between his office and his family home in suburban Bethesda, Maryland. It later emerged that he was a regular patron there, and had frequently strayed from the monogamous ideal, usually with strangers, but sometimes with the wife or partner of a work colleague. Even so, the criminal profilers at the FBI and several other agencies have failed to find a plausible psychosexual theory to explain his actions that day – they may have been cold-blooded.

Arriving home shortly before eight that night, Bishop appears to have first walked into the living room, where his wife Annette was sitting reading a book, and promptly bludgeoned her to death with the hammer. Following that, he went upstairs and similarly slaughtered each of his three sons, aged between 5 and 14, who were thought to have been watching television in their shared bedroom and thus might not have been aware of the sounds from below. Retracing his steps to the living room, Bishop apparently sat down next to his wife's dead body and waited patiently until his mother returned from walking the family dog, and then repeatedly struck her with the hammer, hitting her about the face and neck with such force as to all but decapitate her. Police speculate that Bishop then loaded the bodies of his five victims into the family station wagon and drove through the night to a densely wooded swamp about 280 miles away in Columbia, North Carolina, where he dug a shallow pit in which he lay the corpses side by side and then set them ablaze with petrol.

It was more than a week before, alerted by a concerned neighbour, the authorities called at the home in Bethesda to discover evidence of an obvious homicidal rampage. The five victims' partly burned bodies were unearthed a few days later, and a subsequent search turned up the empty station wagon abandoned some 200 miles away in the car park at the foot of a popular hiking trail leading up to the Appalachian Way in eastern Tennessee.

There has been no credible explanation as to what became of Bishop himself, other than that he possibly took advantage of his State Department passport to slip away and start a new life overseas, quite likely in one of the several Western European countries whose language he spoke. 'A bulletin went out to all points', Clarence Kelley, the Director of the FBI reported in a memo circulated to the US Justice Department on 12 April 1976. 'But suspect [had] escaped at the last moment.'

As with other high-profile disappearances, there have been numerous reported sightings of Bishop over the years, some of them more credible than others. In January 1979, he was apparently spotted by none other than Roy Harrell, the State Department colleague who had last seen him on the day of the murders, standing next to him at the urinal of a restaurant bathroom in Sorrento, Italy. When Harrell greeted his heavily bearded neighbour eye to eye, asking him, 'Hey, you're Brad Bishop, aren't you?', the other party responded in an 'instantly recognisable' voice, 'Oh no', and fled the scene. If true, this would seem to qualify as one of those coincidences shunned by writers of detective fiction but quite prevalent in real life.

In March 2021, a 63-year-old American woman learnt through a DNA test that Bishop was her biological father, meaning that she would have been born at around the same time he had married Annette. Perhaps the key to the whole mystery lies in the perpetrator's complicated private life, or perhaps it was just one of those unfathomable cases in which an apparently well-adjusted individual snaps with such tragic results, becoming what criminologists call a moral atavist, whose primal hunting instincts are no longer moderated by the more conditioned parts of the brain.

Another theory about Bishop's disappearance is that he had shot himself in a belated fit of remorse while wandering around in the Kenyan jungle in the belief that his remains would be consumed by lions – coincidentally or not, a plot device of the British author Berkeley Gray's 1957 potboiler *Conquest After Midnight*, a copy of which was found in Bishop's bookcase. Others believe that he underwent plastic surgery and is still alive today at the age of 89. For Lobelia Bishop, who had always wanted her son to be famous, it might possibly have come as a macabre and posthumous case of wish fulfilment.

THE BLIND MAN ON THE CORNER

On 16 March, in a dramatic gesture, Harold Wilson resigned, telling the nation that he was finished in public life. When the moment came, Wilson informed his Cabinet ministers, most of whom listened to the announcement in shocked silence, that he wanted to go out on top and to make way for a younger colleague (in the event, his successor would be four years older than he was), but he denied the timing of his announcement was specifically linked to the 60th birthday he had celebrated just five days earlier.

On television, Wilson assured his fellow citizens that he was leaving them in robust economic health, although this might have come as news to the currency traders who continued to monitor the pound's downhill progress against the dollar, or the grandees at the Bank of England who had just committed a third of their reserves in a failed bid to support sterling – or, for that matter, the ordinary British consumer still dealing with the day-to-day reality of Weimar-level inflation. Several of the more cynical press commentators referred to Wilson's reputation for deviousness, suggesting there must be a hidden agenda involved, although in the midst of the speculation there was at least grudging respect for his obvious managerial skills so deftly exercised over the course of thirteen years as party leader. 'An incomparable political stunt man,' Bernard Levin called him in *The Times*, who had 'ridden the two bareback horses of Labour Left and Labour Right simultaneously'.

As we've seen, Wilson's departure wasn't entirely illogical, given the pervasive sense of ennui that had increasingly characterised his premiership since last returning to office, let alone the rumours of his fading physical or mental health. Even the prime minister's staunchest supporters had been forced to acknowledge the contrast between the superbly efficient technocrat of ferocious energy and command of even the finest policy detail of the mid-1960s and the stooped, prematurely old man before them now. Wilson seemed to have aged by far more than ten years in that decade. Ken Stowe, the outgoing PM's private secretary, later told a journalist that by 1976, 'Harold had lost both his enthusiasm and his spontaneity, and he wouldn't even receive people in No. 10 without being given a full written text of what he had to say', while less sympathetic observers wondered about excessive brandy intake and failing powers of concentration.

Within four years of leaving office, Wilson would be diagnosed with both bowel cancer and the advanced stages of dementia, and could sometimes be seen wandering in the streets around his London flat or sitting vacant-eyed on a bench in nearby Vincent Square between the homeless people who gathered there.

Most parties, pro and anti, agree that there was a detectable air of *fin de régime* decay about the Wilson administration in the early weeks of 1976, with Wilson himself a sadly diminished figure presiding over an inept and sexually incontinent cabal of cronies, as gleefully satirised in *Private Eye*. An immutable rule of politics seems to suggest that flagrant mistakes can be patched up, individual foibles and even crimes forgiven over time, mere marital indiscretions excused and every other form of moral lapse – bribery, nepotism, falsification of official documents on which hang matters of war and peace – all these can be overcome. But never the point at which an elected leader is revealed as a prize buffoon. There's simply no coming back from there.

A darker explanation also suggested itself for Wilson's departure, one which portrayed him as the victim of a prolonged black-ops campaign conducted by rogue elements in the British security forces in cahoots with like-minded operatives in the United States and South Africa. This might have been dismissed as a mere fantasy on the part of the more imaginative end of Fleet Street, but for the fact that the rumours had one important and singularly well-placed backer: Wilson himself, who frequently complained, both before and after his resignation, that Britain's clandestine services had used their privileged position to seek to influence public opinion against him and ultimately to replace him with a figure they deemed more congenial to the national interest.

The MI5 officer Peter Wright would recall in his memoir *Spycatcher* that towards the end of 1975, he approached senior colleagues in his department's 'K' branch with the proposal that they confront their head of government with evidence of his alleged communist sympathies, if not his direct ties to the Soviet presidium, with the aim of forcing him out. No one has ever produced compelling proof of any such treasonable activity on Wilson's part, although there's plenty of innuendo to that effect. Might he have been indiscreet in his dealings with, for instance, Joe Kagan, the raincoat manufacturer widely thought to enjoy the company of Eastern Bloc intelligence officials? Or what of the curious affair of Wilson's widely travelled former minister and friend, John Stonehouse, who in November 1974 vanished from a Miami beach and remained missing, presumed drowned, for several weeks? (Stonehouse was eventually found in Australia, where he was arrested and flown back to the UK to face fraud charges, along with persistent questions about his apparently close connections with both Wilson and the Czech security services.)

Again, it might all have qualified merely as the sort of ill-sourced gossip that accumulates around political power, but if so, there was some suggestion that it served to fuel what was either a rampant case of paranoia, or salutary disquiet, at No. 10 itself. Wilson's Consumer Affairs Minister Shirley Williams would tell a journalist of a moment late on in the administration:

> Harold took me into the Cabinet chamber. And he pointed to a beam that ran across the room. And he said, 'Look.' I looked up, and there was some sort of peculiar-looking bump. And I said, 'Yes?' And he said, 'That's a bug. They're bugging me.' So I said, 'Really, Harold?' And he said, 'Absolutely. They're listening to everything I say. And they're determined to get me out.'

Again, Wilson's comments could possibly be dismissed as the ramblings of an exhausted mind, but for the fact of the extraordinary interview he went on to give two BBC reporters, Barrie Penrose and Roger Courtiour, shortly after leaving office. Portraying himself as the victim of a carefully orchestrated smear campaign by members of MI5 working hand in glove with US and South African operatives, the discussion soon took an unusual turn. When asked what he saw as his political legacy, instead of the traditional platitudes about peace and prosperity, Wilson said:

I see myself as a spider in the corner of the room. A big fat spider ...
Sometimes I speak when I'm asleep ... You should both listen. Occasionally
when we meet I might tell you to go to Charing Cross Road and kick a blind
man standing on the corner. That blind man may tell you something, lead
you somewhere ...

It remains unclear if this was a striking example of the ex-premier's gift for
puckish allusion and metaphor, or else proof of a once-agile mind that had
been driven more than half-mad under the strains of office.

The following year, Wilson went on to tell a royal commission investigating illegal activities by the press that he and his family had suffered no fewer
than seven burglaries in the early part of 1976. If true, this seems high, even by
the notorious standards of London property theft. He also believed that the
same forces arrayed against him were part of the campaign to smear Jeremy
Thorpe, whose name had recently been linked to a mysterious dog-shooting
incident on a lonely road in Exmoor, which was the prelude to a more sensational charge against the soon-to-resign Liberal leader of attempting to
solicit the murder of his homosexual lover. Wilson was sufficiently moved to
write personally on 12 February 1976 to the new head of the CIA, George
Bush, to enquire whether his agency was in the habit of employing men in
balaclava masks to infiltrate the home of the elected head of a friendly nation
under cover of night. It was a suggestion that caused enough alarm in official Washington circles for Bush to promptly fly the Atlantic to assure both
Wilson and others that this was not the case.

'Harold had a well-developed sense of paranoia,' his Trade Minister Peter
Shore later remarked:

There are politicians who like to go out and press the flesh and draw a large
crowd of friends and admirers around them – the name Bill Clinton comes
to mind – and there are others of more solitary approach. Harold was always
a loner and liked to think of himself as such. This bred a fondness for secrecy
and furtiveness, not to mention a raging persecution complex if things
went wrong.

Was Wilson truly the object of a vast, worldwide security service conspiracy to
force him from office on the basis that he was a closet Marxist, not to be trusted
with Britain's economic affairs or, for that matter, the nation's nuclear button?
Probably not, seems to be the answer, although there was enough cynical talk

and disloyal activity by individual actors to significantly darken the mood at No. 10 during the already fraught final days of Wilson's tenure there.

A further blow to Wilson's reputation for probity followed with the release on 1 June of the traditional PM's resignation honours list. Of the forty-two names published in the *London Gazette*, half a dozen leapt from the page. There was the promotion of Sir Joe Kagan, for one, into Baron Kagan of Elland, while the property developer Eric Miller, who committed suicide the following year while under police investigation for fraud, was knighted. To the dismay of Wilson's left-wing colleagues, several other robustly unapologetic exponents of free enterprise were similarly elevated. Perhaps the most notorious name was that of James Goldsmith, the buccaneering financier who had quite coincidentally just offered Wilson's friend Marcia Williams, herself now styled Lady Falkender, a directorship of his Cavenham Foods, the owner of Bovril and a host of other well-known household brands. More than 100 Labour MPs publicly disassociated themselves from the list, while Edith Summerskill, Wilson's own appointee to head the honours scrutiny committee, felt moved to break the normal bounds of confidentiality and tell *The Times* that she and her colleagues:

> ... were astounded when we read some of the names ... We told the civil servant present that we could not approve at least half of the list, and would he see that this was conveyed to the prime minister ... It astonished us to then find that, with one exception, the original list of recipients was published unchanged.

In a subplot to the whole furore, it was later reported that the list itself had been drawn up in Marcia Williams's handwriting on pastel notepaper, with a few corrections pencilled in by Wilson, which duly allowed the 'lavender list' to enter the language as shorthand for official sleaze.

The suspicion remains that at least some of those named were chosen as much as a reward for past favours to the outgoing administration as for their selfless devotion to the public welfare. In the words of Wilson's biographer Ben Pimlott, 'It was a bad mistake, an error of judgement by a weary man who no longer cared as much as he once did about the feelings of his erstwhile supporters.'

The Cabinet held immediately following Wilson's resignation announcement listened politely to a long recitation of his many achievements in office, and in return dutifully recorded its collective appreciation for his years of untiring public service before moving on to other matters. To judge by his personal copy of the agenda, the prime minister himself devoted much of the two-hour session to doodling a series of caricatures of footballers on the paper in front of him, further evidence, perhaps, of the aptness of his decision to quit.

There was, however, at least one prescient note recorded in the minutes when it came to a discussion of the simmering dispute over the Falkland Islands, where the somewhat chaotic Argentinian government of Isabel Perón, itself to fall the following week in a military coup, had recently revisited the matter of the distant archipelago's sovereignty:

> The secretary of state for defence [Roy Mason] said that our garrison in the Falklands, consisting of no more than a force of 37 marines, would be quite unable to withstand a determined Argentinian assault. Nor could a sudden Argentine move against the area be countered by reinforcement. Apart from South American airfields, which would be denied to us, the nearest usable landing zone was over 3,000 miles away at Ascension Island. There was an airstrip at Port Stanley but this was short and had only the most rudimentary facilities. To defend or recapture the islands in the face of the efficient Argentinian navy would require a minimum of a brigade group, some 5,000 strong, supported by a naval force which would have to include HMS *Ark Royal* … The view of the defence and overseas policy committee was that we should not be drawn into a major and possibly ruinous military commitment of this kind.

After that, all that remained was the matter of Wilson or his secretaries writing a personalised farewell message to ninety-four overseas heads of government. This was no small task in those largely pre-automated days when Bill Gates was still a 20-year-old Harvard maths undergraduate moonlighting in a start-up company he called Micro-Soft, and letters like Wilson's were laboriously banged out by a woman with a furniture-sized Imperial typewriter with a bottle of Tippex by her side.

As usual in the corridors of power, there was the side of government that involved well-intentioned and sometimes even quite intelligent people, who were doing their best to bring a degree of order to a uniquely turbulent world, and then there was the minutiae of whether a particular foreign leader should be addressed as 'Dear Friend' or 'Dear Colleague' or some other variant, and whether to 'affirm' or merely to 'note' the phrasing of some previous exchange of views between them. Not untypical of the general spirit of the exercise was the minute of 18 March sent by the Permanent Under-Secretary at the Foreign Office to Wilson's private office at Downing Street:

1. Three of the farewell letters which the Prime Minister signed contain errors which should, I think, be corrected. I therefore return the letters in question.

2. The first mistake is our fault. Colonel Acheampong in Accra promoted himself to General a couple of weeks ago, and the advice which we offered you about this was therefore wrong.

3. The other two mistakes are typing errors. Some otters have crept into the message to Nyere, and the record seems to have stuck in a groove in the penultimate line of the second paragraph of the message to Tonga, giving the PM's views on the strength of the Commonwealth a somewhat dying fall.

Most of the international reaction to Wilson's valete was at least respectful, and sometimes effusively warm. It was obvious now that even conservative-leaning leaders around the world esteemed this one-time socialist firebrand and champion of state corporatism in a way that few observers had ever suspected. The departing premier was valued, liked and admired. With a few notable exceptions, the world treated Wilson with a respect that was as exaggerated as, a week earlier, it would have been astonishing. Oliver Wright, Britain's Ambassador to West Germany, wrote to No. 10:

Chancellor Schmidt was at the regular Tuesday afternoon meeting of his parliamentary party when the cable about your resignation arrived, but he received me immediately it was over. 'This is a sad occasion,' the chancellor remarked as I entered his room, and sighed deeply after he had read your message. Interestingly, a few minutes earlier he had been on the phone to [French president] Giscard D'Estaing, and said that Giscard's reaction had been 'That's typical of the man. He has just had a success averting a no-confidence vote, and then he resigns.'

In Washington, Henry Kissinger wrote on the night of 16 March:

Dear Harold ... The announcement of your decision to retire has left me with a profound sense of loss ... In addition to the privilege of being associated with you in political life, I have always considered you a close personal friend as well and have had, throughout these many years, tremendous respect and admiration for your vision, dedication and leadership. We will miss you.

In assessing Kissinger's remarks, psychologists might possibly argue that as a young refugee who had grown up thinking of himself as both smarter and more put upon than other people, America's Secretary of State had learned not just how to amuse and impress, but also how to flatter. Even Idi Amin, the Ugandan dictator who expressed admiration for Hitler and once declared himself King of Scotland – with a penchant for feeding his political opponents to his crocodiles – was surprisingly emollient on this occasion. Displaying a hitherto little-known gift for understatement, Amin wrote to Wilson:

When you were elected prime minister the relations between Great Britain and Uganda were not good. But because of your happy and wise leadership you were able to normalise the situation by sending your brilliant man Mr. James Callaghan to Uganda to find out the true facts ... It is my sincere hope that [the] Labour Party will in due course elect your successor who will then be appointed prime minister to lead Great Britain ... Uganda will cooperate with this person, whether he is Welsh, Scottish, Irish or English. It is indeed my desire to consolidate the good relations now existing between Uganda and England, and to work for peace, love and brotherly understanding in the world in order to alleviate all human suffering ... I also wish to extend an invitation to you and your lady wife to visit Uganda at any time convenient. The people here will extend to you their warm traditional hospitality. Lastly, I desire to convey through you my sincere greetings and best wishes to my friends Her Majesty the Queen and the entire people of Great Britain.

With highest regard,

H.E. Field Marshal Al Hadji Dr. Idi Amin Dada, VC, DSO, MC and Bar.

★★★

It proved to be a busy news cycle that week, because on 17 March the *Daily Express* revealed that Princess Margaret and her husband Lord Snowdon were to separate after sixteen years of marriage. Even in those slightly more reticent media days, it was widely reported that both parties had taken the opportunity to test the limits of their wedding vows, and the policy of Snowdon himself on such matters might best be encapsulated in the phrase, 'If it moves, he'll have it.' The news brought another fulsome note from Idi Amin in Kampala, who glimpsed a wider truth in the tragedy of the royal break-up. 'I hope this will be a lesson to all of us men not to marry ladies in a very high position,' he wrote.

Meanwhile, the trial began that week at Exeter Crown Court of 32-year-old Andrew 'Gino' Newton, a sometime freelance pilot who had been recruited as a hitman during a drunken evening at a pub. Recalling the night for the benefit of the court, Newton noted, 'It is a different world after sixteen pints.'

Things did not improve when he sobered up. In October 1975, he had managed to kill the Great Dane belonging to Jeremy Thorpe's friend Norman Scott but failed to do the same to Scott himself. Convicted on a charge of possessing a firearm with intent to endanger life, Newton was given a two-year sentence but loyally declined to implicate Thorpe as the ultimate paymaster in the business. Thorpe, for his part, continued to deny 'the least impropriety in my relations with Mr Scott', an individual whom he 'barely knew', although this claim was somewhat undermined by the publication in the *Sunday Times* of a letter he had once written to Scott, whom he addressed by an unusual nickname, suggesting he seek gainful employment abroad:

> Your message arrived all by itself at my breakfast table at the Reform, and gave me tremendous pleasure. I cannot tell you just how happy I am to feel that you are really settling down. No more bloody clinics ... Bunnies can and will go to France. I miss you. J.

Thorpe resigned as Liberal Party leader on 10 May, still robustly denying 'the least involvement in any scheme to do harm to Mr Scott', until this too was undermined on Newton's release from prison in October 1977, an event he marked by granting an exclusive interview to the *Daily Mirror*, splashed under the headline 'I WAS PAID £5000 TO KILL SCOTT', a matter the Metropolitan Police noted was 'a point of ongoing enquiry' on their part and, perhaps revealing a peculiarly British affinity for their household pets, it was 'especially troubling that an innocent dog' should have become a victim in the case.

Finally, there was the death on 24 March, at the age of 88, of Field Marshal Bernard Montgomery, the hero of El Alamein, whose military and personal reputation conceivably stood higher among the British public than it did with certain of his wartime Allied colleagues, for whom Montgomery's lack of common courtesy, far less diplomacy, came close to matching his undoubted skills as a master of set-piece battlefield operations. Monty's more recent remarks about the domestic and worldwide communist menace had suggested an affinity with various groups who felt that the country had drifted dangerously to the left, that Harold Wilson lacked either the will or the desire to correct this, and that direct action was required as a result.

According to one ill-sourced but popular rumour, a citizen volunteer force, much like that raised at the time of the General Strike fifty years earlier, would join with disaffected military units to stage a *coup d'état* and reimpose law and order on the country. In this scenario, the rebels would seize Heathrow Airport, the BBC and Buckingham Palace, then, with either Lord Mountbatten or Monty himself acting as interim dictator, the Queen would read out a statement urging the public to support the new regime because the civil government was no longer able to keep order.

'All absolute rot,' Montgomery himself assured me, not long before his death at the converted mill where he lived, near Alton in Hampshire. I was there because my father had served under the great man in the latter's role at NATO in the mid-1950s and the two of them had parted on good terms. Monty did admit at one stage in the conversation that there had been a 'fire of indignation' smouldering among some of those, like him, appalled by the recent turn of events in the United Kingdom. But however fiercely it burned, fortunately it still stopped short of reducing the country to ashes.

II

Spring

SUNNY JIM

Harold Wilson's final departure from office on 5 April 1976 may have lacked the elaborate pomp and circumstance of a US presidential transition, but it wasn't without its own sense of ceremony. Before he left, the Queen and Duke of Edinburgh went to dinner at Downing Street, marking the first time the monarch had visited her premier's residence since Winston Churchill's retirement, twenty-one years earlier. Wilson kept a hectic schedule that week, attending meetings, accepting and conferring awards and giving speeches, as well as hosting another well-provisioned dinner for his ministerial colleagues at which the outgoing prime minister took the opportunity to remind those present of the enviable state in which he was leaving the nation's affairs – 'a cabinet meeting with food', as Barbara Castle put it.

Wilson never formally endorsed any of those present as his successor, but was thought to have tacitly lent his support to the candidacy of his Foreign Secretary James Callaghan. In the end, Labour MPs faced a choice between Callaghan and the left's standard-bearer, Michael Foot, known to *Private Eye* as 'Worzel', who was born before the First World War and, to some, almost like a figure out of some sepia-toned *Daily Herald* past, content to be judged on principles rather than his artfully coiffed hair or synthetic charm in front of the camera.

Callaghan received a less than overwhelming 176 votes to Foot's 137 in the final ballot, with Denis Healey having dropped out after the first round. The new leader, who was aged 64, could not contain his emotion on hearing the result. 'Prime Minister! And I never went to university!' Callaghan remarked in between his sobs of joy.

A few minutes later, Wilson gave a short, gracious speech to the staff at No. 10, shook everyone's hand, kissed the garden-room girls on their cheeks and stepped outside in front of a small crowd shouting, 'We love you, Harold!' (along with 'one or two dissentient voices', he later admitted). It was a time-honoured ceremony, which was known for its brevity and said to sometimes lack only the tumbrils in the ruthless haste by which power changed hands. Wilson was then driven in a ministerial car the short distance back to the house at Lord North Street that he and his wife would occupy before taking possession of their new flat at Ashley Gardens.

In the days that followed, Wilson told everyone willing to listen how happy he was and how proud to be the recipient of so many honours 'bestowed on one by the most humble folk up to the very highest in the land'. In the latter category, there was the announcement that he was to be made a Knight Companion of the Garter, an award in the monarch's personal gift, and as Wilson himself reflected, 'not an insignificant thing for the son of a works chemist from Huddersfield'.

The descent from this high world stage to the depths of the widespread ridicule the former prime minister faced just weeks later with the publication of his final honours list must have been painful to one who put such stock in public opinion. To make matters worse, Wilson took the bait by issuing a furious rebuke, denouncing the 'orchestrated vendetta' against him, bizarrely citing anti-Semitism as the only possible reason to object to names such as that of the 'excellent Mr. James Goldsmith'.

The press as a whole were more exercised by the nature of the former prime minister's relations with his private secretary. Several papers, with the help of some tactically deployed asterisks, quoted Joe Haines's story, recalling that he had once been in the premier's office in the Commons when:

Marcia Williams burst in to demand that Wilson accompany her to a function. He wearily agreed, and slipped back out as soon as he could, only for [Williams] to burst in again and exclaim, 'You little cunt, what do you think you're doing? You come back with me at once!'

There was a somewhat schizophrenic quality to Wilson's conduct in the first few weeks following his resignation. He was complaining about being vilified in the press at regular intervals that spring but was also inviting reporters to come and see him, as often as not confirming the rumours of his mental decline when they did so. As Ben Pimlott wrote:

> If Wilson had friends in the mainstream press or in the Labour party [after his resignation] they kept their heads below the parapet. In socialist circles, almost as much as in Tory ones, the 'Wilson years' became an episode to condemn and shudder at, as a missed opportunity, a tawdry sell-out, something that must never happen again.

In similar vein, Christopher Booker wrote in his book *Neophiliacs* that the 'lavender list' fiasco 'could not have comprised a more brilliant epitaph on the whole twelve years during which Sir Harold dominated English life'.

***

James Callaghan enjoyed something of an avuncular image with his kindly, owl-like features and faint air of bumbling, already of nearly pensionable age when he assumed the burden of the nation's highest office. Unlike Michael Foot or Tony Benn, he was not generally one to rattle the teacups of the country's *Daily Mail* readers. At the same time, no one would ever be likely to successively hold all four of the great offices of state without a salutary vein of ambition to advance their claims.

Above all, Callaghan was far from a mere benign extension of his predecessor. Despite sharing a broad view of the need to somehow steer between the Scylla of national bankruptcy and the Charybdis of alienating the unions, the two men had a major personality difference that made them fundamentally dissimilar. When challenges arose, Wilson became intellectually engaged, convinced that the forensic acuity of his mind would convert his enemies; Callaghan, by contrast, became detached, preferring to leave it to surrogates to manoeuvre behind the scenes on his behalf. Wilson's mind mastered the details; Callaghan remained aloof from even some of the major components of issues he faced. Wilson's mathematical lucidity took him straight to the core of any problem; his successor's more intuitive approach led him to see it in terms of appealing to what P.G. Wodehouse called the 'psychology of the individual'.

Speaking some years later of the job he assumed in April 1976, Callaghan said:

I must tell you, there is no other feeling like it in the world, to be sitting in the seat of the prime minister of the United Kingdom … I had no doubts at all about my capacity. I had watched so many others. It's not altogether a very difficult job to do if you use elementary common sense, if you have a knowledge of how your fellow human beings think and feel.

Naturally affable, like all prime ministers Callaghan could also display a sulphuric temper, bordering on menace, behind the scenes. His first order of business on taking office was to send for Barbara Castle, the 65-year-old Social Services Minister, and suggest that she should write him a letter of resignation to help lower the average age of the new Cabinet. Castle angrily refused, preferring to leave him to sack her, which he duly did.

The sight of an elderly woman leaving No. 10 in floods of tears came as an early hint that there might be more to the building's new occupier than his 'Sunny Jim' public persona. Yet when Callaghan in turn left office, he was gracious enough to offer Castle a peerage, which she again refused – 'quite crisply and without undue delay,' she wrote. 'Quite crisply' was not an exaggeration. Increasing age failed to modify Castle's poor opinion of Callaghan, whom she described nearly a quarter of a century later as 'that fat snake lurking in the grass and capable of anything, the most disloyal and damaging man in the government' – and those were just her published remarks.

For all that, perhaps it would be fair to say that Callaghan's strength lay in his simplicity, his judgement, and Barbara Castle aside, his appeal to both sides of his party. He had a rocklike common sense that was neither cluttered by excessive cleverness nor burdened by an unduly reflective mind.

Naturally enough, the Wilson legacy loomed large during the early days of the new administration. First, there were the matters personally involving the former premier and his family. Callaghan was presented with several detailed papers that spring, touching on the security arrangements at the Wilsons' new flat and the question of the car and driver to be paid for, in a break with precedent, from public funds. There was also the long-running case involving Marjorie Halls, widow of Wilson's former Political Secretary Michael Halls, whose affinity for filing lawsuits against her late husband's employer practically amounted to a collector's mania. The stress of dealing with what she described as the 'mad world of Mr Wilson's kitchen cabinet' had brought on her husband's fatal heart attack at the age of 54, she wrote in one such petition. Although ultimately denied the full £50,000 compensation she demanded, Mrs Halls was able to supplement her widow's pension by drawing on a discretionary government fund with the evocative name 'The Endowment for the Relief of Sundry Female Objects in Distress'. To the end of her own life, she insisted that the real aggravating party in the matter was 'that impossible bitch Mrs Williams', whom she claimed had once phoned her 'in a frenzy ... saying that if certain matters concerning her new home were not put right she would bring down the Prime Minister'.

On top of all that, there was the lengthy note prepared by the Cabinet Secretary, Sir John Hunt, that awaited the new premier on his desk in the early afternoon of 5 April. On the whole, the document took a notably differ-ent line on the state of the national economy to Wilson's more rosy assessment of the subject just hours earlier. 'The general picture here is one of *serious imbalance*,' Sir John began, with no preamble, before offering a host of other dispiriting remarks:

> Unless action is taken swiftly, there will be either a continuation of an unacceptably high level of unemployment, or a balance of payments deficit which will be beyond our ability to finance, or some combination of the two ... Inevitably, the underlying problem of how to improve the com-petitiveness of United Kingdom industry remains a matter of grave concern ... There is a complex of issues to be settled over the future of the nation's energy sector, and also outstanding matters associated with the inevitable depletion of North Sea Oil supplies ... The nation's shipbuilding industry faces singularly bleak prospects, with very heavy redundancies likely over the next 18 months ... Our Price Code is under attack, not least by the CBI, who wish to see it abandoned ... The Treasury forecast is that the UK recov-ery in the short term and the medium term presents a depressing prospect ... Employment, inflation and the balance of trade all look very gloomy. Sterling is under pressure ... Elements of the Scots and Welsh are pressing for devolution, with all that entails ... It is true that the chancellor himself was more optimistic about matters at Cabinet this morning ... Perhaps the economic forecasts are exaggerated ... But that is not to say that the going will not be rough. In fact, it is likely to be very rough indeed.

Fanciful as it might be to contemplate the image of armed personnel carriers racing across the tarmac at Heathrow with machine guns blazing, or right-wing paramilitary units bounding up the staircase at Buckingham Palace prior to installing a suitable retired admiral or field marshal at the helm of government, the revulsion against this apparent cycle of national decline and administrative inertia ran deep enough in the spring of 1976 to sustain a heated grass-roots debate about the whole direction the country was heading. In particular, many of the UK's town centres were enlivened each weekend by the interactions of groups like the Socialist Workers Party (SWP) and opposing factions such as the National Front (NF) or its more reputable kindred spirit, the National Association for Freedom (NAFF) in a spirited exchange of views on those questions that lay between them. The author can speak from experience in recalling a regular animated Saturday afternoon discussion held around the normally decorous Cambridge Market Square about the respective merits of the rights of the individual as opposed to the collective, conducted by way of duelling megaphones, once bringing the intervention of a friendly policeman. 'I'd fuck off home, sir, before things turn nasty,' he advised.

A hint of the broader debate about the state of affairs at home and overseas could be glimpsed in the headlines of the factions' rival newspapers that April: 'Why Angola Matters: Solidarity with the Oppressed People of Luanda' from the SWP's *Socialist Worker*; 'Mrs Thatcher, Don't Sell Out to the Union Left' from NAFF's *The Free Nation*. The latter's local readers included a sprinkling of what might be termed young idealists, who were broadly united against the undue exercise of central authority of any kind; several more seasoned conservative-leaning individuals who were disillusioned by the impotence of successive Labour governments in the face of increasingly strident radical-left interest groups, to a background of economic decline, trade union triumphalism and Irish terrorism; and a smattering of former service personnel, some of whom hinted at exotic past duties operating in the nexus of the military–security intelligence worlds.

One middle-aged individual regularly hawking *The Free Nation*, known far and wide only as The Colonel, assured us that he had personally served in Northern Ireland, where he had seen poignant evidence of the province's sectarian strife – 'corpses being picked over by rats in the street' – and whose ongoing troubles could be resolved within a week 'if the Army was given its head'. The Colonel was not pleased by the news that May that nine members of the IRA had managed to escape from the Maze Prison in County Down through a tunnel. 'Those buggers should never have been locked up in the first place,' he said, and slowly drew a finger across his throat by way of signifying an alternative mode of punishment.

Over time, The Colonel also expounded at length on everything from the 'utterly inane' Sunday-trading laws to the inadvisability of permitting 'some twerp in Whitehall to force us to throttle ourselves with a seat belt when out in the car – it's none of their business.' He always had a special note of disdain for the supposed editorial bias of the BBC:

That bugger who stuck a microphone in Mrs T's face on *Panorama* the other night wasn't even wearing a proper jacket and tie, and what was that fungus growing all over his chin? She looked like she was being mugged by the *Socialist Worker* instead of being interviewed by the national broadcaster established by royal charter.

The Colonel laughed bitterly, 'My God, just wait until Maggie takes over and finally sorts that rabble out. There'll be one or two … changes, my boy, mark my words.'

The flip side in this debate between the competing acronyms of the SWP, NF and NAFF was equally convinced that the nation was prey to sinister, rightist forces arrayed against it both at home and overseas. The catalogue of treacherous acts they trotted out was impressive: 'MI5 spooks in Belfast … Spies and infiltrations … Elected prime minister ousted … Peaceful protests wrecked by fascists … Blatant harassment of anyone suspected of deviating … Saboteurs … Nazis …'

A particular cause célèbre on the left that spring concerned Peter Hain, the 26-year-old trade union researcher and anti-apartheid campaigner, who had recently been elected president of the Young Liberals. One Friday, the previous October, Hain had been eating lunch with his wife, Pat, in their small south-west London flat when a police car screeched to a halt outside. It transpired that four schoolboys had earlier that morning seen a man fitting Hain's description hurriedly leaving a local branch of Barclays Bank, having relieved a teller there of £490 in used £5 notes while her attention was elsewhere. The civic-minded young citizens had promptly given chase in the street, where the alleged thief had rather curiously paused to throw the money up into the air before fleeing in a waiting blue car.

Hain was arrested, charged with theft and in April 1976, acquitted on a 10–2 majority verdict by a jury at the Old Bailey. Perhaps the prosecution of Labour's future Secretary of State for Northern Ireland was an innocent case of mistaken identity of a sort not uncommon in the criminal justice system. But perhaps there was more to it than that. Hain remains convinced that he was the victim of an orchestrated dirty-tricks campaign perpetrated by shadowy right-wing factions, which included the South African state intelligence agency BOSS, the CIA, MI5 and 'at least half the mainstream Fleet

Street press', who, over recent years, had come to know him as 'Hain the Pain', among other more private epithets unsuitable to print in a family paper.

Hain told me:

> It was surreal ... I was stitched up for a crime I did not commit – period. I might add I'd also received a letter bomb, which was delivered to my home one morning but failed to explode because of faulty wiring. It was all part of a plan to sabotage the Liberal Party, and a dossier [later] came to light which said the South African operation against me in 1975–76 had 'gone successfully' and was also 'going to plan' against Jeremy Thorpe. So there you have it. The big picture was that BOSS wanted to see a permanent Tory government in Britain, and smashing the Liberal party by discrediting its leadership was the first step to achieving their goal.

★★★

One wet Friday evening in January 1976, Jim Callaghan, then the UK's Foreign Secretary, was preparing to leave his office for Paddington Station to spend the weekend in his Cardiff constituency when a secretary reminded him that he still had one last engagement to fulfil for the day. This was a reception hurriedly arranged at 10 Downing Street to allow senior members of the Wilson Cabinet to make the acquaintance of a visiting US politician who had recently taken to telling anyone prepared to listen that he intended to become his nation's next commander-in-chief and, by extension, Leader of the Free World.

The aspiring president, Jimmy Carter, was a 51-year-old, sandy-haired, former US Navy lieutenant and Georgia State politician, with a distinctive Southern drawl and a smile like that of a young model in a toothpaste advertisement, and he was already well on his way to becoming the surprise Democratic Party choice to face the incumbent Gerald Ford in that November's election. Campaigning as a political moderate and Washington outsider, the sometime peanut farmer and practising Baptist lay preacher had promised to usher in a 'new sense of morality' to US relations with the rest of the world. Carter went on to speak of the 'Nixon-Kissinger-Ford' foreign policy as 'covert, manipulative and deceptive in style', and at odds with 'man's best qualities of Christian goodwill, tolerance and love', as he put it, in one well-publicised speech. The old way of doing business 'runs against the basic principles of this country,' Carter added, 'because Kissinger is obsessed with power blocs, with spheres of influence ... It is a system based on secrecy and exclusion, closely guarded, devious and amoral.' To these broad-based criticisms of his opponents, Carter added his own high-minded, if somewhat quixotic refrain. 'Our foreign affairs should be as open and honest as the great American people themselves,' he repeatedly said.

Callaghan was not best pleased to be reminded that his weekend travel plans would need to be delayed in this way. 'This is never to happen again,' he announced with some heat, as he strode from the rear door of the Foreign Office, accompanied by two young aides, to walk the short distance back across Horse Guards Parade to Downing Street. 'Do you understand me?' he added for emphasis. The pair of hapless flunkies nodded gravely, although they seemed unclear as to how, going forward, they might convince the nation's head of government to arrange his receptions of visiting foreign dignitaries around Callaghan's preferred train schedule.

The Foreign Secretary's mood had not improved by the time he reached the upstairs library at No. 10, where Harold Wilson and some of his ministerial colleagues were already in the midst of entertaining Carter (who, in sharp contrast to his hosts, restricted himself to drinking only water) and his small entourage. 'The only thing this nut farmer and I have in common is our initials,' Callaghan remarked, sotto voce, to his colleague and future party leadership rival Denis Healey. 'You and the son of God,' Healey promptly responded, demonstrating his gift for repartee.

It would be only fair to say that Carter was not initially regarded as an entirely plausible candidate for the executive control of one of the world's two superpowers. On the day he announced his bid for the White House, even his hometown newspaper, the *Atlanta Constitution* ran a headline that proclaimed, 'Jimmy Who is Running for What?' But the Georgian's relative anonymity also proved to be his greatest asset in the coming campaign.

In response to the successive nightmares of Vietnam and Watergate, Americans were increasingly drawn toward leaders who were from outside the Washington swamp. Addressing this need, Carter's slogan, with its artfully placed comma, was 'A Leader, For A Change'. He won the Iowa caucuses held on 19 January, shortly before his whirlwind British tour, and similarly defied predictions a month later in New Hampshire. Suddenly, only a third of the way through the protracted primary-election marathon, the race was all but over. Having started with no national political base or wealthy donors, the former Georgia Governor, who counted Elvis Presley and sundry country and western singers among his friends, had carved out a broad constituency of small-town and rural voters, blue-collar workers, suburban women and disenchanted inner-city minorities. Week after week, winning primaries in the North, South and Midwest, Carter steadily thinned the ranks of his rivals. By the time of his runaway success in the Pennsylvania poll on 27 April, it was clear that he was riding the crest of a wave towards the Democratic Party's nomination.

Carter was one of those anti-politicians who emerge from time to time to inform voters on all sides that their country has drifted badly off course in the hands of the established class, and who transform seemingly fatal political vulnerabilities – total inexperience in national government, in his case – into distinct electoral advantages. The television images of him denouncing the 'Godless Washington power elite' became the symbol of what supporters saw as a campaign of destiny. To others, Carter could seem so obsessively pontifical with all his talk about Christian tolerance and goodwill that people seriously wondered if he were secretly engaged in some absurdist experiment to test the limit of how much flaky behaviour voters could tolerate. One way or another, he was a peculiarly 1976 sort of candidate.

Within only a few months, Carter and Callaghan himself would come to represent the human face of the Atlantic alliance, with all it entailed, while the prime minister would personally prepare a briefing document sent to senior colleagues before the formal visit of the new US head of state the following May. Its title read: 'Main Currents of US Foreign Policy and Pres. Carter's Vision of the Future'.

While Carter focused largely on the political consequences of the successive Vietnam and Watergate tragedies, their cumulative blows to the American psyche helped foster a scepticism towards authority that continues to reverberate throughout much of Western life today. This questioning of the citizen's proper relationship to the government or its agencies often took surprising form.

In April 1976, instructors at the prestigious US Military Academy at West Point, New York, with its motto of 'Duty, Honor, Country', noticed certain striking similarities among the 823 exam papers they were marking for their institution's third-year cadets. The much-vaunted West Point honour code proclaimed that students neither cheated nor tolerated cheating in others, but after a month's review it became clear that there had been a sorry fall from grace on this occasion. By late May, the academy had expelled ninety-four cadets for having used crib notes in their exam, and a further forty-four had quietly departed of their own accord.

The *Washington Post* reported that the scandal was much more pervasive than the authorities were prepared to admit, and it was but one side of what the paper called a wider culture of 'narcissism, instant gratification, disdain for standards and general permissiveness' that in some way seemed to have replaced the old pioneer values of 'devotion to God and others, and unwavering self-discipline'.

In a further twist to the West Point scandal, no less than the US Army Secretary went on to announce on 24 December 1976 that the expelled or dishonoured cadets would be permitted to reapply for admission to the academy in 1978 without any official stain on their academic record – which was either a laudable act of seasonal goodwill on his part or another significant milepost down the road to the laissez-faire culture, largely unburdened by any need to curb one's own desires to better align with outdated societal norms, of the sort whose results we might possibly glimpse today.

DARTH VADER

When President Carter and his Foreign Affairs team later came to consider those areas of concern around the world which might benefit from the new sense of morality at the heart of US policy, they found that they were somewhat spoilt for choice.

At that spring's 25th Annual Communist Party Congress in Moscow, Leonid Brezhnev declared that the Soviet Union 'would never be bribed to permit interference in her internal affairs' by the granting of favourable trade terms with the United States in exchange for nuclear de-escalation and a renewed emphasis on human rights, and that, détente notwithstanding, the Kremlin would continue to support 'national liberation movements around the globe, whatever the fascist objection to them'. As a policy, this was to again fall some way short of the spirit of mutual goodwill proclaimed by the superpowers at the time of the SALT treaty, four years earlier. It continued a trend of Soviet boldness in seizing opportunities for imposing their political blueprint on client states around the world that had repeatedly been ignored or rewarded by the Kremlin's primary ideological foe.

Meanwhile, the genocidal orgy in Cambodia, or Democratic Kampuchea, as it was then known, where at least 1.7 million men, women and children were culled by execution, overwork, disease and famine, continued apace in the service of a class war and a period of crash national rebuilding. In later years, courts would come to hear detailed accounts of forced labour, such as the building of dams and dikes under the threat of death, along with forms of torture ranging from suffocation with plastic bags to the insertion of hot pokers into female body cavities, with public electrocution with live cables of foremen failing to meet weekly construction quotas being a regular Friday-night workplace entertainment. Other, perhaps only marginally more fortunate victims were herded to re-education camps where they were reduced by beatings and starvation to the last waystation before death.

More than forty years later, a small number of elderly former lieutenants of the Pol Pot regime were duly convicted of 'serial crimes against human dignity, and breaches of the Geneva Conventions', which, stripping away the legalese of the indictments, meant that they had participated in acts of assault, rape and murder in pursuit of an ideology which had allowed a man or a woman to be arbitrarily arrested for so-called crimes at the whim of the homicidal maniacs of the state leadership, such as the offence of wearing glasses or liking Western classical music. A foreign teacher in Phnom Penh was bemused one day in May 1976 to hear a ferocious din coming from a recently closed schoolhouse. He entered and saw a group of men wearing distinctive all-black uniform and matching boots made out of tyres smashing a piano with axes.

The Chinese government of Mao Zedong and his new premier, Hua Guofeng, though enduring its own internal ructions that spring, embraced Pol Pot and vowed to join him and his myrmidons in 'resisting the rise of decadent Western imperialism'. In the same spirit, South Korea's President Park Chung Hee announced that 'foreign words are excessive in our life' and as baleful an influence on his nation as 'long hair for men' and, rather strikingly, 'short skirts for women revealing their underclothes or lower cheeks'. A deadline was given to merchants to have their premises 'Koreanized' or else face a mandatory minimum year's jail sentence.

The hardline government in Laos began a similar campaign to root out 'those still adhering to the depraved European way of life', banning all 'foreign hairstyles, clothing, manners and artistic depictions'. Demonstrations broke out that same week against the equally austere Libyan regime of Muammar Gaddafi, and the young protest leaders were publicly executed in a televised ceremony on 7 April.

For their part, troops in India fired into a crowd at the Turkman Gate in Delhi, killing thirty-five unarmed civilians who had objected to the demolition of their homes as part of a road-building project.

Not for the first time, prosecutors in Italy launched a corruption enquiry into their nation's most senior elected officials, including Prime Minister Aldo Moro.

In the US Midwest, a group of fifty baboons escaped from a wildlife park in Mason, Ohio, running amok through the town, gleefully filching food from local restaurants and defecating in the streets until all of the animals were rounded up again a week later.

***

If, in early April 1976, you had somehow been one of the roughly 4,000 Berber tribesmen making your home among the hilltop adobe forts or dried-mud caves around the old French garrison town of Tataouine, in southern Tunisia, you might have been surprised by the arrival there, one Monday morning, of a large convoy of US-style jeeps and other utility vehicles, whose passengers quickly spread out to embark on a riot of frenzied activity, punctuated by intervals of apparent coma that somehow typifies their profession. Ancient dwellings formed by the primeval interaction of wind and sand over the course of the millennia would swiftly be modified by work crews wielding mallets and heavy rollers, their earthen floors levelled and smoothed, while a second unit deployed tractors to fill in giant underground pits gouged out of the surrounding red limestone hills that had once served as granaries for the French Foreign Legion troops stationed on the northern edge of the Sahara.

In short order, other workmen descended from articulated lorries to erect huge wooden backdrops painted in psychedelic shades of purple, pink and yellow, which were in turn illuminated by a row of powerful arc lamps. Set up on poles, their dazzling white light complemented that of the unsparing desert sun beating down on a semi-circle of lean-to tents, electrical generators and portable lavatories. Caterers had appeared next, bearing trays of iced drinks and cakes with coloured sugar, while young men and women with clipboards spoke anxiously to one another about matters of costuming and make-up.

Emerging from the ancient *ksar*, or converted warehouse, where he lived with his parents and three older sisters, 12-year-old Ibn Qatan awoke each morning for the next six weeks to the sound of hammers and saws, the shouted orders and grumbles of men with loudhailers and all the other animation that marked the temporary refurbishment of his family's indigenous homeland into the setting for a major Hollywood spectacle.

The production in question was the original *Star Wars*, which, if nothing else, would come to define the 'high-concept' film whose plot can be summarised in a single sentence: 'We're transported to a galaxy far, far away, where the forces of good and evil clash in an epic struggle' might suffice in this case. To its countless admirers, *Star Wars: Episode IV*, as it retrospectively came to be known, was a groundbreaking cornucopia of dazzling set-pieces, immersive special effects and indelible, if not always fully realised, characters. The film also introduced audiences around the world to the notion of the Force, a mystical energy that binds the universe together, and established the groundwork for the enduring legacy of a blockbuster franchise, now on at least its twelfth incarnation, making the original *Star Wars* arguably the most influential motion picture of the modern age.

To detractors, the same phenomenon marked the very moment when a film's on-screen visuals became a more important component than matters such as a halfway plausible storyline, let alone anything as hopelessly antiquated as drawing audiences in to its characters' inner lives or saying something worthwhile about our common human experience. Possibly, it's enough just to say that *Star Wars: Episode IV*, shot for a then generous but not stellar budget of $11 million, has to date reaped an astronomic $800 million at the global box office, quite apart from launching a sub-industry of themed products including novels, comics, video games, amusement park attractions, posters, buttons, lunchboxes, resin bobble-head action figures, trading cards and clothing – everything from sinister black Darth Vader electronic helmets to a pair of Luke Skywalker faux-suedette boots. If a young fan could wear it or carry it, the *Star Wars* gang were on it.

Perhaps the final word on the matter belongs to the then 62-year-old Alec Guinness, the fastidious and intelligent veteran of more than fifty films, including his Oscar-winning turn as Colonel Nicholson in David Lean's masterpiece *The Bridge over the River Kwai*, who appeared in the original *Star Wars* and briefly returned as a ghostly apparition in its first two sequels. 'The film plods on,' Guinness wrote to his friend Anne Kauffman, while back on the 'relatively civilised terrain' of the EMI studios in Elstree in May 1976:

> I've had a week off while they all blow themselves up electrically, etc, etc.
> I *could* finish by 1 June but suspect 10 June to be more likely, although I
> have only three brief scenes more to play. Play? *Drift* through, aimlessly. I
> *like* Harrison Ford, but doubt if he's going to set the Thames or East River
> on fire.

When finally wrapping his part as the hooded, lightsabre-wielding space wizard, Guinness added in his diary, 'Am more or less flaked out, not ill, just physically incapable of an ounce of energy. Usually I am very resilient after a film, but this one has left me numb.'

***

There were other signs that spring that Hollywood had come to free itself from any prudish notions of self-restraint that had characterised much of its output, a few well-publicised exceptions aside, into the early 1970s. Audiences now merely winked at the lingering full-frontal nudity masquerading as a serious treatment of rape in *Lipstick* or tittered at the cocaine references and pervasive party mood in *Hollywood Boulevard*. Directors who wanted to signal their moral sophistication gave their male characters sterling silver snorting spoons dangling on chains between the buttons of their wide-collared shirts splayed open as if for imminent heart surgery, or women who were increasingly portrayed as independent-minded career types who just happened to have big breasts.

The Rocky Horror Picture Show continued to do sellout business through the spring of 1976 on the premise that a kitsch-slasher-transvestite musical parody, with characters who explore the boundaries defining conventional sexuality, or who dematerialise through solid brick walls, might appeal to a vast worldwide audience eager for a bit of innocent fun. Striking some of the same lubricious tone was, as we've seen, *Carry On England*, whose two chief points of interest were the sight of Judy Geeson in an over-tight military blouse and the absence of the *Carry On* stalwart Sid James.

On 26 April, James was on tour in a revival of the suitably camp *The Mating Season* when he suffered a fatal heart attack while seated on stage at the Sunderland Empire. He was 62.

Time has treated James less kindly than Tommy Cooper or Tony Hancock, but in his way, he was funny almost to a fault. The craggy-faced former South African ladies' hairdresser with the mucky laugh kept the public amused until literally the last moment of his life. James's fellow cast members thought at first that he was playing a characteristic joke when he failed to reply to their prompts that night, and the audience had laughed along, believing it all to be part of the show, at the subsequent time-honoured enquiry, 'Is there a doctor in the house?'

A freelance journalist named Tony Linse, who happened to be enjoying an undemanding night out, hurriedly rang the London office of the *Daily Mirror* with the terrible news. The editor who took the call also initially thought it was a prank. On being told, 'Sid James has just died in Sunderland', the *Mirror* man replied, 'Don't worry, son, everybody dies in Sunderland'.

★★★

Pop music followed an orbit very similar to that of the cinema. At one end of the spectrum there was the thrusting new combo, the Sex Pistols, who were beginning to attract press attention of the simulated shock-outrage variety but not yet much in the way of a dedicated audience, while across the Atlantic, the Ramones released their eponymous debut LP on 24 April, a twenty-nine-minute song cycle of yelped vocals and dentist-drill guitars with titles like 'Blitzkrieg Bop', 'Judy is a Punk' and 'Now I Wanna Sniff Some Glue'.

Somewhere that same spring, it seemed that most songs got angrier and music got faster and more furious. Although there were still plenty of teen-agers in flares kicking up their platform heels on *Top of the Pops*, it's possible to see 1976 as the downhill story of a once-tuneful Hit Parade going on a bender of screwed-up nihilism, with the likes of the Bee Gees and ABBA frantically waving from among the wreckage.

For those who preferred their vocal stars to espouse more traditional values there was still Val Doonican, crooning away about Paddy McGinty's goat to sold-out theatres and on TV spectaculars quite often graced by a royal pres-ence. Or, for that matter, the bell-bottomed Brotherhood of Man sweeping all before them at that April's Eurovision Song Contest with 'Save Your Kisses for Me', a number performed in a peppy, neatly choreographed routine that went on to top the charts in thirty-two countries and sell 6 million copies around the world.

The record-buying public didn't necessarily monitor the shifting cul-tural zeitgeist the way the pundits at *Melody Maker* or *Sounds* did, but, by now, they would surely have come to recognise that the old-time virtues of a catchy chorus and a well-turned lyric of the Barry Manilow school were being challenged by a cast of characters who were seemingly emerging from the basements of charity clothes shops, with a taste for self-laceration and who appeared not to overdo it in terms of visits to the dentist.

In a somehow logical, chronological development, John Lennon and Paul McCartney's last real meeting came on the day of the release of the Ramones' debut album. The venue was the Lennons' apartment in New York's vener-able Dakota Building. The two boyhood friends and their wives started off by chatting about the latter-day Beatles business manager Allen Klein, who was just then suing the Lennons for millions in unpaid commissions. Paul, who had never cared for Klein, commiserated about this and various other legal woes, as well as the recent death of Lennon's father. Later in the evening, the two couples settled in to watch an episode of *Saturday Night Live*, being shot just a mile or two from the Dakota, in which the producer Lorne Michaels famously parodied the then rampant Beatles-reunion rumours by going on air to offer the quartet $3,000 to perform on his show. According to John, 'Paul and I thought it would be funny if we went down there, just as a gag. We nearly got in a cab, but we were actually too tired.' Around one in the morning, the McCartneys left their hosts sitting up in front of the 1960 sci-fi film *The Time Machine*.

Encouraged by the generally good vibes, Paul told his wife Linda that he planned to drop in on John once again the following afternoon. He returned to the Dakota to a noticeably cooler reception. 'Please call before you come over,' Lennon told him. 'It's not 1956. You can't just turn up at the door any more.' Paul and John, who would win his coveted green card three months later, giving an air of greater permanence to his US exile, never met again.

★★★

By the time of Harold Wilson's departure in April 1976, a spirit of sexual parity was at least beginning to pervade the British industrial sector, with the establishment of an Equal Opportunities Commission and a host of similar regulatory bodies intended to end discrimination in the workplace. But there were clearly limits to the wider application of this invigorating new spirit of inclusiveness. Nobody then spoke much about things like gay rights or gender ideology, or for that matter went out of their way to apply the official ideal of office or factory standards to other aspects of national life.

British football, for one, remained a gloriously old-school, often mud-spattered affair contested by mullet-haired young men who enjoyed a post-match Watney's Party Seven and a splash of Brut after performing in front of predominantly male audiences known for their lively interactions with each other on the adjacent city streets. Taken as a whole, the matches of the era had a less cosmopolitan and perhaps even more tribally aggressive quality to them than they do today. As the late historian Tony Judt notes, 'No one who attended games in [the 1970s] between England and Germany, for example, or for that matter Germany and the Netherlands (still less Poland

and Russia) would have been under any illusion about the treaty of Rome and "ever-closer union".'

The obvious reference point for international fixtures was the Second World War, and at least some of the ties pitting British club or national sides against European opponents were vicarious, emotionally charged reruns of the UK's military history. In 1976, it was still something of a novelty to see a woman or girl attending a top-flight league match unless she happened to be employed there pouring the tea or maintaining the deep-frier in what then passed for the average stadium's catering facilities. Liverpool swept all before them in the English First Division, with 25-year-old Kevin Keegan voted the Football Writers' Player of the Year.

In other back-page news, Wales won what was then the Five Nations Rugby Union Trophy, under the captaincy of their moustachioed back-row forward Mervyn Davies, a man who wouldn't have looked entirely out of place in the grizzled cast of a Sam Peckinpah western. Meanwhile, the largely unfancied Rag Trade narrowly pipped Red Rum to the post in the Grand National, which was free of any female jockey participation.

The new spirit of gender empowerment somehow also eluded the organis-ers of the two separate men's and women's World Open snooker tournaments held in Middlesborough that month, with a winning prize of £7,000 for the former and £500 (plus a £50 shopping voucher) for the ladies.

Perhaps it was too soon to say that Britons who had once admired husbands and wives who sustained marriages under difficult circumstances now openly applauded those who ditched their partners, but that day was coming. There were roughly 150,000 divorces granted in the UK in 1976, three times more than in 1966. The average length of a marriage was just less than ten years. Most men tended to divorce between the ages of 45–49, and women between the ages of 40–44. No one legally married or took as a civil partner an indi-vidual of the same sex.

The general feeling was that marriage was hard, and sometimes cruelly so, but if you made the best of it, didn't moan and whistled while you worked, you might find it was still marginally better than the fate of the central charac-ter in the popular Irish toe-tapper 'The Old Maid in the Garrett', or any of the other poor souls depicted in print or on screen bemoaning the lot in life of any female unfortunate enough to still be single after the age of 30.

In her bestselling pop-psychological book *Passages*, published in June 1976, Gail Sheehy celebrated the empowering, almost transformative potential of a good divorce – so much so, she writes, that 'I began to wonder if divorce is now a *rite de passage*. Is this ritual necessary before anyone, above all herself, will take a woman's need for expansion seriously?'

Not only had the laws governing family life in most Western countries changed beyond recognition in the period around 1970–76, but a whole cottage industry of television programmes, films, plays, books and mass-market periodicals had sprung up to give voice to a newly enfranchised network of women's interest groups. Perhaps the best known was the glossy monthly *Spare Rib*, whose contents page typically boasted a variety of bedrock-feminist issues such as abortion, domestic violence and inequality of pay, alongside more traditional features on unwanted hair removal and make-up. The magazine's regular appearance was an editorial feat in itself, given that it was produced in a cramped upstairs room in an alley off London's Carnaby Street, with no fax, no email and no computers. Its one enforced absence from the newsstands came when W.H. Smith and other high-street retailers declined to carry one of its early issues due to the subversive use of the word 'fuck' in a back-page advertisement for the singer Dory Previn's new album.

In 1976, some disparity still existed between what the editors of *Spare Rib* called their magazine's 'vibrant and essential voice', with its mandate to speak for the 'fast rolling feminist tide breaking around the UK and the world', and the perhaps less-progressive attitudes to gender democracy that characterised the grassroots of British life. When the newly formed Women's Liberation Front went for its first annual conference in a windswept Skegness, they found that Joe Gormley's National Union of Mineworkers – the organisation whose strike action had arguably done more than any other factor to bring down the Conservative government in 1974 – was meeting in the adjacent assembly hall. At the end of the Saturday afternoon session, the women's delegates had crossed the street in the hopes of being able to discuss those matters concerning the ongoing class struggle that were of mutual interest to both the feminist and labour element, but found that the union men had a different weekend agenda: a striptease show featuring a generously upholstered local Skegness artiste named Rosita Royce, who emerged from out of a rubber octopus costume to stand on stage agitating a football rattle with her breasts – transformative and empowering, if you like, although on this occasion, the Gormley contingent had largely restricted itself to the more time-honoured hoots of 'Get 'em off!' and its less elevated variants.

***

To judge from the first full session of the Callaghan Cabinet held on 13 April, the nation's priorities were less those of the great fundamental shifts in domestic life and more a matter of obsessive tinkering with the fine detail of policy that characterises so much of the day-to-day business of government. 'The Minister of Agriculture, Fisheries and Food said that the previous evening the House of Commons had passed a resolution disapproving of European Community (EC) measures on skimmed milk powder and aid for the storage of vegetable proteins', we learn:

> The minister had made it clear in the debate that the effect of these measures would be to permit the House to register its disapprobation of such initiatives without necessarily calling into question the fact that the Government had committed themselves, under the terms of the Common Agricultural Policy, to continue to study them in a timely but methodical manner, and that the Community should thus be reassured that the UK Government's declared position on powdered milk, while under review, would for present remain unchanged ...

... and so on, over four closely typed pages. It must sometimes seem that certain Britons have waited their whole lives for a resolution to the debate on their country's relationship with the rest of Europe.

A fortnight later, Callaghan with some pride informed his Cabinet colleagues that 'the House of Commons has received favourably the government's offer to establish a Select Committee on direct elections to the European Assembly, which would work independently but also in parallel to the ongoing discussions in the Council of Ministers', though set against this there were issues concerning the knotty matter of 'appointing the UK minister to said committee ... It could be embarrassing to HM Government if he were to be named Chairman, as this might seem to be a not wholly welcome exercise of UK power'. 'The most judicious course,' Callaghan continued, in a becoming show of British self-effacement:

> ... would be for a Foreign and Commonwealth Office minister to be appointed a member during the committee's interim consideration of matters which are primarily for European decision, such as the allocation of seats among member states, and that he be replaced by a Home Office official at such time as the committee might come to address matters such as electoral arrangements, and that this proposal should in due course be

implemented in light of our commitment to proceed to direct elections to the European Assembly.

It's worth mentioning again that, in keeping with his peers in the private sector, the Cabinet Secretary and his staff recorded the minutes and other voluminous material issuing from Downing Street without the aid of any modern technology.

In 1976, if you happened to work in some editorial capacity at a daily newspaper like *The Times*, your job, late each afternoon, was to rapidly read and if possible correct long, typed strips of text unveiled for you in some upstairs room as if by ancient merchants displaying their wares for an emir. The strips would in turn be cut up and borne away to the basement. At that stage, men in brown overalls would spread long, newspaper-sized white sheets over the illuminated glass top of a light-table and then laboriously manoeuvre the various articles, headlines and photos by hand, until they were more or less properly aligned, at which point each separate piece was glued down.

As night fell, other men, also in overalls, would review the sheets before placing them in a series of long, stiff-backed envelopes and passing them off to other employees, who would take the finished product to the press. If no such facility existed, they would drive it out to the premises of a suburban printer, who, thanks to inflation, was typically charging twice as much for his services in 1976 as in 1971.

In a logistical feat with some of the same general characteristics of the D-Day landings, the goal then was to coordinate a fleet of vans to collect the roughly 500,000 individual copies of the paper and deliver them to their individual points of sale in the pre-dawn hours each morning. There was always the potential for something to go wrong in the whole *grand battement* of composition, printing and distribution of the paper, and it often did.

By the spring of 1976, certain steps were finally underway toward modernising the business of newspaper production. Among them was the introduction of state-of-the-art laser printing technology like the new IBM 3800, capable of producing 45,000 characters a second, which may have been good for management but also served to rekindle certain long-standing grievances on the part of the unions. During one such dispute, *The Times* itself ceased production from December 1978 to November 1979.

In 1976, the traditional office environment of women sitting at typewriters with generous supplies of correcting fluid at their elbows was also coming to be undermined by several restless, tech-savvy individuals tunnelling along their own separate routes from several different directions. As well as the tag team of Bill Gates, his childhood friend, Paul Allen, and their fledgling software company, Micro-Soft, then based in a room above a New Mexico laundromat, a 25-year-old college dropout named Steve Wozniak and his academically unprepossessing colleague Steve Jobs incorporated a company on April Fool's Day 1976 with the aim of marketing what was essentially a microprocessor bolted on to a piece of plywood, which they made available for $666.66, since Wozniak liked repeating digits.

They called their start-up Apple, after Jobs had returned from working on a fruit farm in the US Pacific Northwest, and that first year, they operated out of a modest one-car garage in suburban San Francisco. Eventually, a local electronics shop ordered fifty of the new Apple-I machines, and, building on that momentum, the two young entrepreneurs posted sales of 14,000 units within their first year of trading. In 1977, Apple's earnings surged to $2.7 million, before going on to enjoy an average growth rate of 533 per cent each year until December 1980, at which point they took their business public, with a market valuation of $1.78 billion.

EARTH IN CRISIS

Eight thousand miles away from these high-tech endeavours, an incident occurred in Melbourne, Australia, that, with its cast of lantern-jawed hoodlums with striking nicknames and wide-lapelled lawmen fighting not only the villains but also the pointy-headed bureaucrats, with their absurd rules on police procedure and criminals' rights in general, evoked some of the harder-boiled underworld types of a previous generation. This was the Great Bookie Robbery of 21 April 1976, in which a gang of armed thieves, led by one Ray 'Chuck' Bennett and Ian 'Fingers' Carroll, pulled off a commando-style raid on the premises of the city's Victoria Club bookmakers. It was the settling day after three successive race meetings over the long Easter weekend, and the club's coffers were brimming with takings.

The whole affair began when a workman, later identified as Larrie 'Legs' Prendergast, calmly walked up to the building's front counter and explained that he was there to fix the fridge, while four of his balaclava-clad colleagues waited unobserved at a side door. After a brief discussion on the subject, Prendergast produced a sawn-off shotgun from within his canvas work bag, while his associates swiftly entered the premises, forced open the money cage with sledgehammers and bolt cutters, and helped themselves to an estimated $16 million in cash. (The exact figure remains in doubt, due to certain concerns on the part of the club's management regarding the Australian federal tax authorities.) To emphasise their seriousness in the matter, another member of the crew had shoved his own shotgun into a guard's mouth and remarked, 'I'll blow his fucking head off if anybody moves or says a word.' No one did.

After some more *Sweeney*-like dialogue of this nature, the gang took their leave just ten minutes after they had come. They then pulled what was arguably their masterstroke by not immediately fleeing the area but instead climbing three flights of stairs to an office they had previously rented directly above the scene of the crime, where they locked the proceeds in a safe before changing their clothes and quietly returning to their families.

It proved to be the biggest armed robbery in Australian history to date. The bulk of the money was never recovered, although most of the suspected gang were to die prematurely, some in the execution of other crimes, in the years ahead. The Victoria Club itself, then a bare-walled room with a plain wooden desk at one end and wire cage full of mainly oriental young men and women counting money at the other, is now a Buddhist art gallery.

★★★

At around the same time as the firm led by Chuck Bennett and his associates made off with their ill-gotten Easter gains, a pudgy 22-year-old ex-soldier working as a letter sorter in a suburban New York post office was about to embark on a spree that would make him the most infamous serial killer even by the standards of a city whose residents sometimes seemed to positively wallow in a sea of blood. The man's name was David Berkowitz, and among other grievances, he viewed his mother's death from cancer ten years earlier as final proof of a cosmic masterplan against him. Being an injustice collector of some magnitude, Berkowitz also had several other misgivings about his circumstances in life, and in particular, he seems to have been repelled by what he called the 'stench' he associated with a woman's body, an abnormality he shared with Peter Sutcliffe.

In a somehow familiar development, Berkowitz was not able to get on with his father's second wife, and in short order, the older couple had moved to Florida, leaving the teenager to his own devices in a series of unalluring rented rooms around the Bronx. Howling dogs in the street kept the budding psychopath awake at night, and over time he apparently came to believe that they were in fact instructing him to go out and seek victims to kill. In particular, Berkowitz took orders from a black Labrador retriever owned by a neighbour named Sam.

Rarely could hearing voices have more dire consequences than it did here. Having bungled his first attempt at murder using a knife, Berkowitz then switched to a handgun and began prowling the suburban streets at night, seeking suitable prey – chiefly, long-haired brunettes sitting either alone or with a companion.

In some ghastly way, Berkowitz's year-long reign of terror appeared to be tragically apt for a city then seemingly in the grip of a permanent existential crisis. New York was wracked by a series of allegations of racially motivated police brutality at regular intervals in the summer of 1976 and by the widespread riots that ensued. The Police Department itself was demoralised and underfunded. Garbage was left uncollected in the streets due to a protracted sanitation workers' strike and the dead went unburied when municipal gravediggers similarly withdrew their labour. The city continued to teeter on the verge of bankruptcy. Now detectives seemed powerless to stop a mysterious white man from slaughtering young women.

Periodically, the killer taunted the authorities with chillingly literate notes, such as the one he addressed to Jimmy Breslin, a columnist for the *Daily News*. 'Don't think that because you haven't heard from me for a while that I went to sleep,' Berkowitz wrote. 'No, rather, I am still here, like a spirit roaming the night. Thirsty, hungry, seldom stopping to rest; anxious to please Sam.' (Breslin once remarked, 'He was the only psycho killer I ever heard of who knew how to use a semicolon.') And the situation would soon get worse. A lone nut whose daily existence was a tapestry of LSD trips, insomnia and talking dogs was about to terrorise the world's second-largest city.

We will return to Berkowitz and his nocturnal forays. For now, it's enough to say only that the 'Son of Sam's' rampage took place at a time when the US criminal justice system had come to reassess its traditional role of locking up offenders for the maximum term allowable under the law. Reported violent crime rates more than doubled in the United States between 1969 and 1976, but the total number of criminals in jail actually dropped from a rate of 205 inmates per 100,000 population to 159 per 100,000. Similarly, while the number of homicides in the United States rose from 15,000 in 1969 to 22,000 in 1976, only three men suffered the ultimate penalty provided for first-degree murder, despite the unanimous October 1976 decision by the US Supreme Court reaffirming capital punishment's constitutionality.

According to Amnesty International, just fifteen nations around the world had abolished the death penalty by 1976, and, as we've seen, sanctions were applied on a more arbitrary basis in some countries than others. The world's most prolific state executioners were China, Saudi Arabia and the Soviet Union, with the likes of Egypt, Brazil, India, Vietnam, Malaysia, Japan and Indonesia close behind.

The last judicial executions in Britain had taken place in August 1964, when two young men of significantly below average intelligence were hanged simultaneously at prisons in Manchester and Liverpool. They had driven out one night the previous April to visit a workmate at his home in Seaton, Cumberland, and in short order beat him to death following a disagreement about money. An Act of Parliament sponsored by a Labour MP and wartime conscientious objector named Sydney Silverman led to the death penalty's removal from the statute books a year later.

***

Among the world's best-selling academic books in the late spring of 1976 was a publication by two Florida-based chemistry professors, Thomas Burrus and Herbert Spiegel, called *Earth in Crisis*. Books with 'crisis' in their titles rarely seem to go out of style, but even so, the authors' success was particularly striking in this case. Their admonitory text soon migrated from the classroom and became all but required reading for a mainstream audience. The work's essential message was, as the authors put it:

> Mankind's recent history indicates that we are not adapting to nature, but rather attempting to force nature to adapt to us ... The next several decades hopefully will see attempts to repair the damage we have done to our earth in such a short time. To fail would be catastrophic.

The professors' thesis was in turn taken up by mass-market publications such as the *New York Times*, the *Washington Post* and *Newsweek*, while *Time* magazine warned its 4.7 million readers of a 'looming global apocalypse [if] urgent action is not taken to correct the harm inflicted on our planet'.

Perhaps surprisingly, however, the media's most acute fear at that time was not of global warming, but the coming of a new ice age. It was only in later years that scientists came to update their models to show a trend in the other direction, and the whole existential crisis was restyled as climate change.

Whatever the label, and whatever the underlying data, the takeaway moral was that human beings were destroying the Earth and should take immediate remedial action to reverse the damage.

It was a broadly similar picture in the population-crisis stakes. The total number of humans alive on the planet doubled from 2.5 to 5 billion in the period from 1950 to 1985, with the fastest single growth spurt coming in the years 1974–78. Were such trends to continue, politicians agreed, the Earth's population would exceed its available food supply, with catastrophic results for both the human race and other species. It was only later that the experts became worried about the exact opposite problem, to which they gave the name 'birth dearth', or demographic inversion.

Today, the fertility rate across Europe has dropped below restoration levels – or the average number of children a couple must have to replace themselves in the next generation – contributing to a predicted population decline across the Continent from 745 million in 2026 to 710 million in 2050. Of course, the figures for both climate and population change are subjective and open to different interpretations, but perhaps the one consistent truth to emerge from the data is that something baked into our human DNA as a whole requires us to be anxious about our precarious existence on the planet, and that while the specific facts may change, our capacity to fear remains constant.

★★★

The population of France stood at just under 53 million in 1976, although the annual rate of growth was already in decline, falling from 1.85 per cent in 1966 to less than half that a decade later. The exact number of French citizens who qualified as lovers of fine wine isn't known, but anecdotal evidence suggests a not insignificant ratio of the total figure. As it happened, those same devotees of Bacchus suffered something of a collective shock to their national pride as a result of an event taking place on 24 May at the Paris Intercontinental Hotel, where, in a blind tasting watched over by the world's media, the best French vintages were set in contest against upstarts from California.

'Obviously, the French bottles were always going to win,' says George Taber, then a correspondent working for *Time*'s bureau in Paris at a time when the magazine still ran to such a thing. The event's eleven judges included some of the most-respected names in French gastronomy, among them sommeliers from three Michelin-rated restaurants; the heads of two highly regarded

Bordeaux vineyards; Odette Kahn, the editor of the prestigious *Revue du vin de France*; and Pierre Brejoux, head of the *Appellation d'Origine Controllée*.

At one point, says Taber, a judge – Raymond Oliver, chef and owner of Le Grand Véfour, one of the French capital's great dining establishments – sampled a particular white wine. Some ostentation was involved:

> First he smelled it, then he inspected it, holding it up to the light to luxuriate in its limpid texture, and then he swirled it around his mouth before raising it in salute and, finally, with a deep sigh of satisfaction, said, '*Ah, c'est la France!*'

Except it was a Napa Valley Chardonnay. Of course, Monsieur Oliver didn't know that, and he was not visibly pleased to be informed of his mistake. Nor were his fellow judges of theirs. When the final scores were tallied, the top honours went not to the host country but to a California white and red – the 1973 Chardonnay from Chateau Montelena in northern San Francisco, and the 1973 Cabernet Sauvignon from Stag's Leap Wine Cellars in nearby Napa Valley respectively.

Taber says the results shocked everyone present. When it was all over, Odette Kahn unsuccessfully demanded that her scorecard be returned, apparently not wanting anyone from the outside world to know how she had assessed the vintages on offer. Another judge claimed to be outraged that what he had assumed to be a purely private event 'should be promoted in this way – it was a disgrace'. He was roused to this moral fervour by the realisation that the numerous print journalists and electronic media crews had not been present at the hotel that day for their own amusement.

Taber himself would write a well-received book on the affair, entitled *The Judgement of Paris*, which in turn went on to inspire the 2008 Hollywood feature, *Bottle Shock*. With one or two sour notes, the film exuded a full-bodied robustness that amused even the most discerning critical palates, with an eminently satisfying financial aftertaste and a coveted Seattle Film Festival Golden Space Needle award for its star, Alan Rickman.

***

The mid-1970s might be called a golden age of urban terrorism were the phrase not so inappropriate. Countless left- or right-leaning militant groups were active in both North and South America, Europe, Asia and the Middle

East, with airline hijackings, bombings, kidnappings and assassinations among the tactics of choice. Along with the exploits of the Symbionese Liberation Army and their celebrity frontwoman, Patty Hearst, in the United States and the continuing campaign of the IRA on the British mainland, the era was punctuated by violent attacks of one sort or another on the part of the anarchic Anti-Japan Armed Front; the Palestine Liberation Organisation, with its particular animosity towards the existence of an independent Israeli state and its sponsors; the far-left Montonéros cell, unhappy with the existing state of affairs in Argentina; and the Justice Commandos of the Armenian Genocide, seeking to redress certain historical grievances with the Turkish government. There were also ETA separatists agitating for autonomy on behalf of the Basque Province of north-west Spain, while violent far-left and far-right interplay, with the Red Brigades as its most notorious face, distinguished the Italian domestic politics of the day.

Finally, the ideologically flexible Ilich Ramírez Sánchez, better known as Carlos the Jackal, was a 26-year-old Venezuelan national, whose own corrosive brand of anti-Semitism had recently seen him narrowly fail to shoot dead the Jewish businessman Joseph Sieff while he lay soaking in his bathtub at home in London. He then embarked on a variety of grenade and rocket attacks around Paris and went on to hijack the OPEC oil ministers' meeting in Vienna, an event which left three individuals dead and ended only after the Austrian government had provided a plane to transport Carlos and his crew to Algiers.

Perhaps none of these various individuals or groups, however obsessive in pursuit of their goals, matched the sheer fanatical mayhem that characterised the Red Army Faction (RAF), also known as the Baader-Meinhof Gang, who were active in West Germany for most of the 1970s, in their programme of robbing banks, bombing military bases and murdering policemen, all in the name of overthrowing what its devotees saw as the 'fascist state'. The group's inciting moment came on 2 June 1967, when thousands of students assembled to register their disapproval of a visit to West Berlin by the Shah of Iran. As the protest turned into something more akin to a full-scale riot, police officers charged the crowd, beating them with clubs and shooting dead a 26-year-old graduate student whose wife was then pregnant with their first child. These events, combined with a vehement opposition to the escalating Vietnam War, set the stage for the RAF to unleash its decade-long reign of terror.

A pivotal moment in the RAF's campaign came when the police arrested a young Munich-born construction worker-turned-guerrilla named Andreas

Baader, who was convicted of having fire-bombed a department store in Frankfurt to protest what he saw as the German public's indifference to the 'American genocide in Southeast Asia'. In due course, several of Baader's supporters set about implementing an audacious plan for his release. Among them was a 34-year-old freelance journalist, Ulrike Meinhof, the divorced mother of two young daughters.

Although most of Meinhof's professional duties over the years were monochromatic, some colourful people had come her way. These included several of the pioneer members of the RAF, who found her sympathetic to their cause. Her mission, as she saw it, was simple: to harness her reputation as a reporter to gain access to the library of the Berlin prison where Baader was detained, and then to pretend to interview him. While she did this, two other confederates burst in with guns. In the ensuing melee, Baader and Meinhof both escaped, the latter by jumping out of a window, hotly pursued by the police. The moment she did so, she left her old family life behind her for a career of revolutionary zealotry and nihilistic violence.

Despite trading her typewriter for a gun, Meinhof wasn't entirely to abandon the written word. Later in 1972, for instance, she published a widely read essay defending the massacre at that year's Munich Olympics in which eleven Israeli athletes and a policeman were killed by the Palestinian group Black October. She later wrote, 'What is anti-semitism? The Holocaust [meant] that 6 million Jews were killed and carted on to the rubbish dumps of Europe for being exactly what was expected of them: Money-Jews.'

Andreas Baader was eventually recaptured with two accomplices following a shootout with West German authorities in Frankfurt, and Meinhof soon followed him into custody. The trial of the principal RAF gang members began in June 1975, in a specially constructed maximum-security courthouse complex in Stuttgart. On 9 May 1976, while the proceedings were still underway, Ulrike Meinhof was found dead in her cell.

The official version was that Meinhof had committed suicide by hanging herself from the bars of her window with a strip of towel. Alternative theories surrounding her death still exercise the press fifty years later. An autopsy showed 'pathological modifications' to the deceased's brain, suggesting that an operation she underwent to remove a tumour when pregnant at 26 might have helped tilt the balance of her mind from that of an idealistic young journalist into a bomb-wielding fanatic. All that can be said for sure is that in the period from 1970–76, the RAF took the lives of at least thirty-two men and women they considered enemies of their cause and left perhaps twice that number of children to mourn the loss of a parent. Andreas Baader, in turn, died in October 1977, also by his own hand, in his case by appearing to shoot himself in the back of the head with a gun smuggled in to his prison cell by a supporter. He was 34 at the time of his death.

★★★

It was a time of wholesale change for at least the human face of British politics, which saw the departure of all three main party leaders in little over a year. The transition from a manipulative prime minister, increasingly mired in a paranoia which led him to believe that his own wife might be a Soviet mole, to a more forthright one with an essentially pragmatic view on life did not bring with it any noticeable respite from the nation's seemingly permanent position on the brink of an abyss. The Cabinet meetings of the early Callaghan administration are an exercise in exquisitely controlled expression, but also of a palpable sense of unease about the state of Britain's industrial relations and its national currency. As Denis Healey remarked on 29 April:

> The main reason for the present weakness of sterling, apart from the uncertainty over a further agreement on pay with the Trades Union Congress, is the very high level of the public sector borrowing requirement, which at £12,000 million in the current financial year is £1,500 million more than the previous year and £3,500 million more than in 1974–75. No other country in the industrialised world has a comparable imbalance between its public revenue and expenditure.

Lest any of his ministerial colleagues miss the point, Healey added, 'There is now a very real danger that foreign confidence in the UK's ability to regulate its affairs could collapse if the Government allows our public spending to go unchecked'. The Cabinet 'took note of this state of affairs', the minutes concluded.

While Callaghan struggled to balance the nation's straitened circumstances with a more populist note that might appeal to the public at the time of the next election, his predecessor in office continued his sorry descent into, if not clinical dementia, then at least something approaching eccentric elderly uncle status. The process was in no way relieved by the publication later that spring of an instant memoir by Joe Haines, Wilson's long-time Press Secretary, called

The Politics of Power, which portrayed the Downing Street of January–March 1976 as an only marginally better ventilated version of Hitler's bunker in the climactic days of the Second World War, with Marcia Williams in the role of Eva Braun.

Wilson promptly went on to announce on television, 'I stood loyally by Joe when he was attacked by the press for his grumpy approach to them … People were coming up to me – ministers, very senior ministers – saying I ought to move him, and now this …'

The edifice of governmental solidarity, once maintained so robustly during the Wilson era, now cracked spectacularly, providing the public with the sort of high-end soap opera that never seems to go out of fashion. Speaking to the *Sunday Mirror*, 'not bothering to disguise the venom in her voice', Marcia Williams remarked that Haines had never been comfortable with 'strong, independent women', and actively disliked 'clever, university-educated professionals' – 'a double offence, in my case,' she noted.

On the same day that Williams made these comments, Wilson again summoned the BBC's Barrie Penrose and Roger Courtiour to repeat his opinion that MI5 was riddled with right-wing officers who had done little else with their time over the winter of 1975–76 but 'plot against the Labour government, and, in particular against me as prime minister', and this had certainly been done in cahoots with the US and South African security services. Seeming to confirm their growing doubts about the balance of the ex-premier's mind, Wilson then went on to accuse the two journalists themselves, 'like most of you lot', of having been turned by foreign agents. The net result of the ensuing media coverage, when added to the fallout from the resignation honours list, was to plunge the prevalent public image of the last government to new depths of absurdity.

One way to see the Wilson of around May 1976 is to imagine a pipe-smoking, 60-year-old man hanging around, say, a south London pub, telling people about his life. He relates slightly improbable tales of having once flown around the world with various colleagues, holding meetings with high-powered people in foreign capitals, who control fearsome weapons of mass destruction. He himself has the power to destroy much of the planet by merely picking up a phone on his desk. There are also a series of nefarious intrigues against him back home in Britain, where he oversees a vast political network of incalculable complexity with the power to affect people's everyday lives. Throughout all this, he confronts fiendishly cunning enemies, some of whom were once his friends. Eventually, he comes to see himself surrounded by treachery on all sides and with no option but to retire gracefully into private life, which is how he comes to find himself propping up the bar in his present surroundings. The only difference between this man and Harold Wilson is that while one might be a hopeless bore, the other was a once-revered international statesman and, still to this day, the only British party leader to have succeeded in four general elections.

Britain might have been teetering on the edge of a financial meltdown in 1976, but the Callaghan government still threw itself into what he privately called 'a touch of amelioration in the working man's lot before we, all of us, shuffle off this mortal coil'. The parliamentary clerks charged with updating the UK's ever-expanding statute books were kept especially busy that spring. There were increases in the state pension and rent subsidies for council-house tenants. There was a Fair Employment (Northern Ireland) Act, specifically intended to promote equality of opportunity between those of different religious beliefs in that unhappy province. There were new laws on domestic violence and other aspects of matrimonial life, giving the police the power of arrest for any breach of an existing court order. There was introductory legislation on the metric system. There were increased supplementary benefits, particularly as they might apply to a one-parent family. And there was a significant revision of the 1964 Resale Prices Act, which sought to prevent manufacturers and suppliers from unfairly fixing the cost at which their goods were sold to the retailer and thus on to the ordinary consumer, which Callaghan himself saw as the one imperishable legacy of his government's commitment to change 'the whole climate of national life to the advantage of the common man'.

Lest the record of the first half of 1976 be seen as exclusively one of high-minded altruism on the part of Britain's political class, there was also the Parliamentary Remuneration and Other Pensions and Benefits Act, which brought an MP's basic salary up by 10 per cent to £6,900 (£56,000 today), with a matching increase in secretarial, office and travel allowances. These were figures that, on the whole, compared favourably to the fortunes of professionals employed in other walks of British life. The weekly magazine *New Society* reported that median monthly household disposable income had fallen in the UK from an average of £202 in 1974 and £198 in 1975 to £190 in 1976, with just 5 per cent of those canvassed describing their financial circumstances as 'very strong'. The magazine was left to conclude, 'Sadly, age, class and party did not appear to make much difference ... People seemed to be saying that the country was going to the dogs.'

Among the year's less immediately notable parliamentary business was the seemingly routine Maplin Development Authority (Amendment) Act, which touched on the latest turn of events in the long, Byzantine history of the successive attempts to build a third London airport on reclaimed land near the mouth of the Thames Estuary. In its way, the whole protracted saga was a richly illustrative case study of the sometimes-inscrutable workings of major capital projects of this kind. In March 1971, after what was already an eye-wateringly long and expensive public inquiry into the matter, the Conservative Trade and Industry Secretary John Davies had announced that, on 'environmental and planning grounds', the Foulness site (later known by the more euphonious 'Maplin Sands') was the best of the eighty-four originally studied.

An enabling act was soon pushed through Parliament, which gave the new Maplin Development Authority power to borrow an immediate £250 million, as well as to 'acquire land compulsorily for any purpose connected with its function', and properly compensate 'any person or persons who derive the whole or part of their means of livelihood from the taking of fish or shellfish, or the gathering of white weed' in the expanse of windswept grey mudflats jutting out towards the sea off the coast of Essex around Southend like the deck of a vast naval ship.

The objections to this proposal began virtually before the ink was dry on the original document. The Chancellor, for one, was thought not to be an enthusiastic supporter of Maplin, which was by some distance the most expensive of the four shortlisted options studied by a commission chaired by the High Court Judge Eustace Roskill, which had been in continuous session since 1968. In addition to the economic factors, there was the question of the project's ecological impact, and for that matter, of the precise location of the proposed facility's main runway or runways. The official preference was the cheapest option, 'Site A', which, being closest to Southend, would mean less expensive new transport links. But precisely because Site A lay close to a residential area, ministers rejected it in favour of a more northerly option – Site B – arguing that to do otherwise could risk further delays by forfeiting the support of the local council.

On top of the civilian concerns, the military authorities fired a salvo of their own. The British Army had been testing ordnance around the Maplin area since the days of the Napoleonic Wars and were reluctant to leave. Another lengthy planning inquiry proposed relocating the firing range to Caithness, in the extreme north of Scotland, only for that to be vetoed by local residents who raised issues about the possible damage to the area's many prehistoric remains.

Meanwhile, a protest group composed of local property owners, concerned retailers, county councillors, church officials and assorted trade guilds, such as the Shellfish Merchants Association, came together under the banner of the Defenders of Essex, launching a high-profile campaign to lobby Parliament to oppose the new airport. In time, questions were asked in the House of Commons about the plight of eighteen individuals whose homes might have to be demolished to make way for a proposed Maplin motorway link. Then there was the matter of whether the gravel and concrete artificial island on which the whole enterprise was to be built could withstand the ravages of the inevitable winter storms or would instead collapse back into the North Sea, possibly taking dozens of planes and thousands of innocent passengers with it. And what of the Brent geese? At least 5 million of them made their homes around Maplin Sands. It would only take one of them, perhaps disorientated by the area's notorious fog, to stray incautiously near the intake of a jet engine to risk a dress rehearsal of the drama of 2009's US Airways Flight 1549, or the so-called 'Miracle on the Hudson', but with a potentially less happy outcome all around. Before long, there was an ever-expanding Maplin-themed apparatus of advisory groups and subcommittees convening to discuss whether to consider or merely to record some earlier expression of concern brought to their attention, or how best to administer the terms of reference of the original 1971 enabling legislation as it might apply in each situation where a 'demonstrable concern or inequity should arise in the present circumstances'.

The whole labyrinthine scheme was eventually shelved in 1976, but never quite killed off, and would return from behind its marble slab during Boris Johnson's tenure as Mayor of London, only to be rejected again by the Statutory Airports Commission, and then revived once more, and so on, ad infinitum, the increasingly circular debate polarised between those who felt that the UK should not allow itself to be edged out of the no-frills travel market by large competitive airports elsewhere in northern Europe, and others who believed that holidaymakers in search of a bargain £50 flight to the sun should not be allowed to dictate terms to those who could possibly see their homes and communities demolished as a result.

MAKE THEM GROVEL

By the time the United States bicentennial celebrations began in earnest in the spring of 1976, a degree of soul-searching had already crept in to a country not hitherto known for its introspection, thanks largely to the successive traumas of Vietnam, Watergate and other events that appeared to have touched off a mood of collective self-doubt. It might be tempting fate to generalise, but the consuming internal American debate of the mid-decade could be summarised as one between a culturally conservative core, who looked around them to see a nation characterised by the collapse of educational standards, racial unrest, the discharge of mentally ill patients turned loose from institutions onto the streets, the fracturing of millions of families by divorce, an officially tolerated moral lewdness pervading the public arts, cinema and television and the descent of inner cities into something approaching third world levels of squalor and crime, and the contrary view, of a once-proud, liberal-minded project disfigured by runaway corporate greed and ruinous overseas adventures that justified, if not actually demanded, lawbreaking and, in some cases, elevated this to the status of an eloquent point of principle.

It was a restless period. There was, however, one unifying factor about which most Americans could agree: sport. By 1976, baseball, basketball and American football were all enjoying an unprecedented boom in the United States, with ever more live events shown on prime-time television, the beginning of athletes' taking control of their own careers, greater racial integration and the social revolution that brought more females into the arena, whether as players, coaches, executives or spectators.

The ritual moment of US national renewal heralded by the start of the Major League baseball season came on 8 April 1976, with just over 40 million customers paying to watch one or more of the country's twenty-four professional teams in action between then and the close of play six months later – a figure sports administrators in many other Western countries would kill for. On this occasion, however, even America's relatively pastoral summer game proved not to be immune to the culture wars that swirled around it. A decade of civil conflict had been distinguished by a peace movement that had extended its terms of reference from seeking the end of a conflict that had been effectively concluded the year before to treating America's whole adventure in Indochina as symptomatic of a moral decay that needed to be eradicated, root and branch.

The specific event was the third game of a three-game series between the home team Los Angeles Dodgers and the Chicago Cubs played on Sunday, 25 April. Appearing in centre field for the visitors was 30-year-old Rick Monday, a stocky six-footer with the then standard mullet haircut and, more to the point, a fundamentally patriotic outlook that had led him to volunteer for the US Marine Corps shortly after graduating from college, before embarking on his career with the Kansas City Athletics and transferring to Chicago in 1972. After an hour or so's play that spring evening, Monday had been walking across the warm Los Angeles stadium turf prior to taking up his position in the field when out of the corner of his eye he saw two bushy-haired young men vault over a perimeter wall in the stands and start running full tilt in his direction, shouting, 'Fuck you, America!' at the top of their lungs as they went.

'Sensing trouble,' as Monday later noted with some restraint:

I looked at the two guys and I noticed that one of them had something cradled under his arm. It turned out to be an American flag. They came bar-reling over from the corner of the park towards me, and stood there for a moment in the full glare of the players and that huge Sunday crowd.

That's when I saw the US flag. They unfurled it as if it was a picnic basket ... Then they knelt beside it, not to pay homage but to desecrate it as one of the guys was pulling out of his pocket somewhere a big can of lighter fluid. He began to douse the flag.

'What they were doing was wrong,' Monday continues:

It's the way I was raised. My thoughts went back to the Marine Corps, and the fact that a lot of my friends lost their lives protecting the rights and free-doms that flag represented.

So I started to go after them. I saw them look round at me and then put the match to the flag. It was soaked in lighter fluid by this point. Well, I thought, they can't light it if they don't have it. So I just scooped it up and ran with it. My next thought was, 'My God, is it already on fire?' Well, for-tunately, it wasn't so I kept going ... One of the two men then turned and threw the can of lighter fluid straight at my head. But luckily, he wasn't much of a ball player. It missed.

The three of us kept running like that in a sort of circus chase, until finally we reached the edge of the field and I turned round and said, 'Why don't one of you guys take a swing at me?' because there were fifty-something thousand people in the ballpark, and I only wanted one of them to have a pop at me so I could defend myself and do a job on them ... Instead [a col-league] came off the players' bench and I threw the flag to him. The fight seemed to go out of the two guys after that, and they were led off the field by security.

The first sign that the Chicago player might be among friends that evening came when a section of the crowd then spontaneously broke into a lusty rendition of the Mamas & the Papas' 1966 hit 'Monday, Monday'. Someone else let off some fireworks.

'There was a real buzz in the stands,' Monday says:

People were aghast at what had taken place ... Without being prompted, and I still don't know how or where it started, suddenly 50 thousand people stood up as one and began to chant my name, and from there went on to sing 'God Bless America', and by the end I can tell you there wasn't a dry eye in the house. I still get goose bumps when I think about it. So *that* was America for me in the bicentennial year.

A marginally less charged atmosphere, but a greater shock in terms of the actual sport, came that same week, 5,000 miles away in north London, where Second Division Southampton beat the heavily favoured Manchester United in the FA Cup Final at Wembley. It was Southampton's first ever Cup Final appearance. They had never won a major trophy.

It was all level until the eighty-third minute of play, when Jim McCalliog's long ball dropped over his teammate Bobby Stokes's left shoulder and Stokes slotted his shot past the United goalkeeper. The ball was fired low into the corner of the net from just outside the penalty area and the goal produced both delirium and controversy, with a protracted United objection insisting that at least one of the scorer's colleagues had been offside. No one bothered with video replays in those days, and after waving away the animated deputation of aggrieved red-shirted players, the referee, 39-year-old Clive Thomas from Treorchy in South Wales, advised the interested parties to resume their normal positions in the field, adding a choice intensifier or two to his remarks for emphasis.

Respect for authority figures in general was already quite a hard sell in a mid-1970s culture where deference had been declared obsolete, vituperation and dissent characterised Britain's political discourse and the city streets seethed with sectarian fury, but Mr Thomas carried the day here. A few minutes later, Southampton's captain, Peter Rodrigues, coincidentally also from the Welsh Valleys, went up to the royal box to receive the trophy from the Queen – the last occasion during the remaining forty-six years of her reign that she attended football's set-piece final.

The headline news in cricket that month was the arrival in the British Isles of Clive Lloyd's West Indies team for a series of five Tests, three limited-overs internationals, seventeen matches with the English counties and sundry fixtures somewhat below the first-class against the likes of the Duchess of Norfolk's XI or the Combined Universities. One evening at the end of May, as the tourists were playing out the last rites of a rain-soaked draw with Sussex at Hove, a reporter from the BBC flagship programme *Sportsnight* went up onto the balcony of the small pavilion and interviewed the home team's star all-rounder, 29-year-old Tony Greig, who also happened to be captain of England, about what he thought of the prospects for the summer.

Greig, who was South African-born, qualifying for England thanks to his Scottish father, struck some observers, who still preferred their national cricket captains to be drawn from the ranks of the ancient universities, as a divisive figure. Lean, towering and blond, he had the Nordic good looks that might once have qualified him as the model for a wartime SS recruitment poster. However, the man beneath the somewhat chilly exterior was in fact funny, warm and intelligent, even if it occasionally took time to appreciate his qualities. He was also precociously gifted as a cricketer and, generally speaking, not a martyr to false modesty.

The longer the interview proceeded that evening, the more Greig's impatience grew with a line of questioning that seemed to indicate that England's chances in the coming series were roughly on a par with those of Southampton in the recent Cup Final, but without any realistic hope of a similar surprise ending. 'Look,' said Greig at length:

> I like to think that people are building these West Indians up, because I am not really sure they're as good as everyone thinks they are ... Sure, they've got a couple of fast bowlers [a masterful understatement on Greig's part, as it transpired] but you must remember that if these guys get on top they are magnificent cricketers, but if they're down, they grovel. And I intend, with the help of Closey [45-year-old Brian Close, recently recalled to England colours nine years after his last appearance] and a few others to make them grovel.

It was this last word that proved so explosively provocative to some parties, who seized on it for its apparent racist overtones, while to others it seemed to qualify as an almost wilfully perverse tactic on Greig's part expressly designed to motivate his country's opponents in the series. We will return to the actual outcome of the matches, but for now, it might be fair to say that they did not go entirely as the England captain or his team's supporters might have hoped.

I once asked Brian Close what he and the other home players had made of their captain's remarks at the time. 'I knew what Greig meant,' Close assured me:

We all did. If you got on top of West Indies, the odds were that you'd stay on top. The problem was that Tony, having made his point, never really turned the screw on the buggers once he got on the field. If you don't back words like that up with action you're stuffed. We were stuffed.

✱✱✱

A well-known music journalist said in May 1976:

Perhaps it's me, but it seems like fewer and fewer of the really big hits today – maybe McCartney's the exception – go in for lyrics along the lines of 'I'll love you till the end of time' or 'If you leave me, sugar pie, I'll die' … 'They chopped my baby up, and I don't care' is more like it.

At the heavier end of the rock music spectrum, the journalist's ears weren't deceiving him. Certainly not when it came to David Bowie, arguably Britain's greatest solo star in the pop firmament that spring. As it happened, Bowie had recently parted from his wife, leaving her in their villa in the idyllic Swiss countryside, and had taken the lease on a small flat decorated by the Nazi sculptor Arno Breker in the Schöneberg Quarter of West Berlin, a move that in retrospect proved disastrous to his overall political thinking. Now the man who had enlivened *Top of the Pops* just four years earlier by performing in a multicoloured jumpsuit, with his arm curled limply around his tinfoil-clad guitarist's back, was set to return to play a six-night residency at the Empire Pool, Wembley, in support of his new synthesiser-heavy album *Station to Station*.

Between them, the record and the shows were a major news event. Several hundred fans, as well as reporters from the daily press, were duly present on the forecourt of Victoria Station to welcome Bowie, a confirmed aerophobe, as he arrived from Paris on board the *Orient Express* at around four o'clock on the otherwise uneventful Sunday afternoon of 2 May. A large open-top Mercedes with a uniformed chauffeur was there to meet him.

The idea had apparently been for Bowie himself to give a short speech to those waiting to see him, but the PA system hired for the occasion broke down. A replacement system was quickly brought out but also broke down. As an alternative, Bowie, wearing a waist-length tunic and matching dark shirt and trousers, and concave from drug use, got in the car, stood up and promptly thrust out his right arm. The next day's press photograph of him being driven out of the station in a black German limousine, apparently regaling the crowd with a Nazi salute, achieved near mythological status in the years ahead. *New Musical Express* ran it over four columns, under the headline 'Heil and Farewell'.

Perhaps it was all just an innocent wave or a 'trick of the light', as Bowie himself later insisted was the case, but set against this there was his statement earlier that spring when asked to comment on Britain's latest economic crisis. 'I believe very strongly in fascism,' Bowie remarked:

> The only way we can speed up the demise of the sort of liberalism that's hanging foul in the air at the moment is to speed up the progress of a right-wing, totally dictatorial tyranny and get it over as fast as possible. People have always responded with greater efficiency under a regimental leadership.

Later that month, which also saw the death by electrocution of Bowie's friend, the Yardbirds singer Keith Relf, the Rolling Stones – now known as much for their general air of dissipation as their creative chops, and considered by some to already be hopelessly decrepit in their early thirties – embarked on their own six-night hometown stand at Earls Court. Mick Jagger managed a little 1960s-style outrage by publicly referring to the venue as 'the shittiest toilet I've ever seen', but then somewhat spoilt the effect later that night by inviting Princess Margaret backstage, his fellow band members shuffling up to be introduced like a sick Cup Final team at Wembley. It was not without amusement that the press discovered, as his tastes matured, that when Jagger began to find pleasure in aristocratic society, those who were once the target of his satire became numbered among his closest friends. There was much talk in 1976 of his 'hobnobbing' (a word that was to be slightly fore-shortened in a later biography) with Princess Margaret, among several other well-born ladies.

From the sounds of the ensuing concert, you could tell that there had been a catastrophic breakdown in the chemically based creative process, and as a result, a metallic din was going to be inflicted on the audience for much of the show. Jagger was flying around on a trapeze throughout a good part of the repertoire, which would see Keith Richards perform in front of the Queen's sister and 18,000 lesser mortals wearing a silver necklace with a snorting tube and coke spoon on it.

At a provincial warm-up show in Stafford, Richards engaged in another of those random, long-distance drives which, accompanied by a takeaway fish-and-chip dinner and enlivened by a pounding reggae album in the tape deck, then constituted his idea of a quality night out. Some two hours after leaving the concert venue, Keith was at the wheel of his recently pink-tinted Bentley Continental when he nodded off for a moment, lost control and bounced the car off a guardrail and into a field just outside Newport Pagnell Service Station. It was four in the morning. When the police arrived, they found the hirsute guitarist, wearing sunglasses and wandering up the side of the M1 with his 6-year-old son in tow.

It did not take the officers long in their subsequent search of the Bentley to locate the snorting tube, and other related paraphernalia, squeezed under the driver's seat. Charged with possession, Richards later appeared in the same Aylesbury courthouse where the Great Train Robbers had stood trial thirteen years earlier. Denying everything, he was found guilty on the coke charges, acquitted on others, and given a fine. The author was present on the final day of the proceedings, and it was an interesting experience. The defendant was dressed in a dark suit and spoke in a level, pleasant voice. Nothing really moved in Richards's impressively stony face but his eyes, and when he was moved to anger, they did so with the sudden click of a cocking pistol. Keith told the jury that he never did drugs of any description and had not so much as previously seen the snorting gear introduced as evidence against him. 'It could belong to anyone. I don't even know what it is ... I've never seen anything like it before in my life.' At that point, the prosecution had produced a wall-sized blow-up of a press photograph of the accused wearing a chain and tube identical to the one seized by the police. 'I don't know anything about it,' Keith maintained stubbornly.

A few days later, the Who, another group of 1960s survivors coming to enjoy a 1970s commercial windfall – by no means universally the case – went back on stage at Charlton Football Ground in south London. It poured with rain, but the crowd was lively. Bill Payne and his band Little Feat went on as the night's support act and he still remembers the 'hundreds of bottles' sailing back at them over the footlights. The Who earned an entry in the *Guinness Book of Records* as the world's loudest pop group during their performance, with a 126-decibel reading at 50m, roughly akin to the experience of standing at the end of an active airport runway or operating a heavy-duty chainsaw.

The band played with a primal energy that seemed to take on a comic-strip vitality as the distant cartoon figures on stage landed one musical knockout blow after another; you could almost see the capitalised 'POW!' and 'WHAMMO!' concussion sounds in their spiky little speech bubbles. Characteristically, the Who's drummer, Keith Moon, brought something of the same blithe spirit to the proceedings backstage, where, waiting to go on, his bandmates were surprised by the sight of Moon crashing through the ceiling, having dug a hole for himself in their dressing-room's corrugated tin roof from above.

★★★

Four nights later, violence erupted on the streets of west London, marking the start of what would become a steadily more pressurised summer of soaring temperatures and hot-tempered confrontations between rival groups mutually equipped with smoke bombs, flares, bricks and broken milk bottles to resolve the points that lay between them. The specific flashpoint was the death on 4 June of an 18-year-old Sikh engineering student named Gurdip Singh Chaggar. By all accounts, he was an intelligent and soft-spoken young man, still living at home, a competitive hockey player, turban-wearing, slim with glinting dark eyes and a recent half-hearted attempt at growing a moustache. He had been walking past the front door of the gabled Victory pub in Southall's main street, known to be a lively spot most weekend evenings, at around seven that Friday night, on his way to the cinema, when several white youths, apparently struck by the sight of his turban, accosted him. There would be different accounts of the ensuing exchange, but one way or another, this had soon become 'heated', a jury later heard, and after a scuffle Chaggar fell to the ground with stab wounds to his abdomen and chest. It was said that as the emergency services arrived to attend to him, a middle-aged man had emerged from the pub, calmly assessed the spectacle of a young man lying in the gutter struggling for his life and announced in a loud voice, 'One down, a million to go'.

An hour later, a friend of the victim named Suresh Grover, coming across the drying pool of blood, unknowingly asked a policeman the identity of the victim. 'Just another Asian,' the officer said. Gurdip Singh Chaggar died of his wounds shortly after reaching hospital that night.

Forty-eight hours later, a group of 3,000 predominantly Indian and Pakistani youths took to the street to march to Southall's main police station, while rival factions distinguished by their skinhead haircuts shouted unappreciative comments from across the road. A potential race riot was averted only when Commander Tom Harrison of the Metropolitan Police agreed, after protracted negotiations with the Asian marchers, to release two of their number who had previously been arrested for disorderly conduct. He made the point, however, that he still had to charge one of the two because otherwise he would run the risk of offending his own men. One of the Asian leaders, a recent arrival in the country named Praful Patel, paid the commander an unexpected compliment.

'He is a first-class copper,' Mr Patel informed the press, in terms that suggested he had already adopted some of the *Sweeney* patois of his host culture. 'He took a humane and wise decision. If I had been a copper, I would have liked to have had him as my governor.' But in fact, not all the policemen on duty on the streets of Southall that night were quite as generous when the two youths duly walked out of their station's front door. One of the officers was heard to mutter, 'The bastards have got away', which was mild compared to the references to 'Curry breath' and other satirical comments from the ranks of his colleagues. Mr Patel himself only smiled indulgently in the face of these aspersions, perhaps assuming they were all part of the Met's famously opaque sense of humour. While he gave interviews, some of the opposing factions in the area were setting fire to nearby houses.

There was another demonstration, now some 6,000 strong, the following Saturday night, and this one attracted representatives of interested parties drawn from around the country, such as the International Marxist Group and their sworn ideological foe the National Front. At a climactic moment, when the chant 'PAKIS OUT!' began to issue around the street from crop-haired individuals brandishing loudhailers, the police tried to form a human barrier to separate the members of the rival groups, some of whom broke through the cordon, threw punches, traded insults, smashed windows and managed to overturn a parked car. In short order, the local fire brigade was summoned to train their hoses on demonstrators who attempted to clamber over a locked gate and through the front door of the Southall station house, presumably to try to remove one or more of the young Asians known to be detained there. The dousing didn't entirely deter the rioters, but it impressed a group of innocent passers-by caught in the crossfire, who conferred briefly among themselves and then told the firemen they were wankers.

Broadly similar scenes followed at weekly intervals throughout the summer. Before it was all over, Commander Harrison had deemed it best to have barbed-wire fences erected around his building, while several nearby homeowners had similarly placed broken glass across the tops of their garden walls and local retailers took to nailing large wooden boards over their front windows. Hearing reports of the fortress-like atmosphere of one of the capital city's most densely populated neighbourhoods, the superbly urbane Home Secretary Roy Jenkins came to visit the scene one evening later in July, breaking off from denouncing the 'wholly unacceptable level of disorder on all sides' to quietly enquire of an accompanying journalist where one might get a decent local meal with a drop of red to go with it.

The deteriorating state of community relations in Southall would soon be mirrored in other parts of London, and the country at large, during that oppressively hot summer. No one was ever charged with the murder of Gurdip Chaggar, although two white teenagers later confessed in court to his involuntary manslaughter and each got a three-year prison sentence as a result.

'HE ALWAYS BEHAVED SO NORMALLY AT HOME'

Scanning the British daily press on Monday, 7 June 1976, the reader would have seen the news about the recent outbreaks of factional unrest on the streets of London, along with more mordant comment on the Wilson honours list and the latest turn in the fishing-rights war with Iceland. All the broadsheets carried lengthy obituaries of the American-born oil tycoon, Jean Paul Getty, who had died the previous day, aged 83, at his Tudor mansion near Guildford, just eight weeks after the death of his fellow misanthropic billionaire, Howard Hughes.

As is often noted in screen and print portrayals, Getty was an interesting study in contrasts. Enjoying a net worth of some $4 billion ($30 billion today), and thus with no obvious need to do so, he kept working virtually up to the end of his life, rising early each day, eating a frugal breakfast, chewing each mouthful a precisely counted thirty-three times and then retiring to an oak-panelled study furnished with several suits of armour and heraldic banners, his pride in which was certainly not untainted by an implied, though unjustified, aspiration to ancient dynastic status. There Getty would sit bolt upright at his desk, a pale, sombre figure, his features composed in a default expression of disapproval at the various balance sheets and other data set before him.

It was an unvarying ritual, punctuated only by the arrival of a nurse bringing him a daily hormone shot rumoured to have a strong simian component.

At intervals, a uniformed assistant would appear similarly bearing a telephone on a crested tray and Getty would typically bark out some curt instruction along the lines of 'Buy' or 'Sell', before replacing the receiver with unusual force for one of his advancing years. On summer afternoons, he sometimes liked to potter around his 700-acre estate, in the manner of P.G. Wodehouse's Lord Emsworth, but without the pig, before going on to entertain, if it could be called that, one of his cast of glamorous women friends, all many years his junior, to dinner.

Set against these generally unobjectionable habits and characteristics, there was Getty's famous if not pathological thrift. It permeated every aspect of both his business and personal affairs. Getty often remarked how much he hated to give money away, not only because it was expected of him, but because it was also 'wrong and unrewarding' for the beneficiary. To illustrate the point, he frequently told the story of how he had once declined to pay a number of the more extravagant medical bills for the care of his 6-year-old son Timmy, who had become blind from a brain tumour, or on a more banal note, of the time he had walked around for an hour in a rain-soaked London street in order to get into a local dog show at the reduced evening price.

Each day, an assistant brought Getty a ledger of household expenses, including, for instance, the exact number of eggs ordered by the estate cook or the cover price of the morning papers delivered to him at his breakfast table, down which he drew a long, bony finger, authorising some disbursements and questioning many others. It was said he really had the soul of a shopkeeper straining to express itself as a swashbuckling entrepreneur. Perhaps the most notorious symbol of his parsimony was the fully operational payphone he kept in the entrance hall of his estate, which Getty had installed so that his guests, as he explained it, wouldn't need to feel as if they were imposing on his hospitality.

***

In Oxford, the trial was underway that week of a 39-year-old career criminal who called himself Donald Neilson. A standout homicidal psychopath in a crowded 1976 field, Neilson's early life conformed to broadly the same warped stereotype as Peter Sutcliffe or David Berkowitz. He had been born in Bradford as Donald Nappey, a name which attracted a degree of ridicule at school and which he changed while performing his National Service with the army. His childhood and adolescence were said to be unhappy, especially after his mother died from cancer when he was 11.

Neilson did not adapt well on his return to civilian life, drifting between menial jobs while carrying out at least 400 petty thefts or house burglaries, with a latter-day penchant for robbing sub-post offices around West Yorkshire and Lancashire. His habit of carrying a shotgun with him was to cost three men their lives. At the age of 18, he had married a local Bradford woman named Irene Tate, who would later insist that at no time during their twenty years together did she have any idea of her husband's criminal tendencies, another point of similarity with Peter Sutcliffe's family story.

Along the way, Neilson acquired the nickname of the 'Black Panther'. It came about after the wife of one of his victims said that she had seen him flit across her bedroom dressed in dark clothes, so quick in his movements that 'he was like a big cat'. Neilson himself was later said not to be entirely displeased with the name, which represented a significant step up for him from his previous police sobriquet – chosen for his preference of entering people's homes through their windows – of 'Brace and Bit'.

In the early hours of 14 January 1975, Neilson broke into a detached four-bedroom home in Highley, Shropshire, where he abducted 17-year-old Lesley Whittle from her bed at gunpoint. Some weeks earlier, he had read a newspaper article about the Whittle family, the owners of a modestly successful local transport business, and concluded that they would pay handsomely for Lesley's safe return. After gagging his terrified victim, he took her out through the winter night to his Morris 1300 car, where he tied her up, before blindfolding her and ordering her to lie down on the back seat beneath a foam mattress. The teenager was wearing only her underwear and a short slip throughout this initial part of her ordeal. Neilson then calmly walked back into the house, where he removed £200 in cash and, in turn, left three pre-printed Dymo-tape messages informing the Whittles that their daughter had been kidnapped and would be returned to them for a ransom of £50,000.

Following that, Neilson drove his hostage 65 miles to a lonely spot of his acquaintance in Bathpool Park, near Kidsgrove in Staffordshire. There, he forced Lesley down an iron ladder into the narrow drainage shaft of a reservoir. They navigated this passage together until they reached a shallow protruding ledge some 55ft above what would have been a sheer drop to the ground. At that point, Neilson removed his victim's gag and blindfold, ordered her to undress, placed a hood over her head and tethered her with a coiled wire to the side of the wall, where he left her. It was here that Lesley Whittle was to spend the short remaining time of her life, alone, cold and naked, tied to the side of a dark subterranean utility shaft by a noose around her neck.

Under other circumstances, Neilson's subsequent attempts to collect money from Lesley's distraught family might almost have touched the level of a Peter Sellers comedy – or at least, one of those performances like *Dr Strangelove* that blend farce and nightmare. First, Neilson affected a rather approximate Caribbean accent when phoning Lesley's older brother Ronald to discuss the payment arrangements. The kidnapper then prepared several further Dymo-tape messages addressed to the Whittles, which he placed in a variety of phone boxes across the West Midlands, where they were either overlooked or dismissed as pranks by the disinterested parties who found them. Ronald's subsequent attempt to make direct contact with Neilson similarly foundered when, while driving around Kidsgrove in the dark, he lost his bearings and parked his car in the wrong part of Bathpool Park, as it happened just a few dozen yards from where his sister was being held underground.

A later television appeal by the Whittle family proved fruitless. Neilson encountered a 44-year-old man named Gerald Smith, a store nightwatchman, during one of his Dymo-tape nocturnal tours of local phone boxes and, after a confrontation of some sort, shot him six times with a handgun. The victim died of his injuries some months later.

Fifty-two days after Lesley Whittle's abduction, a chance discovery by some schoolchildren of a lantern-style torch with a scrap of Dymo tape stuck to it led the police to the reservoir in Bathpool Park. The victim's lifeless body was found on 7 March 1975, hanging from a wire noose at the bottom of the shaft. It is not known whether she fell from the narrow ledge where she was held or was pushed by Neilson, but the condition of her body suggested she had been starved for some time before she died. Her killer later taunted the police for their failure to find her sooner, saying, 'Somebody is to blame. I hold you responsible.'

Donald Neilson's eventual capture in December 1975 owed less to the methodical investigation by the 100-strong taskforce assigned to the case than to the initiative of two individual beat policemen in a panda car who saw a man 'scurrying' around a side street in suburban Mansfield, Nottinghamshire. The officers thought they were dealing with what they called the 'local nutter' until the moment the man pulled a gun on them, forced them back into their car and demanded they drive him to the nearby village of Blidworth. About halfway there, the two hostages took the opportunity to confront their abductor and, with the help of some have-a-go members of the public, subdued the man, who identified himself as 'John Motson', which happened to be the name of a popular BBC football commentator. A search revealed two black hoods concealed beneath the suspect's jacket, leading police to believe that they had caught the elusive Black Panther.

At his June 1976 trial, Neilson indignantly denied any responsibility for the death of Lesley Whittle, a tragedy he speculated must have occurred when he had absented himself from his lair in order to continue his fruitless discussions with his hostage's brother. In his account, the 'lovely girl' must simply have slipped off the ledge where he had left her after having first thoughtfully laid on a flask of soup, a bottle of brandy and a book of crossword puzzles with which to occupy her time and insulate her against the frigid temperature. 'My conscience is clear in the matter,' he assured the court.

The jury took less than two hours to return its verdict of guilty, for which Neilson received a whole-life sentence. In July 1976, he was given three further concurrent life sentences for his murder of three sub-postmasters. He remained incarcerated for the remainder of his life and died in December 2011 at the age of 75.

★★★

Some of the same ghastly ingredients of the Lesley Whittle case were also at work that spring some 80 miles away on the darkened city streets of West Yorkshire. In the early hours of Sunday, 9 May, a 20-year-old West Indian-born woman, Marcella Claxton, who was four months pregnant, was walking home from a late-night party in the Chapeltown area of Leeds. A man slowly passed by in a white Ford Corsair saloon, rolled down the window and enquired if she was 'doing business'. Claxton, who had mild learning difficulties, replied that no, she wasn't a prostitute, but that she would appreciate a lift home.

After a minute or two, it became chillingly clear to her that the stranger was taking her in the opposite direction to the one requested, pulling to a stop in a deserted side street near the city's Roundhay Park. Telling the driver that she needed to urinate, Marcella walked to some bushes, where she lowered her underwear and crouched down. It was then that he brutally assaulted her, using either a hammer or a heavy spanner to beat her around the head and upper body, leaving her in a pool of blood, before abruptly driving off. His victim subsequently needed extensive surgery as a result of her injuries. She also lost the child she was carrying.

The West Yorkshire police discounted her impressively detailed description of her assailant, apparently assuming, in the logic of the gulags, that she was either a sex worker who had been confronted by a dissatisfied client or in some other way had contributed to the attack, the result of a perfect storm of official prejudice based on the victim's presumed occupation and skin colour.

The man who assaulted Marcella Claxton was of course Peter Sutcliffe, who would go on to attack or murder at least twenty more women before his eventual capture, in circumstances broadly similar to the arrest of Donald Neilson, in January 1981. In time, Sutcliffe's unchecked reign of terror became so pervasive that, for many, it came to define daily life in the north of England. Women would avoid going out at night or would do so only in groups. Men were stopped in their cars and questioned by police.

A hotline brought in half a million tips from members of the public, some of them potentially helpful, many others seeming to take a perverse delight in steering detectives in the wrong direction, attributing the homicidal spree affecting large parts of the region to everything from an estranged family member to the spirit of the late Winston Churchill. The main investigating police station in Leeds operated a card index system containing over 30,000 individual statements or other files, none of them ever catalogued or cross-referenced, which meant that a significant amount of material was either overlooked or lost.

Even the physical backdrop to the tragedy became synonymous with the horror. The crumbling inner cities and deindustrialised urban wastelands with their acres of dead tramway lines and rubble dumped into the green, still hair-oil of the local canal, sat alongside grim, soiled suburbs whose only points of distinction were their endless one-way systems and rows of pubs and bookie's offices. There was also the expanding motorway network which, it turned out, a man like Sutcliffe could use in order to commit a late-night murder in Manchester and still be back home with his loving wife in Bradford in time for bed.

'I couldn't believe it of him because he always behaved so normally at home,' Sonia Sutcliffe later remarked of the man now thought to have been responsible for as many as twenty-two unsolved murders in addition to the thirteen for which he was convicted. Sutcliffe himself died in hospital while in prison custody in November 2020, at the age of 74. An independent police inquiry led by the former Chief Constable of Lincolnshire, Lawrence Byford, later remarked on the 'progressive decline in the overall efficiency of the major incident room', which, in his measured opinion, 'fell some way short of the optimum standard expected in an investigation of this gravity'.

★★★

Every generation offends the standards of the one that precedes it, but the general dumbing down of mass public entertainment in the mid-1970s became a widely remarked-on truth, even by some of the parties complicit in it. In the words of the 75-year-old US media tycoon William Paley, whose CBS network was responsible for such primetime fare as the lowbrow sitcom *Busting Loose* or the game show *Tattletale*, which encouraged celebrity couples to share details of their sex lives:

> There is a desire on the part of young people for messy TV shows. They don't want it straight. Nor do they want a good beginning, middle and end. They want the damn thing to float around, and they want something there to read into it that the old farts can't or won't see. The cleavage factor should be huge, too.

One of the literally diabolic fruits of the trend Paley referred to was *The Omen*, released in June 1976, with Gregory Peck slumming it in the role of the US Ambassador to Great Britain, whose demon spawn plans to grow up to rule the world in the name of the forces of darkness. The whole film was entertaining enough in its way, if perhaps straining for meaning when it came to the part about the biblical prophecy insisting that the son of Satan would return to the ruination of all mankind when the Roman Empire rises again. Peck nods gravely at this point of the proceedings. 'Yes,' he says, 'That would be the European Economic Community.'

Shot not in Hollywood but around various locations in south London and Surrey, *The Omen* did an initial $40 million worth of business at the global box office, the equivalent of $300 million at current prices. But even those figures paled in comparison to those for *Rocky*, which raked in some $68 million ($540 million today), following its release later that year, giving it an eventual return of 11,000 per cent on its budget. It's been described as everything from a refreshing antidote to the depressing litany of European films of the day in which the main protagonist struggles to come to terms with failure, oppression, institutional and personal corruption and the inability to achieve one's dreams in life, to the worst blockbuster in history. Less lucrative, but more acceptable to serious-minded critics was Roman Polanski's claustro-phobic masterpiece *The Tenant*, an exercise in mental disintegration, whose title suggested that audiences might be watching the story of a man's fragile lease on his own sanity and also worthy of note as the last film Polanski would make before the abrupt fall from grace occasioned by his statutory rape of a 13-year-old girl.

***

On 15 June 1976, the Sex Pistols played a characteristically uninhibited con-cert at the subterranean 100 Club in London's Oxford Street. Things got off to a brisk start when the band's lead vocalist, introducing himself only as John, invited the 300-strong audience to 'Get off your arses', following which the dentally challenged singer writhed and sneered around the stage, his hair a ret-ina-bashing confection of yellow and red, his off-white blazer shredded at the shoulder and held together with safety pins. There was a touch of Richard III and his hunchbacked *confrère* Quasimodo about the performance, with distinct undertones of the sort of knock-kneed Norman Wisdom character who walks the thin line between pathos and comedy. For his part, the guitarist Steve Jones took a defiantly non-technical approach to his craft. 'You just hit the fucking strings, and you've got a riff going,' he remarked.

Even at the time, it was clear that the Sex Pistols were moving the goal-posts of what defined an acceptable form of public entertainment, taking it well beyond or outside even that of the heady early days of the Stones or the Who. There were two or three ad-hoc bouncers at the front of the low 100 Club stage, and as they were shouting at people to not climb up and join the band, the musicians themselves were shouting exactly the opposite, with predictably chaotic results. Many of those who remained on the floor con-tented themselves with pogoing up and down in a series of malign hops, using their point of maximum elevation to spit lustily at the four band members in what appeared to be a spirit of comradeship and respect rather than of critical reserve.

Either way, it was a compelling forty minutes of immersive, mutually con-frontational theatre. After a breakneck rendition of the Who's 'Substitute' and the self-composed 'Pretty Vacant', John the singer glared around the room to enquire, 'Looking at me, are you pro or anti-abortion?' Another storm of applause erupted, though with no definite consensus on the point. Following a climactic version of 'No Fun' by the celebrated American cult band the

Stooges, John tossed the microphone over his shoulder with a clunk, pausing only to treat the audience to a necessarily unamplified but still richly emphatic belch on his way out.

Looking around for a way to capture the essence of the whole spectacle as epitomised by the Pistols, the tabloids borrowed an Americanism that had been around at least since the *Chicago Tribune* first used it in March 1970. They hit on the term 'punk rock' to describe the sort of disaffected youth culture capable of provoking a simulated moral panic in the media that was significantly out of proportion to the movement's actual numbers.

★★★

On a cloudy late summer afternoon in 1976, the blip of an unidentified aircraft flashed up on ground radar just off the coast of the northern Japanese island of Hokkaido. The plane in question had previously been flying a mere 100ft over the water, low enough to avoid detection. Now, suddenly, it climbed to 20,000ft, nearly colliding with an inbound civilian airliner as it did so, before rapidly descending again for an unauthorised landing at the short-runway Hakodate Airport.

The mystery aircraft, identifiable by its markings as a Soviet fighter jet, came in hard, blowing out its front two wheels on touchdown and deploying its drogue parachute. It drew to a stop only yards short of a perimeter fence separating the airport from a busy highway. As groundcrews rushed to meet it, the plane's canopy opened. A stocky blond man of about 30 emerged with a pistol in his hand and fired two shots in the air to warn off the convoy of emergency vehicles heading in his direction. The man's name was Lieutenant Viktor Belenko, of the Soviet Air Defence Forces, he announced, and he wished to speak only to an accredited representative of the Japanese Foreign Ministry before continuing his journey to his stated destination, 'Anywhere permissible in the United States of America'. He was there to defect, he confirmed, and both he and his supersonic MiG-25 'Foxbat' fighter were at the disposal of the Western authorities.

In time, Lieutenant Belenko did indeed settle in the United States, where, with some reservations, he found the land of hope and opportunity he had dreamed about during the years he had grown increasingly disillusioned with the straitened circumstances of his life behind the Iron Curtain. Early in his stay, a US State Department handler showed the defecting aviator around the well-stocked shelves of a supermarket near his adopted home in the Virginia suburbs, where at first Belenko refused to believe that the goods on display were readily available to ordinary Americans. Sometime later in his residency, he inadvertently bought a tin of cat food at a grocery store, not realising it was for pets. When someone pointed out the error, he shrugged and said it still tasted better than the food sold for human consumption back home in Vladivostok.

It turned out that the Foxbat itself was of only limited interest to the Japanese and American experts who successively examined it before returning it, in pieces, to the Soviet Union several weeks later. It was big but slow and sadly lacking in manoeuvrability compared to its US counterparts. Of greater value, though, was what Belenko told his Pentagon debriefers about conditions and morale in the Soviet armed forces. Far from being the relentless fighting machine of popular legend, the typical Soviet soldier, sailor or airman of the day was often a half-starved and ill-paid conscript, forced into cramped living quarters and subject to brutal punishment for the smallest infraction. 'If my regiment could see five minutes of what I see today,' Belenko told a US officer shortly after his arrival, 'there would be a revolution.'

Lieutenant Belenko's story is worth mentioning, not because it conveys the complete and unvarnished truth about life in the United States of 1976 – a country, as we've seen, with a backlog of unresolved social and economic ills perhaps not immediately apparent to the first-time visitor – but because it encapsulated a key argument in the run-up to that year's US Presidential election. In his bid to attract conservative support during his Primary challenge against his party colleague Gerald Ford, Ronald Reagan, the 65-year-old former actor and more recently two-term governor of California, had spoken of the dangers of détente with the Soviet Union, which he equated with a self-inflicted wound on the part of the West. To hear Reagan speak of it, US foreign policy as practised by the president and his slippery Secretary of State Henry Kissinger was principally designed to make 'suspect acquaintances' of 'sworn enemies of the United States like Comrade Brezhnev'.

Reagan also used the continuing negotiations over control of the Panama Canal – transitioning from one of outright ownership to an arrangement that relinquished sovereignty but established permanent US rights of access in the area – to attack the Ford administration for plunging ahead with a 'giveaway'. Panama's leader Omar Torrijos should be told, Reagan declared, to whoops of applause at many of his primary campaign whistlestops, 'We built it, we paid for it, and we're going to keep it'. Ford thought it was not quite that simple and worried about the possible domino effect (or 'nationalist shitstorm', as he privately termed it) that might ensue in Latin America if Washington pursued such a course.

Ronald Reagan ultimately failed in his bid to unseat the incumbent president, although his moment would come at the equivalent stage four years later. He was a likeable and decent man, who his many critics suspected compensated with synthetic Hollywood charm what he lacked in intellectual candlepower. But whatever you made of him, Reagan spoke for a powerful constituency which believed that successive administrations, Democrat and Republican alike, had sold out the nation's interests to the Soviet Union and catastrophically muted America's moral voice to stir the dying embers of détente. Reagan's United States was the one the defecting Lieutenant Belenko experienced as a land of instinctive generosity and unbounded plenty, where it was necessary for the elected officials to have only impulses – patriotism, anti-communism and a desire for peace through strength – rather than policies.

★★★

Perhaps the defining symbol of the United States that star-spangled summer wasn't a great rallying leader or a maverick politician at all, however. Instead, it was a lanky, mop-haired figure, with a pleasing facial resemblance to Harpo Marx, named Mark 'Bird' Fidrych. So called because he shared certain characteristics with the Big Bird character from television's *Sesame Street*, he was just then embarking on his first year as a pitcher for the lowly Detroit Tigers baseball team.

Having grown up on a farm in central Massachusetts, Fidrych was squarely in the storybook tradition of the untutored prodigy who wanders, wide-eyed and shoeless, out of the backwoods to set the world aflame with his God-given talent. When he took the initial phone call telling him that he had been 'drafted' by Detroit, he said in all seriousness that he had assumed he was being recruited into the armed services.

That summer of 1976, he not only electrified his hometown audiences, but captivated much of the rest of the United States as well. Millions of people who never normally went near a sports stadium or followed the minutiae of scores and averages suddenly knew the name, the face and, above all, the mannerisms of Bird Fidrych. His was more than a mere physical athletic proficiency. It was a performance. Among other idiosyncrasies, Fidrych was known to hold animated conversations with the baseball he held in his palm before throwing it at his waiting opponent, and to get down on his knees to carefully manicure the turf in front of him. He would pace maniacally around after each pitch, apparently in a heated debate with an unseen second party, complete with frantic windmilling arm gestures and tortured facial expressions. As people observed, he was a piece of work.

Opinions vary over what Fidrych was really like or how much of it was an act. Perhaps there was a degree of affected comedy or pandering to the crowd. But Fidrych could really play the game, too. He was voted the American League Rookie of the Year in 1976, when he was the winning pitcher in nineteen starts and the loser in just eight, with a league-leading 2.34 average. A cricket fan need only think of the well-known tale of the teenaged Harold Gimblett wandering out to the middle on his first-class debut for Somerset against Essex one spring morning in 1935 and scoring 123 runs in seventy-nine minutes, playing throughout with a borrowed bat, but with a backdrop of patriotic bunting and fireworks and all the other razzamatazz of a major US sports event – sustained over a period of several months – to get some of the feel.

Fidrych became an instant cult hero and fans flocked to fill the previously cavernous stands of the Detroit Tigers' stadium whenever he was scheduled to appear in the line-up. On 28 June, a sellout crowd of 52,000 saw him lead his team to victory against the mighty New York Yankees, and after the game, no one would leave until he came out to take what became a protracted series of curtain calls. Over the course of the summer his face was splashed on the front of *Life*, *Sports Illustrated* and *Sporting News*, and he went on to become the first athlete to grace the cover of *Rolling Stone*.

Part of the attraction was that, like Ronald Reagan, Fidrych exuded a sort of boyish optimism and self-deprecating humour, and was known for his unassuming lifestyle, earning just $16,000 ($125,000 today) a year, living in a one-bedroom downtown Detroit apartment, driving a used car and answering his voluminous fan mail by hand. But part of the appeal went deeper than that. Fidrych preached love of country, the joy of sport in its purest form and the dangers of commercialising what he saw as unadulterated fun. Like Reagan, he believed in the manifest destiny of the United States. He also believed in intuition, psychic phenomena and his ability to communicate directly with a cork-filled, 5oz baseball.

And that, tragically, was it in terms of Fidrych's hour in the sun. No sooner did he come than he went, not only by the same door but almost in the same breath. The monumental brevity of his active career surely adds another layer of poignancy to the whole story. Early in the following year, Fidrych sustained an undiagnosed injury to his throwing arm, which he reported 'just froze' on him one day – only years later, diagnosed as a torn rotator cuff – and things went rapidly downhill from there.

The Tigers kept him on their staff largely for his public relations value but they finally gave him his cards in 1980. At the age of 26, he was finished as an athlete. Now married with a young daughter, Fidrych returned to the farm in Massachusetts, helped serve at a rural diner owned by his mother-in-law, always found time for the fans who made the pilgrimage to see him and operated as a freelance contractor hauling gravel and asphalt around in his ancient ten-wheel dump truck. He died in April 2009 after his clothes became trapped in the spinning take-off mechanism of the truck as he lay doing repairs beneath it. The coroner said that five minutes might have elapsed between the accident starting and his losing consciousness. Mark Fidrych was aged 54 at the time of his terrible death.

Speaking a few days later, Ernie Harwell, the veteran Detroit Tigers broadcaster, said of him, 'Mark was a little naïve, but in a good way. He was just a sweet kid at heart who walked in off the farm, thrilled us for a year, and then walked off into the sunset again.' Part of Fidrych's allure was clearly his technical ability to hurl a baseball accurately, at devastatingly high speed, at an opposing player. But the real reason he brought tens of thousands of customers flocking to any stadium where he played, and had millions more glued to their TV or radio, wasn't merely because he could swing the ball this way or that to make even the most accomplished batter seem like a snake mesmerised by a fakir in his presence. It was because the values Fidrych seemed to embody, among them a fundamental decency, an openness and an unquenchably optimistic outlook that reflected the founding ideals of the United States still resonated with a large proportion of his fellow citizens at the time their nation celebrated its 200th birthday.

★★★

Tony Greig's mission to make the summer's West Indian tourists cower before the might of their English hosts was only partly fulfilled by events at the series' first two Tests, played respectively at Trent Bridge and Lord's that June. The Englishmen had rapidly had to adopt a containment policy during the first of the two matches, in which 24-year-old Viv Richards scored a seven-hour innings of 232. Neither Greig nor the recalled Brian Close offered much in return, although the bespectacled, prematurely greying David Steele – known as 'the bank clerk who went to war' in *The Sun*, and as 'Crime' (as in 'Crime doesn't pay') for his Getty-like parsimony elsewhere – contributed a gritty century of his own. At the end, England were set to score 339 to win in just over five hours, a challenge that was never entertained.

The second Test at Lord's was also drawn, largely because the whole of Saturday was wiped out by rain. Richards was away injured, but by then, a certain disparity in the sheer bowling muzzlepower of the two sides must have been apparent to all but the most partisan home supporter. While the West Indies attack boasted Andy Roberts, Michael Holding and Vanburn Holder, the hosts could offer only Chris Old, the late-career John Snow and Greig, the last with an action, all pumping legs and jutting elbows, which fairly bristled with attacking intent but was only fitfully crowned with any numerical success. Taken as a whole, it put one in mind of watching a fleet of finely tuned Formula 1 Ferraris interacting with a ragtag convoy of steady but slightly ramshackle Ford Cortinas.

The famed West Indies juggernaut, with the likes of Joel Garner and Malcolm Marshall still awaiting their turn, was well and truly on its way. Over the next dozen years, their team won seventy Tests and lost only eighteen, with pace accounting for more than nine out of ten of all wickets taken by their bowlers over the same period, at an average of 21 apiece. With due respect to Tony Greig, on the evidence here, one of his chief characteristics, alongside his undoubted skills as a player, was an unfortunate proclivity for biting off more than he could chew.

***

It was especially perverse that rain should wash out what might have been the critical Saturday, 19 June of the Lord's Test. The downpour not only denied England, who were 68 ahead of their opponents on first innings, a slim chance of victory, but it marked the eve of the UK's longest period of sustained dry weather for more than 350 years, and its driest summer for over 200.

Over the next ten weeks, the iconic images were those of uninhibited young sunbathers plunging into the Serpentine in Hyde Park, while dressed in attire of the most spartan cut (or, in the words of *The Times*, 'no attire at all'), or of bowler-hatted businessmen setting aside their briefcases, rolling up their trousers and splashing their feet in the fountains at Trafalgar Square. In time, whole reservoirs dried up, rivers ran so low that children were able to cycle along the arid bed of the Taff in South Wales and wildfires broke out at Hurn Forest in Dorset with the loss of 50,000 trees. In a further twist that might have been torn from the pages of a John Wyndham science-fiction novel, much of the country was hit by a massive swarm of seven-spotted ladybirds, forced to search frantically for alternative food sources because their normal aphid diet was killed off by the drought.

On each of the fifteen days from 23 June to 7 July, the recorded temperature reached at least 32.3°C (90.14°F) somewhere in the UK, which remained warmer than southern Europe. People began to voluntarily ride up and down the escalators at busy London Tube stations, if not to loiter on the platforms themselves, in order to enjoy the breeze generated by passing trains that also sent newspapers and empty crisp packets eddying around in a mini-pop-up tornado amidst all the broken chocolate-bar vending machines and unemptied litter bins. The ambient smell as the summer progressed was that of human body odour, offset by the aroma of drifting barbeques, and the nightly soundtrack was of the chatter from those sleeping alfresco on neighbouring balconies or in back yards. Add the stifling humidity, absence of air-conditioning and the ever-present miasma of smog, and for long stretches, London or any big city could feel like a particularly unpalatable communal sauna, a bizarre combination of tropical Mediterranean skies and oppressive urban squalor.

As the mercury rose, the value of the pound continued to fall. It traded at $1.75 in the middle of June and reached a low point of $1.62 towards the end of the month, before staging a modest comeback, thanks largely to the £3 billion loan the government took out from a group of other Western nations. With an ebullience that was typical of the man, if not necessarily warranted by the dry arcana of the Treasury's short-term projections, Denis Healey told the BBC current affairs programme *Panorama*, 'We're now in a better position to achieve our economic miracle than at any time since the war.' Within an hour of the markets opening, the pound fell by another two points the next morning.

The Cabinet made no direct reference to sterling's state of health when it met on 24 June, although ministers did express concern about the technical arrangements for the continuing debate of the Aircraft and Maritime Industries Bill then before Parliament, particularly at a time when the government enjoyed a majority of just three seats over all other parties. Summing up the discussion, James Callaghan said that the Conservatives were:

... likely to run into trouble over their highly regrettable attempt to require the Speaker to act contrary to all precedent and use his casting vote against the Bill. [My] general sense of the situation is that the Government should allow time for the legislation to be debated on 29 June, but that it will be advisable first to ascertain how the minority parties are likely to vote ... It may be necessary to proceed with some caution in the matter.

The deplorable turn of events to which Callaghan referred had come on 27 May, when the government by a single vote won a critical division to proceed with a Bill to nationalise the aircraft and shipbuilding industries. In the ensuing furore, Labour MPs on the floor of the House of Commons began singing 'The Red Flag' to taunt the Opposition front bench, while the Conservatives' shadow industry spokesman Michael Heseltine seized the Speaker's ceremonial mace and waved it at his opponents. Heseltine's reputation as a sort of loincloth-clad wild man of Westminster – a political Tarzan – owed a good deal to this gesture, for which he publicly apologised the following day.

Margaret Thatcher sought a private meeting with James Callaghan as a result of these events. Thatcher was not pleased to learn that an unnamed Labour MP had 'broken his pair' – or gone through the government lobby, despite having agreed with an absent Tory MP that neither of them would vote – with the result that a major piece of domestic legislation had been passed by what she regarded as a shameful subterfuge. In their meeting, Thatcher told Callaghan that 'the events of 27 May are in some dispute', although, being a pragmatist, she 'doubted that the facts will ever be established, [as] senior members of both parties would not find sitting in judgement on their colleagues very attractive'.

For his part, Callaghan thought that the best course of action might be to 'ask the two Chief Whips to present to us as soon as possible a report on the contentious vote of 27 May ... This should be a joint account, but it should embody their separate views on the events in dispute, and should be private to the two leaders.' Callaghan went on to 'pledge to give thought to the point Mrs Thatcher had made about the ultimate desirability of enabling the events in question to be further discussed, if need be by recommitting the Bill to a select committee, although this, too, raised significant issues of public perception'.

Such were the enforced legislative compromises and procedural niceties made necessary by Labour's razor-thin parliamentary majority, which shrank further with each successive by-election. With the flexibility of the career politician whose essential motto was 'If it doesn't work out, ditch it and try something else', Callaghan would go on to enter negotiations with the new Liberal leader, David Steel, whose party he had previously lampooned as a rabble of 'sandal-wearing loonies', few of whom, in his view, 'would appear to receive adequate amounts of oxygen to the brain'. Steel and his twelve parliamentary colleagues would duly support the government in return for consultation, via a joint committee, over future policies, coupled with the reintroduction of devolution legislation and a pledge to provide for swift elections to the European parliament, preferably using proportional representation.

In 1876, Gustave Flaubert published *Le Dictionnaire des idées reçues*, a work satirising the platitudes and clichés of public life. An updated version brought out a century later would surely have found room for some of the foibles of contemporary British politics, and in particular, the phrase 'direct consultation', which wafted with it the promise of meaningful collective dialogue, but in fact led only to a series of Maplin-like subcommittees and steering groups. The so-called Lib–Lab pact notionally ran from February 1977 to September 1978, following which Callaghan limped on at the head of a minority government until his defeat at Thatcher's hands in the general election of May 1979. With support from the eleven Scottish Nationalist MPs and mavericks like the Irish Social Democrat Gerry Fitt, the government carried the day by fourteen votes on the final June 1976 reading of the Bill establishing state control of the nation's aircraft and shipbuilding industries – and it remained on the statute book until repealed by the Deregulation Act of 2015.

★★★

A few minutes after its take-off from Athens on the Sunday morning of 27 June, Air France Flight 139, en route to Paris, was interrupted by the sound of shouting from the jet's first-class cabin. The disturbance came from a group of four hijackers – two of them German with Baader-Meinhof connections, two of them like-minded members of the Popular Front for the Liberation of Palestine – who announced that they were armed with guns and grenades and were seizing the aircraft in order to force the release of forty of their fellow freedom fighters who were imprisoned in 'Zionist Nazi' jails, as well as thirteen others held in Western Europe. A ransom of $5 million was also mentioned.

After refuelling in Benghazi, the plane continued to Entebbe in Uganda. On arrival, all 249 passengers and crew members were led into an outlying transit lounge of spartan décor and instructed to sit silently on the concrete floor. The four original terrorists, joined by three colleagues who had been awaiting their arrival, sat in the opposite corner of the room, weapons in hand, while Ugandan soldiers arrived on the scene, also pointing their guns at the hostages. On hardly any other occasion had the rather threadbare airport at Entebbe enjoyed the world's attention, but it had it now.

Uganda's head of state, Idi Amin, appeared several times to personally assess the situation over the next few days. Amin, who had recently been declared president for life by unanimous vote of his parliament, told the detainees – who were denied food, water and medical treatment for the first twenty-four hours of what became a week-long ordeal – how fortunate they were to be in his beautiful country, of which he was sure they would speak in the most nostalgic terms for many years to come.

On the afternoon of 28 June, the hijackers announced that they were separating their hostages into two groups of 'Zionist' and 'other' citizens. Over the next two days, a total of 144 non-Israeli nationals were released and flown out to Paris. The remaining ninety-three passengers and twelve-strong aircrew remained in the unprepossessing and increasingly humid transit building. It was an especially poignant scene for the half a dozen Holocaust survivors among the holdovers, reviving memories of the 'selection' process used by the Nazis in the wartime death camps.

On the morning of 30 June, the Ugandan armed forces examined all the detainees' hand luggage before marching them across the baking-hot summer asphalt to their new quarters in a cinder-block structure on the far side of the airport, where they were subjected to an intimate body search, among other indignities. When a female hostage needed to use the lavatory, she was accompanied by one of the male abductors, who continued to survey her, gun in hand, as she used the facilities. A dinner of bananas, rice and water was served that night.

At seven the following morning, Amin returned again, now accompanied by his fifth and last-surviving wife, a 20-year-old former go-go dancer known by her stage name of Suicide Sarah. He told the hostages that he was on his way to Mauritius for a meeting of the Organisation of African Unity, which he had the privilege to chair, and while there he would take the opportunity to raise the matter of their welfare. Amin added the detail that, far from being merely voted in to office by the Ugandan parliament, he had been personally appointed by God, and the fate of the passengers of Flight 139 now lay in the hands of that same Creator and his mortal instruments in the Israeli government. It was this latter body who would decide whether to release the political prisoners by paying the quite reasonable ransom requested of them. 'I have many good friends in high places in Tel Aviv, and I know they will see reason,' Amin assured the group, before leaving them with a hearty 'Shalom!'

Three thousand miles away from these events, the Israeli state authorities were even now planning a very different outcome to the Entebbe affair.

III

Summer

OPERATION THUNDERBOLT

The UK Cabinet meeting held on the morning of 1 July 1976 had two distinguishing features. The first was the air of almost preternatural calm with which ministers viewed the events of the outside world that day. There was no reference to the unfolding drama in the cinder-block outbuilding at Entebbe Airport. Everything was 'quite satisfactory' in terms of the special relationship with the United States, meanwhile. The prime minister had 'lately had very useful talks with President Ford, whom he regards as a most underrated man who has shown himself extremely friendly to the UK', James Callaghan informed his colleagues, and what was more, he had also recently had 'most cordial discussions on trade with Japanese ministers'. The premier and his Foreign Secretary had found time just the day before to pay a flying visit to Bonn for talks with the German Chancellor, Helmut Schmidt. These, too, had gone:

> ... very well ... During the morning, Herr Schmidt paid a generous tribute to the efficiency of our incomes policy, and it was evident from the exchanges with him and his ministers that there was now a greater understanding on the continent of the success of our efforts to deal with inflation ... It was all highly gratifying.

The second point of note to the Cabinet's discussions was the already palpable air of concern about the matter of the nation's weather. Barely a week after the England and West Indies cricketers had been kept off the field at Lord's by a combination of torrential rain and Stygian bad light, the government was now in the early stages of drawing up an Emergency Bill:

> ... to afford extra powers for dealing with the drought ... the Minister for Planning [John Silkin] regretted that the present law gave no authority to prohibit non-essential and even ostentatious uses of water during any period before more severe restrictions became necessary, and that there were apparently limits to what could be achieved by exhortation ... He therefore proposed a short and urgent Bill which would provide for immediate checks on unnecessary water use, and devise a framework for a rationing system for industrial, agricultural and domestic supply which did not depend on the operation of standpipes.

Such was the 'exigency of the situation', Callaghan noted, that it might even become necessary for Parliament to go as far as to postpone its three-month summer recess, which was scheduled to begin on 30 July, and instead 'remain sitting into the first few days of August ... The matter is potentially most grave,' the prime minister concluded.

No doubt Callaghan and his colleagues were right to express concern about the shortcomings of the United Kingdom's water supplies, although there was something about the tone of their meeting that perhaps reflected a broader truth of the nation's public life. Just as it's wrong to portray young people in the Britain of 1976 as having embarked on a non-stop priapic bender of general licentiousness – living for the moment, not giving a damn and uniformly sporting an ensemble of ripped jeans and Doc Martens, set off by a Mohican haircut and accessorised with a foaming can of lager – it's worth remembering that the nation at large still remained beholden to an almost surreal raft of checks on private conduct and freedom of action that had been introduced at the time of the First and Second World Wars and never withdrawn.

One of the most obvious examples was the enabling clause of the 1914 Defence of the Realm Act, limiting the hours that pubs could sell alcohol, which was gradually relaxed some seventy years after the Kaiser's troops had run up the white flag, but not fully repealed until 2003. Similarly, the main provisions of the Emergency Defence Regulations pushed through Parliament in August 1939 were modified only in December 1964, and even then, the government of the day retained its widespread powers to regulate private industry 'and impose such price controls on goods and services as deemed necessary'.

Even these petty restrictions on day-to-day British life might have seemed compellingly vital to the nation's welfare compared with the entitlement of the Lord Chamberlain's Office to censor or ban any public entertainment, a prerogative first granted it by the Licensing Act of 1737 and still actively in force 231 years later. Nor would the Act's repeal in July 1968 release the iron grip of the state on what constituted an acceptable form of public entertainment.

To give just one example, Dennis Potter's publicly funded television play *Brimstone and Treacle* was hurriedly pulled from the BBC's schedule in June 1976 by direct order of Alasdair Milne, the corporation's Director of Programmes. In Potter's play, a mysterious visitor, who may or may not represent the Devil incarnate – suggestively, he's described as having cloven feet and with a whiff of sulphur about him – performs an unusual holistic procedure on a brain-damaged young woman by raping her, whereupon she promptly recovers. Perhaps it was all a bold attempt at 'challenging conventional precepts of religion by daring to show a benevolent outcome resulting from an evil act', as Potter always insisted. Or possibly, it was the 'unrelieved cornucopia of bare bosoms and heaving rumps', as Milne rather fastidiously put it, that got him in such a froth. Either way, it would be a further eleven years before *Brimstone and Treacle* was finally aired by the UK's national broadcaster, coincidentally shortly after Milne himself had been unceremoniously sacked from his latter-day role as the BBC's Director General.

The hottest day of the year in Britain proved to be 3 July, when the temperature hit an alarming 35.9°C (96.6°F) in Cheltenham. The spa resort somehow forever associated with retired colonels and blue-rinse ladies disporting themselves among the town's bijoux Regency architecture was in for a shock that month as 'buxom beauties frolicked topless' – something of a *Sun* or general tabloid fixation that summer – amidst the croquet lawns of Montpellier Gardens.

No one then really bothered with CCTV, but before long, slightly makeshift-looking 'water detector vans' could be seen cruising the streets of Cheltenham and more southerly parts of the UK in a bid to enforce the terms of the successive hosepipe bans as they evolved through July and August. In a move that stirred memories of wartime rationing laws, 'snoopers' were officially encouraged to report anyone suspected of so much as cursorily sprinkling water on their wisteria or furtively soaping their Ford Cortina. A spokesman for the Thames Water Authority said that they preferred 'education over punishment' in such cases, but those caught persistently defying the ban could face a fine of up to £500. 'If you see anyone repeatedly breaching the regulations, you should let us know via our helpline', the spokesman added – although, as the *Daily Mirror* pointed out, the number given was 'seemingly constantly engaged, and no one answers it anyway after 5pm'.

There was room elsewhere in the *Mirror* for regular front-page photos of well-proportioned young women in bikinis falling into fountains or 'cheekily cooling off in their summer dresses, bereft of undies'. Few of the papers revealed much of the actual grain of the heatwave as it affected everyday life in a major British city – the oppressively packed pubs and restaurants, the sleepless nights and choking scent of stale bodies or the incessant 'Phew! What a Scorcher!' headlines. One way or another, it was a long, drainingly hot summer.

As temperatures rose, tempers flared. Anyone who has encountered the latent hostility of a swelteringly hot day in the city can attest to that phenomenon. Prolonged summer heat can be enjoyable as a memory, but frequently a nightmare to live through. As the sub-Saharan conditions asserted themselves on mainland Britain, the increased outbreaks of public disorder (up 78 per cent in Greater London over the previous year, the Met reported) came as a pointed reminder of the toxic interplay between factors such as hyperthermia, sleep deprivation and excessive carbonated drink intake. On a more institutional level, there was also evidence on many urban streets of the renewed presence of the National Front and their start-up newspaper *Bulldog*, with its uncompromising views on the malign 'Paki's' influence in the community. No respectable politician dared condone, let alone endorse, the Front's sentiments on matters such as the repatriation of Asian immigrants, although Margaret Thatcher would come closer than most when she told the ITV current affairs programme *World in Action*:

> People are really rather afraid that this country might be swamped by people with a different culture … We do have to hold out the prospect of an end to immigration, except, of course, for compassionate cases … Actually, quite a lot of them [immigrants] are fearful that their position might be put in jeopardy, or people might be hostile to them, unless we cut down the incoming numbers.

As we've seen, the fear that the United Kingdom might be overrun by those born under a bluer sky than themselves – Commonwealth citizens, their dependents and asylum-seekers, among others – contributed to a 'not inconsiderable mood of restiveness', in *The Times*'s nuanced phrase, on several British city streets that summer.

In August, that same spirit of restiveness boiled over into full-scale rioting at the annual Notting Hill Carnival in London. The scene was benign enough at first: long rows of boxy 1970s British cars, with an incongruous Cadillac or two tucked in among them, threading their way down dusty, litter-strewn city streets, watched by surly looking black and white youths, to a backdrop of herbal cigarette smoke, ethnic food carts and marching steel bands, in an overall multicultural confection that might have served to fuel the stock racist fables of the Far Right.

The first hint of trouble came when police attempted to arrest a young Asian pickpocket, who was then protectively swarmed by a large crowd. In the ensuing fracas, more than 100 uniformed police officers and civilian stewards were taken to hospital after being struck with rocks and other missiles; at least twelve of them to be detained overnight. Around sixty carnival-goers also needed medical attention. One witness told the BBC of a group of 'coloured lads prowling up Westbourne Park Road, randomly smashing windows' before turning a police van over and setting fire to it, while its two occupants 'beat a retreat', although it was thought that other, white-skinned youths were far from idle during the melee. 'Lusty chants of "Back Britain, Not Black Britain" and "Pakis Out!" echoed down the adjacent streets', the BBC reported, in terms that would be pre-emptively bleeped today.

Many of the following week's broadsheet papers struggled to decide if the increasingly vocal skinhead element on Britain's city streets that summer was merely a sort of innocuous youth fashion statement – like that of the punks, a long overdue, two-fingered riposte to 1960s flower power – or something altogether more sinister, 'a free-form Nuremberg Rally with Herr Bowie as the führer figure', as one horrified reporter in *Sounds* put it.

In the search for good news to offset the otherwise unrelieved gloom of the nation's current economic performance and pervasive social chaos, James Callaghan and his colleagues seized on the providential resource of North Sea oil. For some years, this had seemed to offer the UK a way out of her ruinous dependency on foreign suppliers, following a series of successful fossil-fuel strikes in the region, beginning in 1969–70 and culminating in the discovery of the giant Forties and Brent oilfields, with their steel-latticework production platforms soaring up as tall as the NatWest Tower heralded as the symbols of a new era of national energy self-sufficiency. Such, at least, was the promise of the UK's miracle economic boom. The reality was that it took fully five years for appreciable quantities of crude oil to start coming ashore, and even then, the maximum output of 250,000 barrels a day in mid-1976 remained tiny compared to demand, quite apart from the never-resolved row about whether the bulk of the revenue generated from drilling operations rightly belonged in Scotland or the UK as a whole. Between 1974 and 1978, Denis Healey later wrote:

> We were getting little benefit from North Sea Oil. The capital investment required made it a net drain on our balance of payments ... Even in 1978, it was making good only half the impact of the [1974] OPEC price increase on our bottom-line and was not yet producing any real revenue for the government.

Under the circumstances, it would perhaps be a mistake to confuse the still-unrealised statistical potential of Britain's 'black gold', as the papers termed it, with the practical realities of life as experienced by the average householder or motorist in mid-1976, paying their ever-steeper bills to their local gas board or filling up the family car at what was now an average of 80p (£6.35 today) per gallon, which was double the pump price of just three years earlier.

★★★

For the Israeli War Cabinet, meeting on Friday, 2 July in a secure Tel Aviv government bunker known as The Pit, the central choice over the events in Entebbe was whether to give in to the terrorists' demands and, in exchange for the hostages, free dozens of prisoners captured in previous attacks, even those deemed to have Jewish blood on their hands. Or should they initiate a rapidly planned and high-risk operation on the far side of the world that might turn into a disastrous failure, much like the West German attempt to rescue the athletes seized by Palestinian fanatics at the Munich Olympics in September 1972, which resulted in the deaths of all involved?

In the animated discussion around the conference table that Friday, the Israeli Defence Minister Shimon Peres took the lead in supporting the military option, while his premier, Yitzhak Rabin, concerned at the possible diplomatic fallout of staging an armed assault on foreign soil, urged caution. Adding to the sense of theatre, a long row of ticking clocks on the wall behind them, showing the time in half a dozen foreign cities, reminded ministers that they were rapidly approaching the end of the latest forty-eight-hour deadline set by the hijackers of Flight 139.

It is hard to say what ultimately determined the outcome of the meeting. No formal minutes were released, but several participating ministers would later say that they had been swayed by the unique role played in the crisis by Idi Amin. As Peres remarked to his colleagues, no such act of air piracy had ever before had the 'explicit approval of any president, army or state'. If this was now the case, the game had changed, and any sovereign nation worthy of the name had no real alternative but to send in sufficient troops to rescue their citizens and deliver a clear message of intent to any other leaders around the world who might be tempted to show similar support for radical militants.

Rabin was eventually persuaded by the force of his colleague's arguments, as well as by unofficial backing for the mission by Henry Kissinger, who promised to provide covert assistance such as the use of US Grumman Prowler electronic-warfare planes to help jam Ugandan ground radar. The final motivating factor was a report by the American-born, 30-year-old Lieutenant Colonel Yonatan 'Yoni' Netanyahu, older brother of the future Israeli Prime Minister and head of the elite Sayeret Matkal Commando Unit, who informed the politicians that the raid, code named Operation Thunderbolt, had been hurriedly rehearsed and, God willing, might succeed.

Taking off in the early afternoon of 3 July, in a fleet of four Hercules C-130M cargo planes accompanied by two refitted Boeing 707s, one to serve as an airborne command post and the other as a field hospital, Netanyahu and his team had orders to engage the terrorists and any hostile Ugandan troops they might encounter with lethal force, although to keep civilian casualties to a minimum. On board the six aircraft were a total of 103 commandos, several of them disguised in leopard-print Ugandan Army fatigues, as well as a support team of communications and logistics experts and one full-size black Mercedes sedan bearing official insignia and carrying a hastily briefed Idi Amin lookalike, the better to lull the guards on the ground at Entebbe into believing that they were dealing with nothing more ominous than another snap inspection by their state president for life.

Like all the best such missions, Operation Thunderbolt nearly came to grief. After an unpleasantly bumpy flight, the four Hercules transports landed safely at Entebbe shortly before eleven o'clock on the moonless Saturday night of 3 July, while one of the support planes circled overhead and the other stayed behind on the ground at Nairobi Airport to await any casualties.

Netanyahu and two colleagues alighted first onto the asphalt and made a rapid reconnaissance, running in a crouch from the front of their aircraft to the midpoint of the runway and back. Evidently, no one on duty had seen the Israeli group arrive. The black Mercedes with its Amin lookalike then rolled off the ramp from the lead plane and slowly started down the runway at the head of a silent procession of jeeps carrying personnel wearing both khaki uniforms and Ugandan Army regalia. They could hear the noise of people murmuring from inside the row of shadowy-looking buildings ahead of them.

As the convoy approached the main terminal, a lone bona fide Ugandan soldier suddenly appeared from out of the night and raised his machine gun at them. Two of the Sayeret Matkal team accompanying the Amin double fired at him with their silenced pistols and the man crumpled. He did not immediately die, however. Although mortally wounded, the guard managed to squeeze off a round of automatic fire at the oncoming Mercedes until Netanyahu shot him at close range with an unsuppressed rifle and killed him.

With the element of surprise now forfeited, it was a case of dealing with the chaotic action of close combat. Even as the Mercedes and its crew continued circling the inner airport perimeter, one of the Israeli commandos, Captain Giora Zussman, broke off from the group to make a solo entry on foot into the two-storey outbuilding that housed the hostages. By the light of a torch, he could see the outline of several chairs and mattresses and a table piled with passports, but no sign of either prisoners or terrorists. Just in case, he liberally sprayed the room with a round from his Kalashnikov until his clip was empty, at which point he drew his service pistol.

Zussman later admitted that he had been improvising as he went, but his responsibilities were now shaped to a single purpose: the killing of anyone who might in any way impede the freeing of the hostages. As the Israeli commando doubled back through the maze of darkened passages to continue his search, by now 'pumping with adrenaline', two members of his team ran past him down the hallway, firing as they went. Reaching a room at the far end of the complex that had been used as a makeshift kitchen, they found and killed two Ugandan soldiers.

By now, Yoni Netanyahu and his forward group had abandoned their vehicle at the entrance to the terminal and made their way over the grassy verge beside the runway to join Zussman and the others. A moment later, one of their party located the small, enclosed area next to the kitchen where the hostages, packed together on the floor, were being held for the night. In short order, the room was lit up by the strobe-like flash of gunfire.

The result was an 'aviary racket of shrieking', Zussman later wrote. Into the din, one of the commandos shouted through a megaphone, 'Stay down! Stay down! We are Israeli soldiers here to rescue you!' He repeated the phrase in Hebrew and English.

Failing to follow his instruction – and possibly unnerved by the cries of alarm ringing out all around them – two hostages were killed when their liberators mistook them for terrorists and fired at them. One of the original German skyjackers, Wilfried Böse, was also killed in the ensuing firefight, which took place amidst the bedlam of increasingly shrill screams, while the members of Netanyahu's group threw hand grenades into the adjacent room where Böse's colleagues had until recently been sleeping. Two commandos then entered the room and shot dead any of its surviving occupants.

All the terrorists were accounted for during an attack which lasted just sixteen minutes from the moment of the last Hercules's touchdown. At that, the Israelis shepherded the hostages back out into the jungle-hot, suddenly quiet night and across the asphalt to the planes, which were waiting for them with their engines running to take off without further ado for their rendezvous point in Nairobi.

Slow and painfully vulnerable to air attack, the four transports, perhaps in some measure thanks to Henry Kissinger, made it safely out of Ugandan air space. It was only then that Netanyahu's deputy, Muki Betser, got on the radio to issue the coded message that the mission had been successful. He heard nothing but static in return.

Eventually, a voice came across from the lead Hercules to say, 'Yonni's down, Yonni's down.' Netanyahu was the chief Israeli casualty of the raid, apparently killed by a Ugandan Army sniper's bullet in the act of falling back to the planes, although other survivors insist that Wilfried Böse had fired the fatal shot during the brief firefight that had broken out amidst the chaos of the outbuilding. One hundred and two of the 105 hostages were brought to safety; all eight terrorists and forty-six Ugandan troops died, while the Israelis had suffered a single loss, along with five others lightly wounded. Before the raiders took their leave of the airport they fired shoulder-mounted bazookas that destroyed fourteen Soviet-built MiG fighters parked at the end of the Entebbe runway, which amounted to a quarter of Uganda's air force.

Perhaps the most tragic human victim (or 'incident damage', as the later US State Department report put it) of the Entebbe affair was a 74-year-old British-Israeli grandmother named Dora Bloch. Mrs Bloch had been travelling on Flight 139 to attend her youngest son's wedding in New York. She fell ill during her first day of captivity and had been sent under guard to a hospital in Kampala. Although he always stoutly denied any involvement in the matter, there were to be persistent rumours that Idi Amin had wreaked his revenge on Dora Bloch as the only available target left to him in the humiliating aftermath of Operation Thunderbolt. British Foreign Office files contain a July 1976 memo written by James Hennessy, the UK's High Commissioner to Uganda:

> Mrs. Bloch was seen by a consultant at Mulago Hospital last Sunday, shortly after the Israeli commandos had come and gone. Since then she has not been seen anywhere. Our information is that she was dragged from her bed at hospital screaming.

A second note reads:

> The most likely scenario is that Mrs Bloch was murdered by Ugandan soldiers bitter and dangerous following their disgrace at Israeli hands ... They may have seized on the only remaining Jew on whom to extract a bloody revenge.

Dora Bloch's badly burned body was eventually discovered in May 1979, buried in a shallow grave on a sugar plantation in the Kampala suburbs. Her remains were returned to her older son in Israel, where she was given a state funeral.

On 28 July 1976, 'in the absence of any satisfactory explanation of Mrs Bloch's whereabouts', the British government formally cut diplomatic ties with Uganda, the first time in thirty years that the mother country had resorted to such a measure with a Commonwealth nation. Not even Ian Smith's Rhodesia had merited this sanction. Anthony Crosland said in Parliament, 'The decision is directly attributable to a serious lapse of judgement by President Amin.'

Perhaps predictably, Amin himself was not pleased by the outcome of Operation Thunderbolt. At the end of a lengthy televised denunciation of the 'unprovoked American-Zionist plot' against his country, the Ugandan leader noted, 'We reserve the right to retaliate in whatever way we choose to redress this wicked Jewish attack'. In the meantime, he added that he would be unilaterally adding the CBE, or 'Conqueror of the British Empire', to his already quite formidable list of official titles.

In the end, Amin confined his wrath to ordering the deaths of an estimated 250 Kenyan citizens living in Uganda in reprisal for their country's logistical support of the Israeli raid. A further 3,000 Kenyans deemed it best to voluntarily leave Uganda as refugees.

Amin was deposed by a military coup in April 1979 and spent most of the remaining twenty-four years of his life living in relative comfort in Saudi

Arabia. He remains one of those simultaneously absurd and terrifying fig-ures whom history throws up from time to time. Over the years, Amin was thought to have sired at least forty children with a variety of women. His last wife, Suicide Sarah, who had accompanied her husband on his inspection tours of the claustrophobic terminal building during those hot nights at Entebbe, was running a hairdressing salon in Tottenham, north London, at the time of her own death in 2015.

THE MOUSE IN THE RITZ

The climax of Operation Thunderbolt coincided with the protracted celebra-tions of the US bicentennial that reached their conclusion on 4 July 1976. They took a variety of forms. Half a million people turned out under hazy sunshine on the streets of Washington DC to watch a parade of fifty bands and marching units. Meanwhile, 130 miles away in Philadelphia, Vice President Nelson Rockefeller took the salute at a bunting-strewn parade of US Marine detachments, as military jets trailing red, white and blue smoke flew over-head. He drew less attention than Telly Savalas, TV's *Kojak*, who drove by in a vintage car, doffing his hat to expose his distinctive bald pate and sucking on one of his trademark lollipops, to the delight of crowds who were themselves munching hotdogs, popcorn and ice cream and waving miniature US flags.

The only note of discord came when a small contingent of the National Socialist White People's Party, conspicuous by their all-brown uniforms and swastika armbands, showed up to stage a counter-rally, protesting 'the rise in national life of the negro' in the years since 1776. In the nuanced words of the *Washington Post*, 'One individual, evidently a right-wing sympathizer, was taken into custody by the police after leaping over a barrier to engage with a college-aged youth carrying a sign reading "Nazis are pigs".'

The most spectacular single event of the day was the gathering at New York of 212 tall ships from thirty-four nations, with a supporting flotilla of 15,000 brightly flagged small craft sailing around the southern tip of Manhattan in an animated piece of choreography like that of a vast aquarium.

Elsewhere in the USA, there were street parades, traffic jams, concerts, county fairs, rodeos, laser shows and fireworks. The Queen was on hand in Washington to help Britain's former colonial subjects commemorate their independence, even as *The Economist* suggested that the UK might be better off reunited with 'our American brethren as the 51st state'. In the event, the monarch restricted herself to thanking the founding fathers for 'teaching us a very valuable history lesson', which earned her a sustained round of applause. She added, 'We learned above all to respect the right of others to govern themselves in their own way and by their own means.' Another burst of approval erupted. 'It is the sovereign people of the United States who have earned this respect through their combination of hard work, enterprise and ingenuity demonstrated over these many years,' the Queen concluded. The roar this time was truly deafening; she had clearly struck the most responsive possible chord.

★★★

That same night, the more modest setting of the Black Swan pub in Sheffield witnessed the punk-rock equivalent of the wartime Allied leaders coming together at Yalta, when the Clash gave their first-ever public performance, appearing as the warm-up to the Sex Pistols. It was a fast-paced night's entertainment, taken as a whole, played at the tempo of the scotches and pints the musicians downed throughout to calm their nerves. The support act played a total of five songs, including a reggae-infused cover called 'Pressure Drop', a bold choice for a northern pub of that era, and the headliners followed with a further ten, for a combined running time of just over an hour.

Perhaps the brevity of the night's repertoire was all to do with a taste on the part of both bands for stripped-down songs whose key ingredients were a clangorous rhythm section in tandem with a pair of energetically scrubbed guitars, typically coming in at around the two-minute mark. Or perhaps there were other factors involved besides both the punk ethic and the hospitality of the bar. As the Pistols' vocalist John Lydon, now known as Johnny Rotten for his carious teeth, later reflected:

> There was something of a fad for amphetamines in those days. Personally, I loved the stuff. I was doing a ton of speed before I went on stage most days. I'm normally a very slow person, and it made me feel more alive, like I didn't need anyone else … I liked speed because it made everything more intense.

★★★

Somehow, neither the Pistols nor the Clash made it onto the agenda when the Cabinet met thirty-six hours later in Downing Street. Perhaps James Callaghan and his ministerial colleagues, to the extent that they thought of them at all, took the long view of the sort of bands whose music, clothes and attitudes helped rouse a sleeping generation, swapping consensus for dissent and making an icon out of the humble safety-pin. Perhaps, too, some of the Cabinet were *du jour* enough to understand that the so-called new wave was really the old wave bushwhacked by the press. Thirteen years earlier, there had been the same widespread sound of fans braying and screeching, MCs or other authority figures sternly asking for order and police chiefs rumbling 'Disgraceful!' in response to the threat to public morals from a group from the London suburbs named the Rolling Stones, with their objectionable clothes and disastrous haircuts. The headlines had followed suit. 'THUGS ... CAVEMEN ... APES' was the consensus, thus eerily foreshadowing the simulated media panic of a generation later.

Or possibly Callaghan and his team simply denied themselves any consideration of the punk aesthetic, preferring to concentrate, in common with almost all post-war Western democracies, on frantically pulling the levers of decline management, and above all, the need to avoid national bankruptcy.

The minutes note bluntly:

The Chancellor of the Exchequer said it was essential to keep both the economy and the contract with the trade unions afloat. He was especially concerned with the recent terms of foreign trade, and the J-curve effect of sterling's decline overseas meant a further likely deterioration in our balance of payments ... Commodity prices were also rising higher and faster than expected, and invisible earnings were likely to be lower next year than this. The trade deficit in 1976 was now forecast to be about £500 million, while in 1977 it would be up to £2,000 million on present policies, and there was no sign of any improvement on the horizon.

It went on like this over four pages of uniformly grim economic data that would have tested even Denis Healey's innate faith in the ability of his fellow citizens to recognise and respond to a crisis when they saw one. 'It was clear we were not headed toward a brave new world of industrial productivity and growth, as I had thought in 1974,' Healey once told me. 'Where we were headed was toward a cliff.'

***

Sociologists would spend years puzzling over the strange disparity between the apocalyptical gloom of the official Treasury projections of the day and the fact that many, if not most ordinary Britons experienced their lives as budget conscious, certainly, but still of unimaginable comfort compared to those of twenty years earlier. In 1956, more than a third of all British citizens lived in houses without a flushing toilet and more than half lacked basic amenities such as central heating or their own phone. By 1976, phones, televisions and cars were owned by 85 per cent of families. By and large, people now simply got on with life rather than dwelling on the latest anguished report issuing from the government.

In November 1939, a 38-year-old Iowa farm boy turned advertising executive named George Gallup sailed for England, where over the next six weeks he enlisted a small team of regional helpers to knock on a total of 6,200 doors in London, Birmingham, Manchester, Glasgow and, rather curiously, the area around Mamble in Worcestershire, in order to ask residents about their attitudes to everything from the recently declared war to the advent of tinned tomato juice on British breakfast tables. Only 12 per cent of those canvassed said 'yes' to the question, 'Do you think public officials are too detached from what most matters to you?' That response rose to 37 per cent in a comparable poll conducted in March 1961, before reaching a total of 71 per cent in July 1976.

Perhaps it was a case of post-Watergate alienation and the wholesale forfeiture of trust in authority, wherever it manifested itself, that tainted so much of the fabric of Western life in the mid-1970s. But perhaps it was more a matter of the British genius for simply shrugging and carrying on, undaunted by unpalatable facts. With real wages rising steadily, whatever the larger economic context, most families could – and did – allow themselves a few modest luxuries. In the same Gallup poll in July 1976, 74 per cent of all 31–49-year-olds strongly agreed with the proposition that it was 'important to enjoy yourself while you can'. According to Gallup, most people, of all ages and from all walks of life, were either oblivious or indifferent to the great macroeconomic trends swirling around them and simply wanted to invest their extra money as they pleased.

One of the most immediately obvious beneficiaries of this spending power was sport. People, by and large, had bread; now they wanted circuses. Record crowds attended in person and millions more tuned in on television for that July's 105th Open Championship at Royal Birkdale, where the American

Johnny Miller cruised to a six-stroke victory over his countryman Jack Nicklaus and a teenager from northern Spain named Seve Ballesteros.

The tournament that year was also notable for golf's own Eddie 'the Eagle' Edwards prototype in the form of 46-year-old Maurice Flitcroft, who made news by carding a round of 121, the worst in Open history. By trade, Flitcroft was a crane operator from Barrow-in-Furness, but this did not satisfy his higher ambitions in life. He had only turned his hand to golf for the first time in 1974, not on the basis of any innate talent for the game, but because 'I noticed the players individually on TV, and there was this exciting theme tune, boom, de boom, ba de *boom* ... and I remember thinking how marvellous it would be to be a part of it.'

After taking a few lessons, Flitcroft tried to register with the Royal and Ancient Club (R&A) as a professional player, but was thwarted by their churlish insistence on seeing evidence of even modest playing ability on his part. Undaunted, he applied to enter the qualifying competition for the 1976 Open, which was due to be played not far from his home. The entrance sheet required a box to be ticked next to the word 'amateur' or 'professional'. 'I ticked "professional" – I couldn't play as an amateur because I wasn't a member of a club and I didn't have a handicap certificate,' he recalled.

A man of immense bonhomie, Flitcroft shared certain physical features and radiated a faint air of haplessness not dissimilar to the inept Irish builder in *Fawlty Towers*. He managed to get lost while on his way to Royal Birkdale, and made straight for the bar when he arrived. Due to an apparent administrative oversight, the R&A accepted Flitcroft's entry form, a decision they soon came to regret considering his abysmal qualifying score, banning him from all further such competitions. His round of 121 had put him 49 over par and was 38 shots more than taken by the next worst player.

But Flitcroft, who made up in persistence what he lacked in technical skill, now had the scent of the greens in his nostrils. He continued to apply for entry to the world's most prestigious tournaments, employing such aliases as 'Swiss Superstar Gerald Hoppy', 'James Beau Jolly' and one 'Gene Paychecki', often with the result of audiences being entertained by the sight of his being chased off the course by blazer-wearing officials. 'The punters were cheering for me, not the gin-and-tonic brigade who ran the sport,' Flitcroft later explained with unaffected pride, making him one of those enjoyably perverse cult heroes the British sometimes take to their hearts.

Flitcroft died in March 2007, aged 77, although his family brand would live on in the person of his twin sons, Gene and James, respectively a golf caddy who traded under the name 'Troy Atlantis' and a disco-dancing champion, as well as allegedly being the joint recipients of the UK's first-ever antisocial banning order for sword fighting with each other in the street.

There were capacity crowds, too, if less in the way of surrealistic pranks, at that summer's Wimbledon Championships, where the singles titles went to Björn Borg and Chris Evert, and a transgender player named Renée Richards was deemed ineligible for both the men's and women's competition.

The British Grand Prix on 18 July at Brands Hatch was won in controversial fashion by the Austrian Niki Lauda, after the home favourite James Hunt had crossed the line first, only to be disqualified later on a technicality. The world's two leading Formula 1 drivers respected each other's technical ability but had little else in common. Already the *enfant terrible* of the motor racing world, with the sobriquet 'Shunt' – and other close rhyming derivatives – thanks to some uninhibited driving in Formula 3, the 28-year-old Hunt was another one of those forces of nature who enliven their chosen sport. He was intelligent, articulate and forthright, and often unconventional in manner and dress. Asked what apparently winning the 1976 race meant to him, Hunt had looked out over the assembled spectators and replied, 'Nine points, $20,000 and a lot of crumpet', before good-naturedly cadging a cigarette off someone in the crowd.

Meanwhile, the wheels now spectacularly came off Tony Greig's ill-fated 'grovel' prediction in the summer's third Test with the West Indies at Old Trafford. The tourists went in first for a total of 211, which looked modest enough, until it came to be set against the England reply, which lasted all of 32 overs, of 71 all out. David Steele, with 20, was the only home batsman to reach double figures and the only one to beat the number of extras.

It seemed to many of those in attendance, or watching at home on TV, that the English batsmen were embarked on a private agenda – bodily survival being its most obvious component – that was only tangentially connected to any overall strategy, let alone to the interests of the paying public. West Indies then made 411–5 before declaring soon after tea on the third day to give their pace quartet ninety minutes' exercise before the close.

What followed was an exhibition of explosively fast and hostile bowling, directed largely at the 45-year-old Brian Close, who was equipped for the occasion with no helmet, no chest pad and no arm guard, contenting himself with a small strip of towel tucked over his front thigh to try and minimise the bruising. Close had been sent in to open the innings for England only after asking his captain what was wrong with Bob Woolmer, who was the regular opener. 'We don't want Woolmer killed off. At his age, there's still a lot of Test cricket left in him,' Greig had said.

Close stubbornly held on for a score of 20, but it was a forlorn hope. Set 552 to win, England fell 426 short. It did not go unnoticed that the tourists' bowlers seemed to add several yards to their run-ups whenever Greig himself appeared at the wicket.

To his credit, the embattled England captain responded with a typically robust first-innings century in the summer's next Test at Leeds. At stumps on the fourth day, England were 146–5 in pursuit of 260 and – with thunderstorms, ironically, in the forecast – any one of three, or even all four results were possible.

Although the full admission of £1.10 was charged, some 9,000 customers paid at the turnstiles on the final morning. In the event, the rain held off, the pavilion flags snapped gently back and forth in a warm breeze and on the grassy hill in front of the food area, well-lubricated groups of suntanned male spectators under an assortment of novelty hats and naked to the waist tossed beer cans around them as if they were peanut shells.

England's hopes were dashed this time not by Holding and Roberts, but by 20-year-old Wayne 'Diamond' Daniel of Barbados, who took three quick wickets, all caught off the outside edge, in his first four overs. West Indies won by 55 runs, giving them an unassailable 2–0 lead in the series.

The Summer Olympics were reaching their climax that week, 3,000 miles away in Montreal, where Princess Anne suffered a concussion after falling from her horse in the eventing competition. Fourteen-year-old Nadia Comăneci scored the first perfect 10 in Olympic gymnastics history, a sporting landmark to stand alongside the likes of Geoff Hurst's 'They think it's all over' goal in the 1966 World Cup Final, Red Rum's serial triumphs in the Grand National, the building excitement and flying finish of Gareth Edwards's try for the 1973 Barbarians against the All Blacks at Cardiff, or Roger Federer pretty much any time he walked on court for a Grand Slam tennis match. Comăneci's achievement was so exceptional that Omega, the company responsible for the timing and scoring of the Montreal Games, had no means of displaying the figure 10.00 on the stadium's digital scoreboards, which could only accommodate a maximum of three numbers and a single decimal point. The best Omega could do for the Rumanian prodigy was to award her a perfect 1.00.

***

'It's been a melancholy summer in London,' the *New York Times* reported in August:

> The drought has withered the grass on Hampstead Heath, emptied the sprays on Trafalgar Square and sparked restrictions on washing dishes and taking baths ... There was the worst racial violence in years near Portobello Road, the pound has begun to drop again and the British government was asked by Pakistan to return one of the most valuable gems in the world, the 109-carat Koh-i-Noor, which was set in Queen Victoria's crown and served, in its own dazzling way, to symbolize British imperialism[1] ... *Watch It All Come Down*, the title of John Osborne's dreary new play, seem to be the summer's bywords. An American woman saw a mouse scamper across the bar of the Ritz Hotel. The man who was proclaimed the Brain of Britain – after responding, with ease, to an alarming quiz on the BBC – found himself without a job. 'The fact that I'm unemployed rather symbolises the national malaise,' said Thomas Dyer, a teacher and scientist. 'As a nation, we don't really know what to do with our brains'.[2]

Amid this apparently unrelieved slough of despond, a character now emerged to significantly add to the nation's gaiety. He was 59-year-old Tom Keating, a former south London delivery boy, housepainter and naval stoker who had gradually regressed from the entirely reputable trade of art restoration to the more equivocal one of actually reproducing the work of various household-name artists from scratch. By 1976, Keating had long been in the habit of selling his pieces to gallery owners, who proved surprisingly incurious when it came to the provenance of hitherto obscure Gainsboroughs, Constables, Holbeins, Brueghels, El Grecos and Matisses, brought to them by the heavily bearded figure with a taste for cockney rhyming slang, typically arriving at their premises on a loud motorbike with his latest canvas tucked under his arm. Keating was well paid for his troubles, but always insisted that he turned to forgery not for his own gain but as an act of vengeance on a snobbish and effete art world on behalf of his illustrious predecessors.

---

1   As of today, the Koh-i-Noor remains on public display in the Jewel House of the Tower of London.

2   It's thought that Thomas Dyer was eventually able to find suitable work behind the counter of his family's drapery business in Ilminster, Somerset, although after 144 years of selling men's and women's clothing and housewares, the shop closed its doors for the last time in 2014.

'It seemed disgraceful to me how many of them had died in poverty,' Keating wrote in his picaresque autobiography, *The Fake's Progress*. 'All their lives they had been exploited by unscrupulous dealers and then, as if to dishonour their memory, those same dealers continued to exploit them in death.'

The time had come for the heirs of these venal art establishment figures to learn a lesson, Keating believed, and the poverty he had once shared with his fellow toilers with the canvas and brush uniquely qualified him for the job. 'I was determined to avenge my brothers, and it was to this end that I decided to turn my hand to the Sexton Blaking.'

Opinions vary over whether Keating conformed at all times to his popular image as a roguish cockney geezer determined to strike a blow against the toffee-nosed art world, with its spotted bow ties and faint but discernible air of condescension or was perhaps embarked on a more narrowly commercial enterprise. *The Observer* caught some of the debate when it spoke of him as a 'cuddly and eccentric *bon viveur* [who] looks like everyone's idea of Father Christmas'. Set against this benign depiction, there was the married Keating's relationship with his personal and professional partner, Jane Kelly, twenty-nine years his junior – she was 16 when they met – who later portrayed him as a malodorous old roué whose prolific use of attractive models for his Old Masters' 'pastiches', as he called them, was by no means confined to a strictly aesthetic appreciation of the female nude.

What all parties agreed on was Keating's obvious talent for artistic mimicry, as well as the industrial efficiency with which he turned out the end product. It's thought that he was responsible for producing more than 2,000 imitation masterpieces over the years 1955–76, a rate of roughly one every four days, with a particular fondness for the work of the French and German impressionists.

To add to the air of intrigue about the whole exercise, Keating always took the trouble to leave what he called 'time-bombs' in the works he and Kelly sold at market – whether by deliberately adding an anachronism like a wristwatch worn by a character in the background of a painting ascribed to the seventeenth century, or writing the word 'fake' on the back of a canvas in lead-based paint which would show up under an X-ray. The idea seems to have been to encourage 'experts' in the field to discover his deception. For some fifteen years, none of them did.

In fact, questions were first asked of Keating only in February 1970, when Geraldine Norman, the young auction house correspondent for *The Times*, reported the sale of a work attributed to the nineteenth-century English landscapist Samuel Palmer, which changed hands for £9,400 (£85,000 today), a record for that artist, through the office of a prestigious gallery in London's Bond Street. A month later, the same newspaper published a letter from a reader unequivocally stating that the picture was a fake.

Nothing came of the matter, however, for a further six years, during which Keating continued to flood the market with his 'Sexton Blake' homages to Rembrandt, Goya, Degas, Monet, Tintoretto, Klee and many others. He did not grow conspicuously wealthy as a result of his subterfuge and later insisted he had given away several of the works to local tradesmen in lieu of paying their bills, although he was at least able to abandon his family home and relocate to a riverside cottage at Dedham, on the Essex–Suffolk border, in the heart of Constable country.

In the stifling heat of July 1976, Geraldine Norman tracked Keating down to these new premises, which lay close to the scene depicted in the real John Constable's 'The Hay Wain'. A series of front-page exposés followed in *The Times* at intervals over the summer. With disarming frankness, Keating himself came clean about what he had done, if always maintaining the purity of his pose as the selfless Robin Hood figure of the art world. 'I swamped the market with "the work" of Palmer and many others,' he later wrote, 'not for gain – I hope I am no materialist – but simply as a protest against merchants who make capital out of those I am proud to call my brother artists, both living and dead.'

This being the silly season of immoderate temperatures and good-natured pranks like that of Maurice Flitcroft at Royal Birkdale, Keating's activities quickly became a much-discussed source of fun and satire and were hotly debated by millions of people who never normally went near an art gallery. Was he, in fact, the quintessential working-class hero, a harmless and avuncular old buffer with a talent for imposture and a seemingly inexhaustible supply of cockney wit, who had jovially pulled the rug from under the Burlington Berties? Or just another plausible chancer intent on claiming a spurious altruism with which to cloak his nefarious gains?

The austere figure of Sir Norman Skelhorn, Britain's Director of Public Prosecutions, inclined to the latter view of the matter, and both Keating and Jane Kelly were duly arrested and charged with conspiracy to defraud. The couple's trial at the Old Bailey was not without interest. The jury heard stories of uninhibited young artist's models and paintings carried through the desert by camels to the palaces of Saudi princes in exchange for carrier bags stuffed with cash, among a variety of other unusual practices.

In due course, Kelly turned Queen's Evidence and was given an eighteen-month suspended sentence. Keating pleaded not guilty, and when his case was dropped because of his poor health, in part the result of his having fallen off his motorbike while on the way to give evidence, he emerged from the court-room a celebrity.

In later years, he somehow rallied to publish his autobiography and host his own Channel 4 television series in which he pottered amiably about his studio, dressed in an old-fashioned smock and with a hand-rolled ciga-rette clamped to his lip, demonstrating to viewers how to paint Constable's wagons or Modigliani's long-necked nudes. Keating's running commentary became something of a masterclass in itself, frequently serving to puncture the assumed erudition of those like the art historian and public aesthete Sir Kenneth Clark, whose own thirteen-part BBC series *Civilisation* had aired some time earlier. 'Although Renoir's first impulse to paint came from an almost naïve sensuous delight,' Clark had intoned, 'he never imagined that the more graphic depiction of visually agreeable objects might be the end pictorial result.' Keating, for his part, took the more direct approach to the matter. 'The old boy [Renoir] loved young girls,' he told his appreciative TV audience. 'Don't we all?'

In a further subversive twist, Keating and his pastiches brought the very definition of a work of art under greater scrutiny. 'If anyone enriches the world by giving us something as good as the original we should be grateful,' a correspondent wrote to *The Times*. 'That they have to sign the piece under an alias is our fault. If Mozart's real name was Fred Smith, if Van Meegeren painted the Vermeers and Keating drew the Palmers, good luck to all of them.'

If you happened to have walked into a pub somewhere in Britain around late July 1976, alongside the idle chat about the price of petrol or the news of England's latest batting collapse, you might well have found yourself engaged in a lively exchange of views about the mystery and awe of creation as illus-trated by the Keating affair. Even the tabloid press found room for it amidst all the coverage of the heatwave. In 1983, Keating himself added to this debate by sending 137 of his pictures for auction at Christie's in London, who accepted the pieces as signed by Keating but 'in the style of' other artists. Every one of the consignment sold in a single day, raising £74,000.

A fatal heart attack in February 1984 meant that the artist barely lived to enjoy the proceeds, although his tale continues to cast its spell. There are now fakes of Keating's fakes in circulation, and it's widely believed that cer-tain historical paintings still displayed in some of the world's most reputable galleries were actually produced by an anarchic, ex-naval stoker in his south London garage.

***

Life wasn't all a case of black comedy that summer. Shortly after 9.30 a.m. on Wednesday, 21 July, a black Jaguar XJ 42 drove through the wrought-iron gates of Glencairn House in the south Dublin suburbs. The car carried the UK's newly appointed Ambassador to Ireland, Christopher Ewart-Biggs, and his small private staff, who were on their way to the nearby British Embassy.

Ewart-Biggs, a war veteran who had lost his right eye fighting at El Alamein, had been advised to always vary his route while driving to work in this way, but at that juncture outside his official residence there was only a choice between turning left or right. He chose right, and 300 yards further down the road a watching IRA cell detonated a bomb hidden in a water culvert. The ambassador and his 26-year-old assistant, Judith Cooke, were killed outright in the blast, which left the car's two other passengers seriously injured. Ewart-Biggs's wife Jane had originally meant to be at her husband's side that morning, but instead had taken the overnight ferry to Fishguard and was driving towards London, where she planned to buy some curtains for the family's new home, when she heard the news on her car radio.

'These miserable men are the common enemy of both governments, and indeed of all decent people who wish to live in peace and amity,' James Callaghan informed the Commons later that afternoon. As well as his widow, the ambassador left behind three children, aged between 8 and 15. Jane Ewart-Biggs dedicated the rest of her life to the cause of improving Anglo–Irish relations. Thirteen members of the IRA were subsequently questioned in connection with her husband's murder, but to this day, no one has ever stood trial for the crime.

SPECIAL RELATIONS

In the early afternoon of 21 December 1956, 41-year-old Waffen-SS Colonel (Rtd) Joachim Peiper walked out of Landsberg Jail in West Germany a free man. It happened to be exactly thirty-two years to the day since Peiper's former commander-in-chief, Adolf Hitler had emerged from serving a nine-month sentence in the same institution after being convicted of treason in the wake of the failed Beer Hall Putsch in Munich.

Peiper's own crimes were of a gravity that might have earned a nod of respect from even his old boss and his inner circle. A decade earlier, the SS man had been sentenced to death for orchestrating the murder of eighty-four US soldiers of the 285th Field Artillery Group, who had been taken captive near the Germany–Belgium border during the Ardennes Offensive of December 1944. The GIs had been on their way to reinforce their colleagues in the 7th Armoured Division around the village of Malmedy, when a superior force – Joachim Peiper's men – brought them to a halt.

It was snowing hard, and the US soldiers, who were lightly armed with carbines and service revolvers, had already slithered on foot through the mud and slush for the better part of two days without sleep. They quickly realised on being confronted by the enemy that they had little choice in the matter but to surrender. In short order, the Germans – who revelled in the nickname of the 'Blowtorch Battalion' – lined their prisoners up in a corner of the field where they had been captured. The GIs stood twenty abreast and several rows deep, completely unarmed, silent and with their hands raised.

Within moments, two German tanks pulled up to the edge of the field and an armoured personnel carrier parked between them. Without a word, a German soldier in the middle vehicle stood up and fired two pistol shots, and two Americans fell. At that, machine guns on the flanks opened up, methodically sweeping from left to right and back again. After fully three minutes of continuous fire, two SS officers walked briefly through the men lying dead or dying in the snow, finishing off with pistol shots or rifle butt anyone who showed signs of life.

Sergeant Kenneth Ahrens was one of the few who, almost incredibly, survived the bloodbath, which he did by the expedient of lying motionless in the snow, pretending to be dead. 'The Germans were having a hell of a good time laughing and joking while the [American] boys were praying,' he later recalled, adding the detail that he had heard the thud of bullets striking his comrades and their cries of pain. In time, some of the survivors had managed to pick themselves up and stumble away to take shelter in a café a few hundred yards away at the Baugnez crossroads. At that, the pursuing Germans had promptly set the café on fire with flamethrowers, shooting dead every US soldier who escaped the inferno.

Joachim Peiper, a character seemingly out of Nazi central casting with his chiselled jaw and ice-blue gaze, had not personally been present at the

Malmedy massacre. As he was later at pains to point out, he had left the scene in his staff car a few minutes earlier. Peiper had, however, only recently taken the trouble to read out an order received from Sixth Panzer Army Headquarters, signed by its commanding officer, SS general Sepp Dietrich. It instructed all German troops in the area to fight 'with no regard for Allied prisoners, [who] must be shot if the situation compels it'. Peiper had added to the official order by reminding the men under his command that they were engaged in a death-struggle with the enemy, and as a result, should 'not pay any attention to unimportant goals, nor to prisoners of war'.

Following the slaughter at Malmedy, Peiper's troops would go on to rape and kill several Belgian women in the surrounding villages whom they believed had impeded their advance, again applying their flamethrowers to their victims' homes before leaving the area. Medals and badges were distributed throughout the battalion by General Dietrich for their 'outstanding contribution' to the German war effort. Peiper's battle group was eventually held responsible for the deaths of 362 prisoners of war and 111 civilians.

Captured by US forces in May 1945, Peiper was unrepentant. 'All Jews are bad and all Poles are bad. We had just cleansed our society ... we moved these people into camps, and you let them loose!' he informed his Allied interrogators. Sentenced to hang at his subsequent trial, where his essential defence was that he had been following orders, Peiper was spared the noose and released on parole eleven years later, in part due to pressure by the West German Chancellor Konrad Adenauer. Adenauer had urged the wartime Allies to establish 'an immediate machinery for clemency' for Peiper and several other convicted war criminals, warning the US State Department of the 'considerable psychological and public opinion problems in Germany' caused by the continued agitation of veterans' group organisations.

On release, Peiper found employment with the Porsche company in Stuttgart before moving with his wife to Traves in eastern France, where he rented a house from a former Wehrmacht colleague and did freelance translation work. He remained unashamed of his former career. 'If I am here,' Peiper informed a reporter from the Paris newspaper *L'Humanité*, 'it is because in 1940 the French were without courage.'

Perhaps unsurprisingly, these were not views that conspicuously endeared the former SS officer to his local community. Peiper's life in exile took a turn for the worse in early July 1976, when leaflets were distributed throughout Traves and the surrounding villages, declaring, 'Attention: A war criminal is living amongst us!' and calling for his immediate expulsion from France.

Swastikas soon appeared, daubed on the walls of Peiper's home, which was perched on a high bluff above the River Saône and partly hidden from the nearby road by a thick screen of bushes. A sign in French and English at the front gate read, 'Keep Out', and it was thought that the occupants had also taken the trouble to furnish themselves with one or more guard dogs to deter unwelcome guests.

On the morning of 13 July, Peiper's wife left the house for a long-standing arrangement to visit friends in Germany. A swell of discontent with their notorious new resident had been growing in the village all week. Later that evening, Peiper wrote a letter to Rudolf Lehmann, the former head of the 1st SS Panzer Division and a personal friend, in which he said that his 'quiet haven' had recently become 'an entrenched camp' and he would 'move in the autumn if the Communists and Jews allow me to wait until then'. Again, he would not seem to have taken the opportunity to modify his views on Germany's former adversaries.

When his landlord, Erwin Ketelhut, came to visit him the following morning – Bastille Day – Peiper told him that he was not unduly worried about his safety since the French as a race were cowards, and besides that, he was armed with both a revolver and a rifle. Ketelhut offered to lend his tenant a Remington twelve-bore shotgun, which he accepted, and to keep an eye on the area as darkness fell from the balcony of his own property further up the hill. The two old comrades parted at about ten o'clock on that warm holiday night. Shortly afterwards, the first celebratory fireworks exploded over the town and lit up the curve of the river that wound through the sun-baked fields below the Germans' enclave.

Four hours later, Ketelhut was rudely awakened by the wailing of the village siren and from his back window saw flames leaping from the roof of the house below him. The local volunteer fire brigade reached the scene at 2.15 in the morning, but found that there was insufficient water pressure at the hydrant to fill their hoses. When the blaze eventually burnt itself out towards dawn, the authorities discovered a badly charred body in the remains of the study. Due to the intense heat generated by the fire, it had shrunk to a length of just 2ft and was barely recognisable as that of a human being. When Ketelhut was shown the corpse later that morning, he said, 'It is Peiper, but he is diminished [réduite]'.

A subsequent investigation found that the perimeter fence around the property had been partly cut away with pliers, and that Peiper had evidently confronted his intruders by firing all three of his weapons at them. The police concluded that several individuals had broken into the grounds of the house under cover of dark, shot the guard dogs and set the building alight while Peiper had continued to defend himself by barricading himself in his study until he was overcome by smoke inhalation. No one has ever been charged in connection with his death.

***

Four hundred miles away in Nice, a group of individuals took advantage of the same extended French national holiday to relieve the Société Générale bank of 46 million francs, or the equivalent of roughly €25 million (£120 million today), in an elaborately planned operation with some of the same general characteristics of the plot of *The Great Escape*.

The gang responsible evidently spent months preparing the job, using rubber rafts to navigate the sewer network beneath the city streets to gain access to the spot where they dug a 30ft tunnel and installing hundreds of yards of electrical cables to provide lights, leading directly upwards into the bank's vault. Investigators later determined that the men had taken several weeks to conclude their excavations. Police even found glossy pictures of nude women hung across the walls of the tunnel, which were reinforced with concrete, as well as picnic tables and the remnants of meals, empty wine bottles and discarded packs of Gauloises cigarettes.

The thieves were thought to have made their entrance to the premises in the early hours of Friday, 16 July, and bank employees finally discovered the loss only the following Monday afternoon. It had taken them several additional hours to do so because the gang members had taken the trouble to weld the front door of the building shut from the inside. Before leaving, they had spray-painted a message on the wall: '*Sans armes, sans violence, sans haine*', which roughly translates as 'No weapons, no violence, no hate'.

The police eventually detained 44-year-old Albert Spaggiari, a local chicken farmer and right-wing activist, as the suspected mastermind of the crime. Spaggiari had powerful political connections in the area and had been on an overseas trip with the Mayor of Nice when the warrant was issued for his arrest. He was taken into custody on his return with the municipal party at the airport.

During a recess in his trial, Spaggiari jumped out of an upstairs courthouse window, bounced off the top of a parked Renault and fled the scene on a waiting motorbike. President Giscard d'Estaing admitted in his memoirs that he had been 'grudgingly impressed' by this part of the story. The owner of the Renault later received 5,000 francs in the post with an anonymous note apologising for the damage to his car's roof.

After undergoing plastic surgery, Spaggiari spent most of the rest of his life in Argentina, surreptitiously visiting France at intervals to see his elderly mother at her home in Hyères, 90 miles along the coast from Nice. She discovered her son's lifeless body in bed there one morning in June 1989, a victim, apparently, of lung cancer at the age of 57. No one has ever accounted for the Société Générale's missing cash.

★★★

In that same news-intense week of July 1976, Jimmy Carter was officially nominated as his party's candidate for president by a vote of 2,239 of the 3,000 delegates at the Democratic National Convention in New York.

If Carter had any illusions about the global challenges of the job he sought, they would have been dispelled by events that day in Angola, where thirteen US and British mercenaries were tried and convicted of choosing to fight for the wrong army in the country's three-sided civil war. Nine of the convicted men were given lengthy jail terms and the remainder were summarily shot. Angola's communist President António Neto declined appeals from both the Queen and Prime Minister for clemency on behalf of the Britons among the guilty parties.

The Soviet Union, meanwhile, continued to actively explore the opportunity to export its political ideology to central Africa. Henry Kissinger later remarked tartly on the internal power struggle at the heart of the Ford administration that had now allowed Angola to become the latest domino to fall into the Marxist-Leninist camp. 'Looking back,' Kissinger wrote:

> Our best strategy would have been to invest as much money and manpower as we could in order to bring about a radical change on the ground, and stop the Soviet escalation in its tracks. But [CIA chief] William Colby and his successor George Bush both spent half their time on Capitol Hill defending their agency before congressional committees, and either couldn't or wouldn't commit to the cause until it was too late. The best Colby could do was to urge the mercenaries to buy their weapons on the open market, with funds we had given them, rather than have us supply them direct. As I said at the time, the difference in virginity eluded me. It still does.

In the weeks ahead, William Colby would tell the US Congress of various hair-raising details of covert CIA operations, including the use of LSD in several bungled mind-control experiments designed to kill or neutralise foreign adversaries, as well as the deployment of lethal dart guns and exploding cigars that seemed to combine the worlds of James Bond and Groucho Marx. He went on to display to a fascinated Senate Select Committee bottles of deadly shellfish toxin and cobra venom taken from the CIA storeroom.

After being replaced as America's spy chief, Colby would argue with a convert's zeal for deep cuts in the nation's intelligence budget, believing the money could be better spent on poverty relief programmes. He died in May 1996, aged 76, after apparently suffering a heart attack while out by himself in a canoe drifting down a secluded stretch of river behind his Washington home.

It must seem to many Americans that the threat or reality of worldwide communism has been the bane of post-war life. Certainly, Ronald Reagan made it the centrepiece of his primary election challenge to Gerald Ford, which ended in the latter's favour only on 19 August, when Ford was narrowly renominated at the Republican Convention in Kansas City. To Reagan's mind, and those of his like-minded fellow Americans, any policy of cooperation with Moscow was a chimera that owed its existence to an unholy alliance between liberal appeasement and orthodox conservative thrift with the nation's finances. In this view of the world's affairs, détente should be replaced by a retreat to the strategy of confrontation between two irreconcilable 'camps', while what was most needed at home, Reagan announced, was 'a clean sweep of the old foreign policy establishment [who] have sold our country short to the Reds'.

Leonid Brezhnev, for his part, took the opportunity of a rare Kremlin press conference that month to claim that 'constraints' were placed on his own flexibility when it came to making an accommodation with the West by a Soviet public opinion that he knew to be mythical.

While the two superpowers traded largely idle barbs over what life should ideally look like for their respective citizens, the actual flashpoints of the Cold War came about in proxy conflicts conducted among states less concerned with the nuances of global stability than with subverting the status quo they identified as being at the heart of their national frustrations. Such conflicts had occurred or continued in places like Somalia, Lebanon, Rwanda, Cyprus, the Congo, Nigeria, Argentina and Uruguay. And those were just the set-piece clashes, with a more or less coherent set of competing political or ethnic objectives. There were also those strange, sometimes semi-farcical but none-theless deadly incidents that can take place when two bitterly opposed armed factions are brought into proximity with each other.

One such event occurred on the morning of 18 August, around Panmunjom in the demilitarised zone (DMZ) between the two Koreas. There had already been a certain amount of ill will engendered between the US and North Korean troops stationed only a few dozen yards away from one another at what, along with Berlin, amounted to one of the perma-nent crisis points of the Cold War. Earlier in the year, an American GI had had his arm broken by North Korean troops after he inadvertently drove his jeep a few feet over the border into their territory while patrolling the DMZ. As a result, the local US forces under the command of Lieutenant David 'Mad Dog' Zilka had fallen into the habit of banging loudly in the dead of night on the walls or windows of buildings close to the main North Korean guardhouse or treating their country's declared ideological foe to bursts of heavily amplified rock music. According to Private Mike Bilbo of the US Army 10th Support Group, 'Once or twice we caught a Red where they weren't supposed to be and kind of cooled them off, maybe roughed them up a little. Nothing too serious. That's how the game was played in those days.'

These actions on both sides may have contributed to the incident on 18 August, which came about when a group of US and South Korean sol-diers decided to trim the branches of a poplar tree standing in the DMZ, which they had complained was obscuring their view of the border. The North Korean forces strongly objected to this initiative, and used clubs and axes wrenched from the hands of the landscaping party to bludgeon two American servicemen to death. The next day, a large US Army contingent drove out to fell the offending tree with chainsaws, while hostile troops sat silently observing them a few yards away, at the far end of the Bridge of No Return that had divided the Korean peninsula since 1953, with machine guns at the ready.

Back in Washington, Henry Kissinger wanted to take more direct action to 'teach those bastards a lesson about power'. The incident saw him in one of his more bellicose moods. 'You know my preference last week was to hit the [North Korean] barracks as hard as we could, but that was overruled,' Kissinger told a high-level meeting at the State Department on 25 August. Some talk then ensued around the table about a possible retaliatory air strike on other selected North Korean targets. According to the minutes:

Kissinger: What kind of defences do they have there, anyway?

George H.W. Bush [CIA]: They have superb defences, and any action would involve a very high risk. They have excellent coastal radar. It would be a very high risk measure. Very high indeed.

Kissinger: What would we have achieved if the North Koreans didn't know who did it?

Bush: The advantage would be the element of doubt … And our own assistant general counsel says you would not have to report [it] under the War Powers Act.

Kissinger: But congress will say we have to report, and if we don't want to lie we would be forced to take a no-comment line which would in effect be admitting we did it.

[Deputy Secretary of Defence] Bill Clements: I like the plan. We should probably proceed with it. George?

Bush: I think it would be terribly risky, but I know you don't need my advice on that now.

Kissinger: Right. Develop the plan.

In the end, the United States declined to bomb any North Korean targets, however, and the Pyongyang regime issued a statement remarking that it was 'unfortunate that two persons [had] accidentally died', but insisting, 'Our side will never provoke first, but take self-defensive measures only where provocation occurs'. President Ford accepted this as an adequate expression of regret. The bodies of the two slain US soldiers were initially flown to Saigon, where the newly formed Provisional Revolutionary Peoples Government of Vietnam formally returned them to US authorities for burial with full military honours in the United States.

Kissinger later remarked in private that the voices of caution in terms of an armed US response to the DMZ incident had consisted largely of Gerald Ford, George Bush and several prominent congressmen such as the Democratic Senate Leader Mike Mansfield, with the South Korean President Park Chung Hee also 'not unreasonably worried' about the potential for any military strike to escalate into full-scale war on the peninsula. The more hawkish element in the debate was represented by the voice of Ronald Reagan and Kissinger himself at home, and several NATO leaders, most notably James Callaghan, overseas.

Kissinger's view of the British premier remained untainted by any possible concern over their differing political philosophies. 'Jim combined an avuncular personality with abundant good sense,' Kissinger later wrote, proving that his gift for flattery extended to friendly foreign leaders as well as to the current occupant of the White House:

> He was neither a strategist nor a geopolitician, and he knew it … But when it came to tactical matters, Callaghan could be relentless, enveloping us in joviality while his skillful experts bombarded us with briefs designed to move us in the direction of British preferences.

In turn, Callaghan 'quite liked Henry personally', but was wary of US expansionism. He later wrote:

> Their foreign policy was like an octopus that held the world in its tentacles, or tried to … It [was] one thing to take direct action where your subjects are being murdered, like [Panmunjom], but quite another to be constantly prodding your opponents with a sharp stick, then to complain should they rear up and strike back.

★★★

Callaghan's own priorities that month prominently included the continuing British drought, which now had its own minister in 52-year-old Denis Howell, a former professional football referee turned Birmingham City Councillor and latterly an MP. Howell caused some perhaps unintended mirth by promptly inviting reporters to his constituency home, where he revealed that he was doing his bit to help conserve water by sharing baths with his wife, Brenda.

Meanwhile, the heatwave continued to assert itself in the daily life of the nation. The tabloids competed with each other to publish the most striking images of young women in bikinis; the high-end broadsheets were more circumspect, but worried about the potential for reduced productivity; the House of Commons bar staff walked off the job in protest when officials refused to allow them to remove their traditional heavy green jackets; above them, Big Ben suffered its first and to date only major breakdown due to metal fatigue, and was out of order for the next three weeks as a result; sales of lager soared, even at the gouged price of 50p a pint; major British roads were strewn with broken-down cars that had burst a radiator and given up the struggle; and the Metropolitan Police dealt with 300 more daily domestic disturbance calls than normal as tempers frayed in the heat.

When, on 25 August, Manchester City hosted Aston Villa in what was then called the First Division, it was found that the City players had collectively lost 4 stone in weight over the course of ninety minutes. The home team's last manager, the fedora-wearing Malcolm 'Big Mal' Allison, had left the club amidst some acrimony to take over at Third Division Crystal Palace. But this arrangement, too, ended abruptly after Allison saw fit to invite the glamour model and *Men Only* columnist Fiona Richmond to join him in the bath at the club's training ground, an event gleefully recorded for posterity by a *News of the World* photographer. This seemed to the stuffed shirts at the Football Association to be taking the government's water-saving initiative to uncalled-for extremes, and a formal charge of bringing the game into disrepute followed, as did Allison's departure from the club.

Surveying the agenda set before him at the Cabinet meeting of 3 August, James Callaghan remarked mordantly to Denis Healey that life just then seemed to be a case of 'one damn thing after another', with the problems simply refusing to line up to be addressed in an orderly fashion, although at least the long-running Cod War seemed to have been resolved by a compromise which allowed Britain to keep a maximum of twenty-four trawlers within the disputed 200-mile limit, but otherwise gave Iceland everything it had demanded.

Callaghan took advantage of the same Cabinet meeting to set out his proposals for an urgent reduction in Britain's public expenditure, both at home and abroad. Delivered to his ministerial colleagues in bullet-pointed form, the list made for stark reading:

To consider new ways of funding our short term overseas debt.
To introduce emergency legislation to cut housing subsidies at the same time as reducing tax relief on mortgage debt.
To get a firm grip on local authority manpower.
To look at the cost to the public sector of educating children in the private sector.
To drastically reduce our presence in Cyprus.

Total government spending on the three elements of the 'social wage' — healthcare, education and welfare benefits — reached a post-war high of 24 per cent of total national income in 1976, before falling steadily over the next decade. There were still some 6 million people living on the breadline in the UK, or about 11 per cent of the population, just 1 per cent less than in 1961.

The level of poverty had not changed much in those fifteen years, but its character had. Those struggling to pay their bills or to make ends meet were now far more often to be found living in urban areas than in the country. In the nation's biggest cities, the number of poor was even more striking. Depending on the terms involved, London was home to close to 1 million men, women and children living in a 'state of scarcity' in 1976, which most government statistics defined as those with an income less than 140 per cent of the basic National Assistance level. As just one example, there was the case of the Jamaican-born teenager and future Oxford University lecturer Patricia Daley:

> At [that] time we lived in a two-bedroom flat in one of the 1930s blocks on the Pembury Estate in Hackney. The estate's residents were primarily white working-class. Often, someone would daub 'n*****' or 'NF' on the stairwell and we would have to sidestep dog shit to get to our front door ... I sometimes wondered about the architects who designed such places and their views on the humanity of the people who lived in them.

Oddly enough, the level of urban poverty in the United States rivalled or exceeded that in Britain, particularly in the black or Hispanic majority ghetto neighbourhoods, even as the US middle class (said to be 68 per cent of the total) took advantage of luxuries that were unheard of across the Atlantic: air-cooled cars, their dashboards trimmed in afrormosia teak veneer, luridly branded velour jogging suits, $50 designer tennis shoes, locally harvested microgreens, cage-free eggs, low-fat oat milk, miso soup sprinkled with kelp flakes, and organic truffle pizzas. Alongside the clothes and food, there was also a growing number of pop-psychology movements to help middle-class Americans come to terms with their guilt pangs about seemingly having won the lottery in life. Perhaps the most notable was Erhard Seminars Training, or EST, which for only a modest fee promised its clients a lifelong sense of personal empowerment. Within only weeks of opening its doors, sufficient numbers had enrolled with the group to ensure long waiting lists from coast to coast.

EST workshops typically took place in intensive weekend getaways, where 'trained moderators' first berated attendees for their beliefs and then raised their spirits through guided meditations and repetitive readings. At the end of each session, participants either got it and experienced a transcendent life change, or walked away, dazed, confused and several hundred dollars poorer. The movement's founding father Werner Erhard, a former car salesman, described the process as a form of 'Socratic interrogation', although to critics it was just another evanescent cult primarily designed to separate gullible Americans from their cash. Erhard himself deemed it best to leave the United States during a period when the federal tax authorities were investigating his affairs, although it should be stressed that he was later cleared of all suspicion of wrongdoing.

ERIC'S SUMMER PADDLE

Even by rock music standards, Eric Clapton was something of a protean character in those days, if not a human chameleon. Born in the south London suburbs in 1945 and raised in one of those character-shaping households where he was led to believe that his grandparents were his parents and his young mother was his big sister, as a teenager Clapton had discovered the appeal of blues music for its relatable sense of struggle, heartbreak and resilience. An obviously gifted guitar player, who honed his craft by constant practice, his all-consuming heroes in those days had been US pioneers of the form like Robert Johnson and Muddy Waters. It was as much an act of projection as professional respect, allowing him to visualise himself not on the dreary suburban Guildford streets but sashaying around Memphis or hopping a box car through the Southern cotton fields.

In time, Clapton developed a romantic association with self-destructive performers of the Charlie Parker school, whose lives were haunted by the demons that eventually destroyed them, and he himself nearly died of heroin addiction as a result. 'I was one of the greediest and most selfish bastards who ever lived,' the guitarist later recalled of the period around 1970–75.

But by August 1976, Clapton was back, now a drunkard rather than a junkie, and with a pervasive new role model: Alf Garnett, the celebrated screen bigot, who supported West Ham, the monarchy, the Tory Party and the Church of England, and who intensely disliked immigrants, feminists and anyone who disagreed with him. As portrayed by Warren Mitchell in TV's *Till Death Us Do Part*, Garnett made people laugh, but he made people think, too. And he also quite often made them angry.

This was the backdrop to the events of 5 August 1976, when a visibly intoxicated Clapton chugged on stage as part of what he called his 'Summer paddle' at the not entirely full 2,400-seat Birmingham Odeon. The first number he performed was barely coherent. But the words which the guitarist addressed to the audience once it ground to a halt were painfully clear.

'Do we have any foreigners here tonight?' Clapton enquired. 'If so, please put up your hands … So where are you? Well, wherever you are, I think you should all just leave. Not just leave the hall, leave the country … I don't want you here in the room, or in my home.'

Striking a further variant on the traditional 'Hello Birmingham!' salute normally favoured on these occasions, Clapton was only now getting into the gist of his address. 'Listen to me!' he continued. 'I think we should send the whole lot back. Stop Britain from becoming a black colony. Get the foreigners out. Get the wogs out. Get the coons out. Keep Britain white ... The fucking Saudis are taking over London. The black wogs and coons and Arabs and fucking Jamaicans don't belong here, and we don't want them here. This is England, this is a white country, we don't want any black wogs and coons living here. We need to make clear to them they aren't welcome. England is for white people, man ... This is Great Britain, a white country. What is happening to us, for fuck's sake? Throw them all out. Keep Britain white. For fuck's sake ...'

To a growing backdrop of boos from the crowd, Clapton went on from there to offer a ringing endorsement of the maverick ex-Tory and latterly Ulster Unionist MP Enoch Powell, ending with a further impassioned plea for Britain to 'stop [from] becoming a wog colony'. He then finished a set described by the local *Evening Mail* as 'lacklustre', before exiting to catcalls from the house.

Clapton later rationalised his speech by noting – lest it not already be apparent – that he was 'quite drunk at the time', and also, 'a foreigner had just pinched my missus's bum before I went on, and I proceeded to lose my bottle'. It would therefore – he implied – be quite wrong to ascribe his remarks that stiflingly hot August night to any innate prejudice; we can also note the long list of African American musicians to have benefitted from his patronage in the years since 1976. But at the time, Clapton's outburst was made all the more shocking because it seemed to be of a piece with other major rock stars who took an ambivalent attitude to racial politics. First, it was David Bowie, then it was John Lennon, complaining from New York about the Labour government's spending priorities 'doing bugger all for the average Englishman', and now it was Eric Clapton. Was something really going on in the lively arts that summer to reflect the sort of pervasive mood that in its most extreme expression had brought violence to the streets of Notting Hill or killed the young Gurdip Singh Chaggar?

Bigoted public remarks may not have been new, but only rarely were they validated, mainlined and presented as reasonable by high-profile popular entertainers with vast and often impressionable legions of fans at their disposal. Either way, Clapton's comments at Birmingham proved sufficiently inflammatory to kick-start the Rock Against Racism movement, as well as to bring a public rebuke from the organisation's founder, Peter Bruno. 'Come on, Eric,'

Bruno wrote. 'What's going on? You've got a touch of brain damage. You're going to stand for MP, and you think we are all being colonised by black people. Own up. Half your music is black. You are rock's biggest colonist.'

Before moving on, it's worth touching again on the mysterious ways of artistic creation. Just a week after his hate-filled meltdown on the Birmingham stage, Clapton was back at his Italianate mansion, close to where he had grown up, in more threadbare circumstances, in rural Surrey. Waiting for his partner Pattie Boyd to join him downstairs so they could leave for a party, he started to hum. Within a minute, he was closeted with his acoustic guitar in the small room he used as a studio, and within five more, recording the basic track for what became his ubiquitous hit single 'Wonderful Tonight'.

Released the following year, the song sharply divided critical opinion. *Rolling Stone* called it an 'exquisite paean conveying emotion with a tender clarity', while more jaundiced observers came to believe that one of the ultimate compensations for death might be the ending of the obligation to ever listen to it again. As of this writing, 'Wonderful Tonight' has been downloaded more than 500 million times on streaming services and accompanied many elevator rides in all parts of the world. So, possibly it was a mixture of all these qualities, good and bad, and another example of a ballad whose 'beauty' and 'authenticity' speak to many people and leave others cold. Coming so soon after Clapton's ill-chosen remarks at Birmingham, perhaps it's enough to say that the song truly was a case of a creative mind passing rapidly from the ridiculous, or offensive, to the sublime.

Either way, Clapton and his established rock music peers operated at some distance from the still small but fast-growing number of punk bands thrashing away in their provincial polytechnic common rooms or inner-city basement clubs. It's been said that the new-wave aesthetic unleashed on the world in 1976 was a backlash against the classic 1960s ethos of flares, beads, flowers, peace and love. In their place came distressed leather, decayed teeth, ripped vests, snot and anger. For all that, it's possible the visual element of the punk phenomenon may have owed less to what *The Atlantic* called 'the fruit of a situationist subversion of cultural norms [which] made the safety-pin the symbol of a self-lacerating generation' than some critics supposed. The Sex Pistols' Johnny Rotten always offered a more practical reason for the accessory, claiming it prevented 'the arse of your pants falling out'.

Although still a novelty in August 1976, the profusion of mohawks, studded chokers, aggressively dyed hair and torn fishnets, with the odd swastika armband thrown in, would soon act as a magnet for American tourists drawn to Britain both by the favourable exchange rate and the pursuit of anthropo-morphic data about this exciting new youth movement. The chance to see the Sex Pistols in action typically cost you between 40–50p that summer, although even at those prices the band and their ilk would have struggled to fill most venues had they stapled a free packet of Benzedrine to the ticket stub.

There were between fifty and sixty-five paying customers when the Pistols played at the Lesser Free Trade Hall in Manchester on 4 June, although the list of those who did attend famously included future founding members of Joy Division, the Smiths and Simply Red. The band members themselves pulled up to the rear door of the hall in a ragtag *Mad Max* convoy of ramshackle tran-sit vans and motorbikes and left it again less than an hour later amidst a shower of freshly expectorated saliva as a parting tribute from their newfound fans. As Joy Division's Peter Hook later remarked, 'The takeaway message was that if they can do it, so can we. That night started it all.'

***

As we've seen, the fledgling punk movement was not an issue that troubled James Callaghan's government that summer, but there was no shortage of the sort of disorderly problems the prime minister had complained of to his chan-cellor. Among other things, there was the continuing heatwave, which was fast becoming an established reference point for almost every discussion where two or more parties were gathered.

There were more racially charged disturbances on the streets of London, Birmingham, Wolverhampton and Bradford, where the representatives of the National Front lost few opportunities to insert themselves in the debate. There was the matter of sterling's exchange rate against the dollar. And then there was the fact that the nation's social fabric was sufficiently fragile for the prime minister to place a phone call to Gerald Ford in the Oval Office, informing him that there was 'not a cat in hell's chance' of the Labour Party agreeing to the full severity of the spending cuts Washington was urging on it to 'ensure Britain can meet its defence obligations as a full partner in our common secu-rity enterprise'. 'The question is, Jerry, who is going to be out of office first, you or me?' Callaghan had enquired, again demonstrating the sliver of ice that lay under the sunny exterior.

On 6 August, after a sixty-eight-day trial, the former Labour Minister John Stonehouse was sentenced to seven years for fraud. As we've seen, beset by financial problems, he'd neatly folded his three-piece suit on a Miami beach, walked into the sea and apparently disappeared into thin air, perhaps the first example of a real-life political drama inspiring a sitcom – *The Fall and Rise of Reginald Perrin* – before being arrested a month later by police in Melbourne, who at first believed he was the missing Lord Lucan.

Six days after Stonehouse's guilty verdict at the Old Bailey, his former parliamentary colleague, Tom Driberg, latterly Baron Bradwell, suffered a heart attack while in the back of a London cab and died at the age of 71. An unreliable witness of undoubted charm and with the morals of a bisexual alley cat, Driberg had once contracted a marriage to a society lady, with a well-attended reception to follow in the House of Commons, while going on to enjoy a series of assignations with young soldiers, sailors and airmen. Like Stonehouse, he kept questionable company in terms of his overseas intelligence service contacts. It remains a moot point whether he was a British agent, a Soviet mole or just a gossipy free spirit of no fixed ideological abode who liked being the centre of attention. A notable maverick in a crowded political field that year, Driberg had even once come close to persuading Mick Jagger to stand as a Labour MP.

On the day of Driberg's funeral, three children aged between 2 and 8 were killed when a hijacked car ploughed into them and their mother, who was left with a permanent brain injury, on a street in suburban Belfast. The driver of the car, an IRA man on active service, lost control after being shot by the British Army patrol which was chasing him. Later that week, the children's aunt and a family friend joined forces to found the Peace People movement and soon organised a 20,000-strong march through the streets of Belfast, sharing the following year's Nobel Peace prize for their initiative.

In sport, it was the month in which Niki Lauda, leading the German Grand Prix in his Ferrari, hit a slippery patch at 140mph, spun out, broke through a metal fence which snagged his helmet, then careened off an embankment and bounced back onto the track, where he was hit by several following cars. Lauda's ruptured fuel tank then burst into flames, which engulfed him in the cockpit. Despite suffering extensive burns to his head and face and losing most of his right ear, the 27-year-old Austrian returned to the Formula 1 circuit just six weeks later and won the following year's Drivers' World Championship, only retiring from competitive racing in 1985.

The last rites of the summer's Test cricket series were played out that week at the Oval, where the baked plains of south London provided the setting for England's third successive defeat at the hands of the West Indies. Having begun the series by promising to make his opponents grovel, Tony Greig ended it by crawling on his hands and knees in comic supplication before the tourists' supporters as their side wrapped up a decisive 231-run victory. Few people had ever previously witnessed batting as masterful as that of Viv Richards or bowling as consistently fast and hostile as that of Michael Holding, who took 14 wickets in the match. The start of Holding's superbly fluid run-up – dead straight, ball tucked in close to his stomach, white toecaps glinting in the sun – before the climactic delivery leap was always the signal for dead quiet in the crowd.

★★★

Early on the Friday afternoon of the week that England's cricket captain was abasing himself on the Oval outfield, one of those peculiarly British industrial disputes was gathering steam about 10 miles away in north London. This was the walkout and subsequent strike at the large Grunwick mail-order film-processing works in Chapter Road, Willesden, which was finally settled only in June 1978 following a full-scale judicial inquiry and a plethora of competing lawsuits. Along the way, the site became an attritional battleground, with long periods of relative calm punctuated by spectacular outbreaks of violence on the picket lines stationed at the factory gates, and crowds in the tens of thousands arriving to demonstrate their support for one or other of the competing factions. At the height of the mayhem, there were regular pictures at the populist end of the press of policemen's helmets flying and of 'secondary pickets' like the miners' leader Arthur Scargill being led away in handcuffs under such eye-catching headlines as 'Gestapo!', while to the likes of the *Daily Mail*, by contrast, Grunwick became 'the Ascot of the Left – the place to be seen in order to signal your virtue, or impress the union shop floor'.

If you had wanted to show a curious alien what life was really like in Britain in 1976, you could have done worse than to take them to Willesden on most Saturday afternoons during the late summer and autumn months. It all touched on the great unresolved question of British life of the era – how much of the nation's political and economic power was the government's, and how much of it the unions'?

Like many of the most acrimonious disputes, the Grunwick matter had modest beginnings. At around one o'clock on the sweltering Friday afternoon of 20 August, the plant's duty manager Malcolm Alden had an exchange of views with a 19-year-old temporary employee named Devshi Bhudia. Bhudia was told that he would need to work through his lunch break that day to process a backlog of customers' orders needing to be sent out before the weekend.

The teenager was not pleased either at Mr Alden's directive or the tone with which it was delivered.

'There was a scene,' as the later official report put it, and the hourly paid worker was sacked on the spot. He had hesitated for a moment while on his way out, apparently reconsidering his position, but Alden's booming baritone had insisted. He had a business to run, and his need to satisfy his customers was matched only by his impatience with his obstinate young temp.

Seeing what was happening, two of Bhudia's colleagues spontaneously decided to walk off the premises in sympathy. A number of the plant's remaining employees were thus called upon to work overtime, and at that stage, in a demonstration of what geopoliticians call the domino effect, 43-year-old Jayaben Desai, a £30-a-week film processor, and her son Sunil, who had found temporary summer work in the same department, also walked out in protest, to be followed in turn by five of their disenchanted colleagues.

There were no windows on the main floor of the Grunwick factory and conditions in the building that summer struck many observers as akin to a sweatshop. The walkout by Jayaben Desai and the others had therefore not come as 'a completely unforeseeable development', a court later noted, 'and to some extent reflected long-held grievances exacerbated by the intemperate heat'.

The respective parties dug in over the intervening weekend. Surveying the placard-waving strikers who had begun to assemble outside his premises on Monday, 23 August, Mr Alden, a Jaguar-driving employer of the old school with a military manner and a side parting to his hair so sharp it was as if someone had drawn a white chalk line across his scalp, went on to remark that the largely Asian workforce gathered at his gates reminded him of 'chattering monkeys'. Jayaben Desai replied, 'What you are running here is not a factory, sir, it is a zoo. But in a zoo there are many types of animals. Some are monkeys who dance on your fingertips. Others are lions who can bite your head off … we are the lions here.' Mrs Desai, who stood only 4ft 10in tall, was later arrested for pushing a male manager (not Mr Alden) to the ground during a scuffle at the Grunwick front gate, a charge the magistrate who heard the case dismissed as 'risible'.

As the dispute escalated, with ever-growing numbers of walkouts, it became clear that there were really three separate but related issues involved: the original clash of wills about working terms and conditions in the Grunwick plant; the management's refusal to allow its factory-floor employees like Mrs Desai to join a trade union; and the more pervasive desire on the part of newly arrived immigrant workers, many of them women, to be treated with respect by some of the more Alf Garnett-minded school among the local community.

It took a further year for the government to set up a court of inquiry into the whole Grunwick affair, which by then had become a proxy party-political battle, with James Callaghan and Margaret Thatcher frequently exchanging views about the respective rights of management and labour. The dispute eventually ended in defeat for the strikers. No one got their job back, and the House of Lords upheld the right of Malcolm Alden and his colleagues to not permit union membership for their workforce. Following that, the picket lines gradually drifted away.

The Grunwick company prospered and expanded after the strike, and at one time employed over 500 staff, spread between two north London factories. Having survived the defining industrial dispute of the decade, the firm eventually succumbed to the market pressures of changing digital-camera technology and closed its gates for the last time in 2011.

★★★

With a certain inevitability, Britain's long, uninterrupted dry spell came to an abrupt end over that year's August Bank Holiday. With rain falling, cold temperatures, gusty winds and the possibility of thunder and lightning in the forecast, the meteorological misery that seems to roll around every long week-end played to type again in 1976. Nevertheless, many seaside resorts, often the scene of unwonted displays of St Tropez-like flesh that summer, reported record attendances. Blackpool was 'as crowded as ever', despite the 'dubious conditions', with trains and motor coaches 'full of tourists and day-trippers, and guest houses packed to overflowing'. Brighton saw 'unprecedented numbers making their way through the town', while, along the coast, Eastbourne was inundated by 'vast hordes'. At Clacton, it was noted that the weather 'had no noticeable effect on amusements and relaxations', which included 'amateur boxing and wrestling bouts, bumper cars and freak shows'.

On 30 August, play was completely washed out in the scheduled one-day cricket international at Birmingham, although the teams managed to get on the field to complete a contest shortened to 32 overs apiece the following afternoon. The tourists won by 50 runs. Viv Richards was, for once, out cheaply, but his captain Clive Lloyd clubbed 79, more than two-thirds of the runs coming in boundaries, and England were never seriously in the chase after that. A 20-year-old named Ian Botham was making only his second appearance for his country, and to the delight of the crowd bowled three consecutive bouncers to Michael Holding, the last of which the batsman managed to hook onto his stumps.

That effectively concluded the eminently successful West Indies summer tour, and after the medals ceremony, Lloyd and his men lined up on the Edgbaston pavilion balcony, where the crowd saluted them in vocally resonant if not especially tuneful style. The steady drizzle mocked their high spirits. When all the figures were added up, it was found that the Test and County Cricket Board were £950,000 (or £7.5 million) better off than they had been when the tourists arrived the previous May, a jackpot from which the players themselves earned £140 apiece for each full five-day international – the backdrop to the leaked announcement the following spring of the Australian media tycoon Kerry Packer's World Series Cricket. Overnight, it was bedlam. 'Cricket "Circus" Threat to Test Matches', ran the comparatively subdued headline in *The Times*, while extra bold, war-is-declared type and multiple exclamation marks typified the coverage elsewhere. It turned out that Tony Greig himself had acted as Packer's principal recruiter, thus abruptly bringing his England Test career to an end. A much-travelled writer and broadcaster on the game in his later years, he died in a Sydney hospital in December 2012, after being diagnosed with cancer. He was 66.

INTO THE WHIRLWIND

Shortly after 4 p.m. local time on Thursday, 9 September, martial music began to blare out over the loudspeakers in Beijing's Tiananmen Square. In short order, several thousand people, many wearing black armbands and some weeping, gathered in front of the imposing neoclassical façade of the Museum of the Revolution, whose red flag was lowered to half-mast. In time, the music gave way to the staccato tones of a disembodied male voice reading out what was described as 'news of the first gravity', addressed to 'the whole Party, the whole army, and to people of all races throughout the nation', which it was his duty to impart, even though his soul was 'fiercely shaken' and his eyes 'flowed with a sea of tears'.

Following that, the announcer came to the point.

'Mao Zedong passed away at 0100 hours today because of the worsening of his health,' he began. 'All victories of the Chinese people were achieved under the wisdom of the late Chairman Mao,' the voice continued, in eulogising the man who had led the communist takeover of his country in 1949 and then guided it from backward isolation to the status of a nuclear power with a burgeoning industrial base, purging rivals, defying Soviet ideological leadership and winning a seat in the United Nations. The announcer went on to note that China would 'continue to carry on the Great Helmsman's revolutionary line and policies in home and foreign affairs resolutely', and to urge the country's 930 million citizens to 'deepen your criticism' of the 'Right-deviationist former first vice premier Deng Xiaoping', who had been toppled in the power struggle that followed the death the previous January of Mao's closest comrade in arms Zhou Enlai.

The voice concluded that there would be eight days of memorial ceremonies to mark the Great Helmsman's passing at the age of 82, and added that no foreign leaders, whether 'capitalist governments, fraternal parties or friendly personages', would be invited to Beijing for the funeral. A reverent hush fell over the crowd following the spokesman's remarks, although in the distance, factories could soon be heard sounding their sirens in tribute. 'The Internationale', the nineteenth-century French battle hymn adopted as the worldwide socialist anthem, echoed over the Beijing streets as darkness fell that evening, while tens of thousands of men and women began to make their way home from work on bicycles.

Addressing the Cabinet at eleven o'clock the following morning, Britain's Foreign Secretary Anthony Crosland told his colleagues:

> The death of Chairman Mao, coming so close on the heels of Zhou Enlai, must be expected to lead to a period of uncertainty in China, in which the moderate and radical elements will compete for leadership ... But no change [is] likely in China's foreign policy or in her attitude towards the West.

Crosland was right about the first part of this summation but mistaken about the latter. Within a few weeks, China's so-called 'Gang of Four', the leftist rump that included Mao's widow, Jiang Qing, a former pin-up model who had wielded significant power in her husband's declining years, had themselves been violently purged. The four were lured into the Chungnanhai compound of Beijing's Forbidden City on the pretext that an urgent meeting was about to be convened. Once there, they were unceremoniously arrested and jailed. Newspapers and radio stations were seized and key universities where the four had influence were surrounded by troops.

Overnight, the previously revered Madame Mao became a pariah. It was rapidly made apparent that many people in all walks of Chinese life in fact despised this once-eulogised figure in a way few had ever imagined. The official organs of the state treated Mao's widow with a contempt that was as extreme as, a few weeks earlier, it would have been shocking. Among other unappreciative terms, Jiang Qing was described in the central party newspaper as being 'malevolent as a demon, treacherous as a serpent and savage as a mad dog'. And that was just the relatively restrained official opprobrium. To the ordinary Chinese citizen, as expressed in the fliers denouncing the nation's former First Lady stapled to the wall in every public building, she had taken an 'inappropriate ideological perspective' and become 'a witch' ... 'slime' ... 'coprolite' ... 'fossil of dung' ... 'no better than fecal matter under the shoe'.

The Gang of Four were eventually put on trial in 1980, and perhaps not entirely surprisingly found guilty of anti-party activities, all to be given lifetime sentences. Jiang Qing allegedly committed suicide while in custody in May 1991, at the age of 77.

During the lengthy period of internal turmoil following Mao's death, Deng Xiaoping returned from exile and would go on to dominate China's government for the next two decades. His rapid rehabilitation into public life was the mirror opposite to Jiang Qing's trajectory.

It would be wrong to portray the Deng era as one of uninterrupted mutual peace and goodwill in Sino-Western relations, but there were nonetheless to be significant developments in that direction. Deng effectively ended China's role as an exporter of revolution and people's war, signalled that he was open to discussions on the future of Hong Kong and that he was in no especial hurry to revisit the thorny issue of Taiwan. As a moderniser, he proved willing to open China to the influence of foreign technology, management techniques and investment, but not to the accompanying winds of social change. Sometimes described as the acceptable face of Maoism, he was also the hardliner who imposed martial law on his country in May 1989 and subsequently ordered the imprisonment or exiling of his critics. On his own death in 1997, the familiar staccato voice that had denounced him twenty-one years earlier now returned to the loudspeakers in Tiananmen Square.

'The passing of Deng Xiaoping is an immeasurable loss for our party, our army, and the people of all ethnic groups throughout the country, and will cause tremendous grief around the world,' the announcer intoned, before adding that the Chinese people would certainly 'hold high the principle of the late paramount leader's cause of building socialism with unique characteristics, firm and unshakable and full of confidence ... Eternal glory to comrade Deng Xiaoping,' the voice concluded, as the factory sirens once more sounded in the distance.

At first planning to attend Mao's funeral in September 1976, Henry Kissinger decided to travel to Africa as an alternative. On the 15th of the month, he met with President Julius Nyerere in Dar es Salaam, before travelling to Lusaka, Nairobi and finally on to Pretoria where, by happenstance, Rhodesia's renegade Prime Minister Ian Smith was scheduled to be in town to watch a rugby match.

Kissinger met Smith for two hours on 19 September. It's possible that America's relentlessly calculating Secretary of State was genuinely motivated by a high-minded desire for, as he put it, 'a new order in southern Africa, achieved not by the strength of arms, but that of the human spirit'. Or equally, he might have been concerned that the Soviets, following their recent success in Angola, were eyeing Black Africa as a lucrative sphere of influence of their own, especially as the civil war in Rhodesia escalated. In either case, the Pretoria talks proved to be only a mixed success.

Kissinger presented Ian Smith with a five-point plan that included a two-year transitional government in Salisbury under a council of state with two white and two black members, following which 'a full and free vote including all people, regardless of race or ethnicity' would take place to determine the country's future. By way of incentive, Kissinger also quietly handed Smith a paper prepared for him by the CIA, which predicted that as things stood, the Rhodesian economy would be crippled within a year and the civil war was unwinnable by the current regime. Communism would take hold, Kissinger warned, if there were no immediate negotiations to permit moderate black representatives to take their seats in the government.

Smith studied both documents in silence for some time. 'I see,' he said at length, levelling his gaze back across the table at Kissinger. 'You want me to sign my death warrant.'

Smith duly did sign, but that did not end the war in Rhodesia. A conference in Geneva that November to discuss the fine detail of the transition to majority rule broke down in acrimony. The leaders of the African front-line states – Tanzania, Zambia, Mozambique and Botswana – would only consider a settlement on their terms, and Smith refused to make any more concessions in the matter. Terrorist activity in Rhodesia continued unabated for a further three years. The parties would meet again at a conference held over the winter of 1979–80 at Lancaster House in London, which would set a new path for what eventually became Zimbabwe.

As the nomadic US Secretary of State pursued his signature tactic of shuttling tirelessly around the world, domestic politics were heating up back home in Washington. On 22 September, a Gallup Poll reported that Jimmy Carter, the Georgian farmer widely mocked as 'Jimmy who?' only a year earlier, now enjoyed a 30 per cent lead over Gerald Ford in that November's presidential race. The following day, the two candidates met for the first of three ninety-minute televised debates at a music hall in Philadelphia. The live broadcast attracted 70 million viewers, the same number that had tuned in to watch the iconic first Beatles US TV appearance twelve years earlier, and who endured a lengthy technical breakdown in the transmission, leaving the candidates to talk quietly between themselves. The conversation soon turned to foreign affairs. Carter expressed his doubts that the Soviet Union would ever over-reach itself and provoke a war, as 'the people in charge there are too sensible'. Ford shook his head violently in disagreement and bet his opponent a dollar 'that the Soviets will be on the move again somewhere in the world by the end of the year'.

The debate itself largely went Ford's way. The president strode onto the stage wearing a dark, three-piece suit, and at 6ft 1in with a football player's solid build, cut a more obviously impressive figure than his slightly toothy opponent who couldn't seem to keep his hands still, first resting one on top of the other on the lectern, then rapidly switching their position, and finally, as if giving way to his preacherly tendencies, going on to repeatedly chop the air in front of his chest in order to illustrate a point. Ford set the tone with his opening rebuttal:

> I don't believe that Mr Carter has been any more specific in his remarks just now than he has been anywhere else … I noticed particularly that he didn't endorse the spending bill that is included as a part of the Democratic plat-form. I am not surprised. It would add $30 billion each year in additional expenditures by the federal government. That bill would be met by the American taxpayer.

Ford immediately rose in the overnight opinion polls, in some instances by as much as fifteen points. Worse was to follow for Carter, just twenty-four hours later, with the publication of his long, free-ranging interview with *Playboy* magazine.

Hugh Hefner's publication reached 27 million readers each month at the time, its pretensions to be seen as a serious chronicler of contemporary culture, with its profiles of such power players as Jean-Paul Sartre, Bertrand Russell, Muhammad Ali, Germaine Greer and Miles Davis, set against its eye-catching pictorials of absurdly curvaceous nudes with pouting expressions and unfeasibly pneumatic breasts. If the devoutly religious Carter saw his appearance in *Playboy* as part of a counterintuitive strategy to endear himself to a mainstream audience, it seems not to have immediately worked.

Among other bones of contention, there was the candidate's aside, adapting the words of Matthew 5: 27–28, that he was in no position to judge a man who 'shacks up' and 'screws around', because he himself had 'looked on many women with lust' and thus 'committed adultery in my heart'. The political cartoonists and late-night talk show hosts had a field day with remarks that perhaps qualified as 'too much information' by the political orthodoxy of 1976, leaving Carter's aides scrambling to make clear that their man was not a serial adulterer or sexual maniac. As if fuelled by a reverse Viagra, the challenger's poll numbers sank vertiginously over the course of the next week. On 30 September, Gallup reported that the race had narrowed to just 47–44 in Carter's favour, with 9 per cent undecided.

***

On 10 September, Denis Healey told his ministerial colleagues that Britain's economic affairs 'did not currently give rise to complacency', which, under the circumstances, showed considerable restraint on his part. 'Sterling has been edgy [and] the cost of fighting off bouts of selling has meant that £1,100 million of our £5,300 million standby facility has now been spent,' Healey was forced to admit. There was also the troubling matter of a seamen's strike, which, the prime minister noted, 'could begin to adversely affect stocks of major foodstuffs such as grain and wheat within 2–3 weeks', alongside an 'unsettled industrial relations landscape generally', possibly a reference to Grunwick. Also at issue were the lingering effects of the summer's drought on domestic and commercial water supply and 'urgent business relating to pressure of individual events throughout the United Kingdom'.

These events included a major prison riot at Hull, which put the entire facility out of commission for the next year; a series of sometimes violent marches and counter-marches on the city streets of Northern Ireland; the mid-air collision between a British Airways Trident and a Slovenian DC-9 in the skies over Zagreb, with the loss of all 176 passengers aboard the two aircraft; and, on a lighter note, the arrest for kerb-crawling of George Wigg, the 75-year-old Labour peer and former minister with the general air of a dissipated bloodhound, who had once played a leading role in exposing his political opponent John Profumo as an adulterer. Accused of driving his red Triumph Herald late at night through the Park Lane area of London, and stopping to approach six women with whom he exchanged pleasantries through the car window, Wigg told the magistrate hearing his case that he had merely been in search of a late-edition newspaper from a vendor outside Marble Arch Tube Station, a defence which gave rise to a *Private Eye* cartoon showing a dishevelled-looking Wigg leaning out of his car with the speech bubble, 'I'm desperate for a quick *Evening Standard*'.

In later years, the story gained circulation that Harold Wilson might have personally arranged for the police to frame his former ministerial colleague, for reasons buried somewhere back among the intrigues of their thirty-year personal and political association in what Wilson called 'the green-eyed jungle' of Westminster. Tony Benn went further: 'George Wigg was a fantasist whose passion was secrets, and the story I heard was that Harold had taken this step as an insurance policy against some future smear at Wigg's hands.'

James Callaghan did at least try to pursue a proactive domestic agenda, as opposed to dealing in perpetual crisis management, during his first year in office. On the spending side, it's true, he did not really ask for much. For all the furore they created at the more traditional-minded end of the press, the budgets and other financial measures of this period were mild manifestos devoid of conspicuously revolutionary purpose. They did not seek to 'tear up the existing fabric of society' (the view of the *Daily Mail*), or even to accomplish the 'more equitable distribution of state funds [and] social programmes to those most in need' called for in the prime minister's first major address to the party faithful after replacing Wilson. Callaghan wanted to reorder fiscal priorities, but he had no intention of imposing a radical socialist blueprint on the country.

The Supplementary Benefit Act of 1976, for instance, applied a careful touch on the tiller to the existing provisions relating to the taxable income of the parent in a one-parent family, and gave every low-paid worker over the age of 16 the right to claim a modestly calibrated state allowance. Similarly, the amended Race Relations Act enshrined in law the principle that it was wrong for an employer to discriminate on the grounds of an employee's skin colour, religion or national origin.

Much of our present-day health and safety apparatus can be traced to 1976, with new laws including the Woodworking Machines (Protection of Eyes) and Coal Mines (Respirable Dust) Acts coming amidst a host of other such regulations. The Police Act established a formal review board to deal with complaints by members of the public.

There were attempts to reduce child poverty and to restore the free supply of school milk, although Shirley Williams, the go-ahead former Consumer Protection Minister, appointed in September to replace 'my eminent predecessor, Mr Mulley' as Education Secretary, later privately conceded that the ambitions of most state school staff of the day had extended only 'to teaching kids to read, write and add up, and if possible to stop them from stabbing each other'.[3]

James Callaghan led the applause at the early Cabinet meeting at which Mrs Williams announced her determination to recruit more immigrant women into the teaching workforce. In broadly the same spirit of diversity, Callaghan publicly declared himself 'delighted' at the news of the opening late that summer of the UK's first purpose-built Buddhist temple, somewhat incongruously located immediately adjacent to the All-England Club at Wimbledon, which he saw as welcome relief from 'the dreary recitations of certain C of E vicars whose views one has to endure.' The prime minister's spirits may have been further depleted by the visit to Downing Street on 14 September of the incumbent Archbishop of Canterbury, Donald Coggan, favouring the premier with his thoughts on the ordination of women.

Margaret Thatcher was less impressed by the tenor of recent legislation, either on narrowly political or more broadly social grounds. The country was in decline, both economically and culturally, she informed a loudly appreciative audience in Birmingham on 18 September. 'We have begun to forget who we are as a people,' she added, to further applause.

***

The definition of acceptable public behaviour again came to the fore that month, when 66-year-old Mary Whitehouse, the founder and leading light of the National Viewers' and Listeners' Association (NVLA) and a tireless campaigner against moral collapse, awoke one morning to find a large envelope on her doormat. Opening it, she discovered the latest copy of *Gay News*, with an anonymous note attached drawing her attention to a specific page. Thumbing through – one imagines with some distaste – the intervening pictorials,

---

3 Fred Mulley (1918–95) was a man of impeccable working-class credentials, a bona fide war hero and a master synthesiser of otherwise irreconcilable political views within the Labour movement, who will always be best remembered not for his many legislative achievements but for falling asleep while seated beside the Queen as members of the armed forces paraded in front of them.

Mrs Whitehouse came to a poem entitled 'The Love That Dares to Speak its Name', by a widely respected academic and Fellow of the Royal Society of Literature, James Kirkup. The subject matter was striking, if not deliberately provocative, detailing the crucifixion of Christ as witnessed through the eyes of a homosexual Roman centurion, and illustrated by a picture that similarly strayed far from the orthodox depiction of the event. This exceeded the bounds of any reasonable exercise of artistic expression, according to Whitehouse, who, by then, already had form with certain members of the gay community who had invaded her 'Festival of Light' at London's Westminster Central Hall. On that occasion, some of the infiltrators, dressed as nuns, had kissed and fondled one another, while others had released mice in the aisles.

Mary Whitehouse remained a polarising figure. The NVLA's recent attacks on the TV comedian Benny Hill, for his suspender-clad girls, and on Alf Garnett, for his default use of the word 'bloody' in *Till Death Us Do Part*, had seemed to some to cast the organisation's founder as a meddling, petty-minded battleaxe. Others found her to be a woman of affectionate nature, courtesy and sincere beliefs.

Mrs Whitehouse also used the law aggressively, now bringing a rare private prosecution for blasphemous libel against *Gay News* and its editor Denis Lemon for its 'revolting graphic attack upon Our Lord'. The case was taken over by the Crown, whose counsel's opening statement to the court cut to the chase of the matter, 'It may be said that this is a love poem. It is not, it is one about buggery.' When later coming to sum the case up, Justice Alan King-Hamilton dismissed any suggestion that blasphemy might be a 'dead letter', noting that a law's antiquity – in this case, dating back to the time of the English theologian John Wycliffe in the fourteenth century – did not stop it from being valuable and relevant. The jury returned a guilty verdict. Denis Lemon was given a nine-month suspended sentence and his publication fined £31,000 for its perversion of the biblical story.

Whatever one thought of her, Mary Whitehouse proved impressively resilient in the face of sustained attacks from all quarters of permissive society. Students howled obscenities, intellectuals affected a lofty disdain, satirists pilloried her, and it was even said that a one-time BBC Director General purchased a naked portrait of her – presumably drawn from imagination – adorned with six breasts, and amused himself by throwing darts at the image, shouting with delight if he made a hit. It is hard to think of a more widely reviled public figure in 1976, not excluding the serial rapists, murderers and sectarian terrorists who were so prominent a part of British life at the time, nor one who maintained her essential dignity to the end. Mary Whitehouse died in November 2001 at the age of 91.

***

It seems reasonable to assume that Mrs Whitehouse was not among those investing their admission money to see the Sex Pistols' latest incident-laden tour of Britain, beginning on 11 September in Whitby. The band's manager Malcolm McLaren lied brazenly to reporters, assuring them that the dozen or so provincial theatres and clubs involved had been sold out long in advance. It was not immediately clear if the makeshift arrangements and zigzagging itinerary were a brilliant masterplan on McLaren's part to reach disaffected youth across the UK, or the result of a clueless desperation to get a gig anywhere. Either way, the Pistols continued to divide opinion: you either loved them for their 'sod it' attitude, cartoonish antics and winning gutter appeal to the socially marginalised in society or loathed them for much the same reason. As always, the shows themselves blended chaos with spectacle. Headlining at the 100 Club Special in London's Oxford Street, the Pistols proved to be a tight, ferocious live band, even if their lead vocalist occasionally tended to wander off-piste, interrupting songs with ad-libbed insults to the crowd, which served only to further animate the proceedings.

Perhaps the true spirit of the occasion was captured by the 19-year-old Sid Vicious, né Simon John Ritchie, then a rather approximate drummer with the whimsically named group The Flowers of Romance, who threw a pint mug at a rival band while they were performing at the 100 Club. When it shattered against a pillar, sending glass shards into the face of the lead singer's girlfriend, Vicious was arrested, subsequently spending several weeks at a remand centre in Ashford. There was aggro there, too. It has to be said that the flying-glass incident wasn't entirely unrepresentative of Vicious's chosen role as a leather-clad human destruction machine. His friend Chrissie Hynde, later of the Pretenders, recalled of the era, 'I saw Sid pull a long link of chain out of his jacket and spin it around to clear an entire dance floor. If anyone got in the way, it was tough shit.'

The Sex Pistols did not make a conspicuous contribution to the topical ideal of European harmony with their first-ever overseas trip that month, to the Chalet du Lac Club in Paris. By all accounts, there was something of a culture clash between most of the audience members, who dressed in attire suitable for a disco-themed venue with a large mirror-ball hung from the ceiling drenching the stage and the elegantly framed posters of Edith Piaf and Charles Aznavour in specks of eerie, wriggling light, and the band members themselves, with Johnny Rotten performing in a black bondage suit cut in the style of a straitjacket.

There was still some question in September 1976 about whether punk was all about the healthy release of youthful energy by anyone who knew a couple of chords or could keep up a relentless beat like that of a wind-up monkey banging a tin drum, or part of some larger situationist movement impatient to destroy the last vestiges of the Woodstock ethic of the 1960s. It was a point of some debate among the highbrow critics who came to witness the proceedings at the Chalet du Lac that warm September night. Some saw the show as a searing indictment of cultural vacuity, others found vacuity in the performance itself.

Still clad in his bondage suit but now also adorned by a red beret, tilted back at a rakish angle over his rag-doll barnet of spikes, Johnny Rotten was asked to comment on the matter over breakfast the following morning at a pavement seat of the Deux Magots café. Rotten replied in unorthodox but expressive fashion, first shifting his weight from side to side before letting rip with a fart that was as impressive for its pungent fallout as for its eloquent summation of the punk ethic. It was left to the French public intellectual Jean-François Lyotard to conclude that his country's first exposure to the Sex Pistols qualified as a 'superbly inarticulate commentary on the cognitive human myth and textual subject matter', which might have come as news to the band members themselves.

Of course, it wasn't all a case of edgy interactions between pervasive mid-1970s cosmic disillusionment and rampant youthful ennui, as channelled through punk's snarling practitioners. The same pop landscape that embraced the cloaca-tongued burlesque of Johnny Rotten also played home to the likes of Leo Sayer's 'You Make Me Feel Like Dancing', the Bee Gees' 'You Should Be Dancing', ABBA's 'Dancing Queen' and, extending the motile theme, KC and the Sunshine Band's '(Shake, Shake, Shake) Shake Your Booty', as well as the enticing lilt of Bob Marley's new album, *Rastaman Vibration*.

But if reggae, disco and family-friendly favourites like ABBA were one response to the confusions of a sardonic era, a back-to-the-roots approach was another. The members of the band Dr Feelgood, four self-styled Canvey Island geezers, all well tasty, typically arrived for their gigs looking as though they had come direct from robbing a bank, with one Wilko Johnson on guitar. He was an arresting figure. Clad totally in black, pudding-bowl haircut, eyes staring out across the audience like searchlights, about twice a song Johnson would suddenly take off like an overwound Energizer Bunny and go lurching across the stage, side to side, back to front, all the while keeping up a stark, percussive rhythm with a chopping right hand interspersed with a few demented solos that seemed to be more the product of a semi-tuned chainsaw than a traditional musical instrument, a routine he varied only by periodically lifting the guitar to his shoulder and peering down it as if to strafe the audience. Dr Feelgood's live album, *Stupidity*, quickly went to No. 1 in the chart that September.

Representing the older generation, the Rolling Stones had wrapped up their summer European tour by performing to 200,000 fans at the Knebworth Fair in Hertfordshire, following which the BBC crew sent to record the event for posterity were surprised to spot Mick Jagger's wife Bianca standing alone by the side of the road where her car had broken down, attempting to hitch-hike back to London. Although happy to oblige, it struck them as odd that rock's most glamorous consort should find herself stranded on the outskirts of Barnet while her husband went on ahead of her by limousine and helicopter. The show itself was a shambling parody.

That same week, an only fitfully promising band of teenagers, then called Feedback, gave their first public performance to an audience of school friends, before going on to bigger things as U2. Elton John revealed that he might be bisexual, and Queen performed to over 150,000 fans in London's Hyde Park. Across the Atlantic, 41-year-old Jerry Lee Lewis managed to shoot his own bass player non-fatally in the chest with his new .357 Magnum. The incident was officially ruled a case of friendly fire, the result of some birthday party hijinks, although just a month later, Lewis was arrested for waving the gun around outside the front gate of Elvis Presley's home in Memphis, loudly insisting that it was he, not Elvis, who was the true king of rock and roll.

Television was still less a case of youthful energy bursting through the psychic dam of the 1960s than a package of largely conventional police or hospital serials, formulaic domestic dramas and imported US sitcoms whose stock plot developments were as dreary as watching a traffic light change. News bulletins were introduced by Soviet-style theme music, and fronted by reassuringly old-school presenters capable of conveying the right note of concern when reading an account of the latest terrorist outrage and feigning egalitarian good cheer when it came to the broadcast's lighter moments.

At prime time on a Saturday night, British viewers could choose between half an hour of *The Two Ronnies* (BBC 1), the early Roman Empire saga,

I, Claudius (BBC 2) or *The Many Wives of Patrick*, an undemanding series in which a middle-aged playboy and antiques dealer repeatedly tried to divorce his sixth wife in order to remarry his first (ITV). For the more hardboiled, Monday evenings were enlivened by *The Sweeney*, with its authentic smell of mid-1970s Britain conveyed by coppers in kipper ties chasing villains ('You're nicked, sunshine') around the less salubrious parts of London, a world in which people still used call boxes, smoked real cigarettes and drove petrol-guzzling cars down largely empty streets before parking immediately in front of their destinations.

There would also be a modest instance of transatlantic cultural exchange in September 1976 when Thames Television bought a week of programming on WOR-TV in New York in the hope of selling the likes of *George and Mildred* or *Magpie* to a lucrative US audience. Much to their surprise, the only successful transplant proved to be *The Benny Hill Show*, which went on to claim the distinction – in the words of its eponymous star – of 'putting knockers on Midwestern telly'. In time, the show took on an almost talismanic quality, the subject of tetchy highbrow reviews and sermons from church pulpits, even as 35 million viewers tuned in each week from coast to coast.

The programme's initial 1976 ratings were more modest: a mere 1.3 per cent share of the greater New York market, which was roughly on a par with the audience for a typical public-service broadcast explaining how to apply for a passport or inoculate your children against whooping cough, while the sole reference to the show from the influential *Village Voice* came in the form of an indignant letter deploring a sketch in which Hill had simulated suffering a cardiac arrest after patting a young woman's obligingly displayed bottom. 'There is nothing the least bit comic about a heart attack,' the correspondent noted, reasonably enough. Most viewers still watched their chosen programmes in real time, although exotic new video recorders roughly the size of a family suitcase were beginning to come on sale for around £275 or £2,200 in today's money.

For those not wedded to the Benny Hill school of entertainment, the cinema offered the latest remake of Dorothy Parker's *A Star is Born*, the Watergate saga *All the President's Men* and John Wayne's screen swansong, *The Shootist*. Your high-street bookshop would have displayed rows of what Anthony Burgess stigmatised as 'abject drivel, with neon-pink covers and infantile lettering' to help while away the remnants of the summer. But you might also have noticed more elevated titles on the shop's 'just published' table, such as Saul Bellow's *To Jerusalem and Back*. An acute observer of people and places, the 61-year-old,

Chicago-based Bellow was in some ways an unlikely looking author. Small, white-haired and always impeccably dressed, he struck *Time* magazine as an 'amiable and placid gent who might have caught the number 37 bus in to his accountancy office each morning, [but] who happened to be a great writer'.

Bellow's new book offered readers a *tour d'horizon* of the troubled politics of the Middle East, along with asides on the likes of Mozart, Stendhal, the metaphysical poet George Herbert and the humour of the Marx brothers. He was a master of the sardonically comical, with the gift of being simultaneously highbrow and drily jocular, leavening his analysis of geopolitical currents in the Holy Land with an acute novelist's eye for detail, often conveyed in a few deft brush strokes: an old barber in the King David Hotel, with his 'senile strength and cheer', a self-consciously bohemian Jewish poet with hair 'in long and random tufts', and a nose 'nobly hooked and slender'.

As a rule, Bellow had little time for the fashionable platitudes of the left. 'A great deal of intelligence can be invested in ignorance when the need for illusion is deep,' he wrote in *To Jerusalem and Back*, although even this paled in comparison to the explosively provocative question he asked of a journalist who had pressed him on a point of cultural relativism. 'Who is the Tolstoy of the Zulus? The Proust of the Papuans? I'd be glad to read them,' Bellow said, which was enough to reduce him to Mary Whitehouse status on certain US college campuses, which promptly banned his work from their syllabuses.

Despite his contempt for academic liberals, 'swingers' who ingratiated themselves with the cultural elites, Bellow insisted that he was merely an objective observer commenting on the self-sustaining myths of the left. 'When you have free speech without any debate what you have is a corruption of free speech, which very quickly becomes demagogy ... As a onetime anthropologist, I know a taboo when I see one,' he wrote in September 1976. 'We can't open our mouths without being denounced as racists, misogynists, supremacists, imperialists or fascists. It is a bad moment in the history of the world.'

★★★

In a crowded field, the prize for the defining symbol of Britain's perennial 1976 economic crisis probably came on Tuesday, 28 September, when the Chancellor Denis Healey turned around at Heathrow Airport as the pound embarked on yet another freefall on the foreign exchange markets. Healey had been due to address a finance ministers' meeting in Hong Kong and may not have been entirely displeased to thus miss the annual Labour Party Conference, held that year in Blackpool, where James Callaghan faced a vocally hostile barrage of objections to his government's industrial relations policies and handling of the economy in general.

When Healey left his office at the Treasury at 9.30 that morning, sterling was trading at 1.68 against the dollar. By the time he reached the Heathrow VIP lounge forty-five minutes later, it had sunk to 1.63, on its way to a full 6 per cent loss for the day. Still managing to smile for the cameras waiting for him at the door of the terminal, the Chancellor was in reality far from happy, nor even entirely sure what to do about the reigning state of affairs. 'If I took the plane,' he later recalled, 'I would be cut off from all contact with London for seventeen hours.' If he turned around, however, it could signal to the global markets that the British government had panicked, a possible death blow even for an administration that had survived a series of flagrant tactical errors and individual foibles since its return to office in March 1974.

Healey turned around. Later that evening, he formally applied for a further £2.3 billion IMF loan, which he did with the promise of higher taxes and interest rates, as well as the deepest cuts in public spending since before the Second World War.

Even as his Chancellor was returning in some haste back down the M4 to his office in Whitehall, James Callaghan was delivering his first keynote speech as prime minister to the Labour Conference in Blackpool. In its way, it marked as profound a reversal of party orthodoxy as Nikita Khrushchev's denunciation of the cult of Stalin from the stage of the Great Hall of the Kremlin twenty years earlier.

'For too long,' Callaghan began:

… we have postponed facing up to fundamental choices and fundamental changes in our society and in our economy … We have been living on borrowed time … The cosy world we were told would go on for ever, where full employment would be guaranteed by a stroke of the chancellor's pen – that cosy world is gone … We used to think that you could spend your way out of a recession [by] cutting taxes and boosting government spending. I tell you in all candour that that option no longer exists.

Now we must get back to fundamentals. First, our labour costs must compare with those of our major competitors. Second, we must significantly improve the productivity of both labour and capital. And third, we must stop printing what Denis Healey calls 'confetti money' to pay ourselves more than we produce. To do otherwise is to spell doom for our future as a sovereign country.

It would be fair to say that the prime minister's remarks were not well received in the hall, and as the full enormity of what he was proposing – a reversal of basic Labour economic policy as it had existed since July 1945 – struck home, there were shouts of 'No!' and 'Resign!' from the floor.

Denis Healey then attempted to fly to Blackpool, but on arrival at RAF Northolt in west London, he found that the base's runway, recently declared unfit because of the deep cracks that had appeared in it during the heatwave, was currently unusable after being flooded in an overnight thunderstorm – a case of 'one damn thing after another', the station's commanding officer observed. Hearing this, the Chancellor may well have found himself wondering at the parallels to his own situation.

Healey eventually reached Blackpool by train late on the afternoon of 30 September, and having recently been voted off his party's national executive, was given a precisely timed five minutes to address the assembled delegates from a seat on the floor, not the stage, on the subject of Britain's possible imminent collapse into bankruptcy and social chaos. His remarks took place amid an atmosphere that displayed much the same level of decorum as that of a *Fawlty Towers* fire drill. Some delegates rose and tried to shout supportive remarks, as many others stood and shouted the opposite, while Healey, sweat pouring down his face, continually punched his arms aloft as if to illustrate his role in the coming gladiatorial struggle for the nation's survival.

Speaking on television later that night, James Callaghan was characteristically more subdued in tone, if no less blunt in his overall message:

> If we were to fail in our discussions with the International Monetary Fund,
> I do not think that we or any government could proceed. Such a develop-
> ment would lead down the path to a totalitarian takeover by the left or the
> right … Those are the stakes before us.

When the exchange markets opened the following morning, the pound quickly fell a further three points against the dollar.

Sid James in somehow characteristic pose; the *Carry On* stalwart died on stage, literally, one night in April 1976. (Trinity Mirror/Mirrorpix/Alamy)

Maurice Flitcroft comes as close as he ever would to the Open golf trophy. Flitcroft's qualifying round for the 1976 tournament put him 49 over par, the worst in the event's history. (Trinity Mirror/Mirrorpix/Alamy)

Jimmy Carter (left) and his running mate Walter Mondale, come-from-behind winners in the US presidential election. (Library of Congress)

The ABBA phenomenon started in earnest in 1976, and still shows no sign of ending anytime soon. (Anders Hanser/Wikimedia Commons)

The IRA disrupt service on the Dublin–Belfast railway line, part of a terrorist campaign that continued throughout 1976 both in Ireland and on the British mainland. (Trinity Mirror/Mirrorpix/Alamy)

Joachim Peiper, the Nazi war criminal and sometime car salesman who made the perhaps unwise choice to settle in the French countryside, only to die violently there one night in July 1976. (Bundesarchiv, Bild 183-R65485/CC-BY-SA 3.0)

Denis Healey; the British chancellor's habitual good cheer would be sorely tested by events that year.

The defining symbol of the United States in its bicentennial summer – not a politician or a Hollywood star, but the mop-haired Detroit Tigers baseball pitcher Mark 'Bird' Fidrych, who enjoyed a brief, but spectacular, time at the top. (Archive PL/Alamy)

If you wanted to show a curious alien what life was really like in Britain in 1976, you could have done worse than to take them to the streets of Willesden, north London, where the labour dispute at the Grunwick film-processing works saw lively interactions between protesters and the police most Saturday afternoons. (Keystone Press/Alamy)

The actors Dennis Waterman and John Thaw illustrate their roles in the popular TV series *The Sweeney*. Nothing summed the show up quite like Thaw's world-weary Detective Inspector Jack Regan with his trademark admonition: 'Shut it!' (Trinity Mirror/Mirrorpix/Alamy)

Eric Clapton in his widely regretted 'Summer Paddle' phase. (Matt Gibbons/Wikimedia Commons)

England's cricket captain Tony Greig. Precociously gifted and not, generally speaking, a martyr to false modesty, Greig assured a reporter that he and his teammates intended to make the visiting West Indies side 'grovel' in the summer's Test series. Events proved otherwise. (Trinity Mirror/Mirrorpix/Alamy)

A representative scene of the British heatwave, which saw packed beaches, incessant 'Phew! What a scorcher!' headlines and even a few makeshift-looking 'water-detector vans' patrolling the streets in an effort to enforce the latest hosepipe ban. (PA Images/Alamy)

Freddie Laker, who finally won his six-year attritional battle with the UK government to operate a cut-price air service across the Atlantic. (PA Images/Alamy)

Mary Whitehouse, a tireless campaigner against moral collapse, leaves court. (PA Images/Alamy)

The former naval stoker Tom Keating, whose 'Sexton Blake' homages to the Old Masters earned him an arrest for fraud, but also a cult following among those who applauded him for pulling the rug from under the stuffy art establishment. (PA Images/Alamy)

Three emblematic political figures of the year – Margaret Thatcher, James Callaghan and Harold Wilson – in close proximity to each other at a Westminster reception for the visiting president of France. (PA Images/Alamy)

Idi Amin, whose steady stream of correspondence with the British government included a note on the tragedy of Princess Margaret's divorce. 'I hope that this will be a lesson to all of us men not to marry ladies in a high position,' the Ugandan dictator wrote. (Dan Hadani collection/National Library of Israel/The Pritzker Family National Photography Collection/Wikimedia Commons)

Fans and police await the arrival of David Bowie at Victoria station. (Trinity Mirror/Mirrorpix/Alamy)

Fourteen-year-old Nadia Comăneci, whose achievement in scoring a perfect 10.00 at the Montreal Olympics defeated the organisers' efforts to display the figure on the stadium's digital scoreboard. The best they could do was to award her a perfect 1.00.

Operation Thunderbolt, complete with its decoy Mercedes, gets under way in Tel Aviv. (IDF Spokesperson's Unit/Wikimedia Commons)

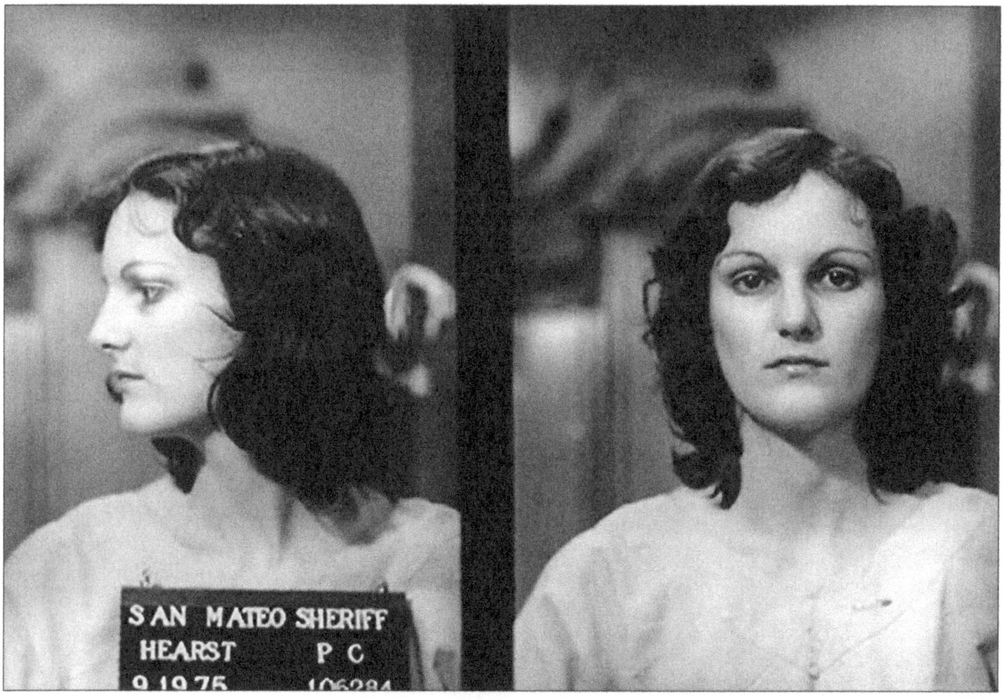

The San Francisco media heiress Patricia Hearst, whose trial on bank robbery charges polarised American opinion in 1976. Some news outlets portrayed her as a wayward brat who had willingly chosen to join her sometime kidnappers in a life of crime, while, by contrast, the Hearst press preferred to see the whole matter as a tragic case of an innocent young woman who had succumbed to Stockholm Syndrome. Hearst eventually served twenty-two months in prison.

Gerald Ford, Leonid Brezhnev and Henry Kissinger in a rare moment of mutual levity. (Gerald R. Ford Library/ NARA/Wikimedia Commons)

Ronald Reagan, who failed to become US president in 1976, but fatally damaged Ford's prospects in his race against Jimmy Carter. (NARA/Wikimedia Commons)

The former child star Sal Mineo, whose life ended violently in a darkened alleyway behind a Los Angeles apartment building. (Allan Warren/ Wikimedia Commons)

The Sex Pistols, who accepted a possibly ill-judged invitation to appear live on Bill Grundy's teatime television show, with somehow predictable results. Although the segment in question lasted barely two minutes, it was enough to spell both the overnight arrival of the Pistols as an international talking point and the effective end of Grundy's career. (Koen Suyk/Nationaal Archief, Den Haag, Rijksfotoarchief: Fotocollectie Algemeen Nederlands Fotopersbureau)

Steve Jobs (left) and Bill Gates. In 1976, both men were just starting to tunnel along their separate routes to revolutionising the way the world does business. (Joi Ito/Flickr)

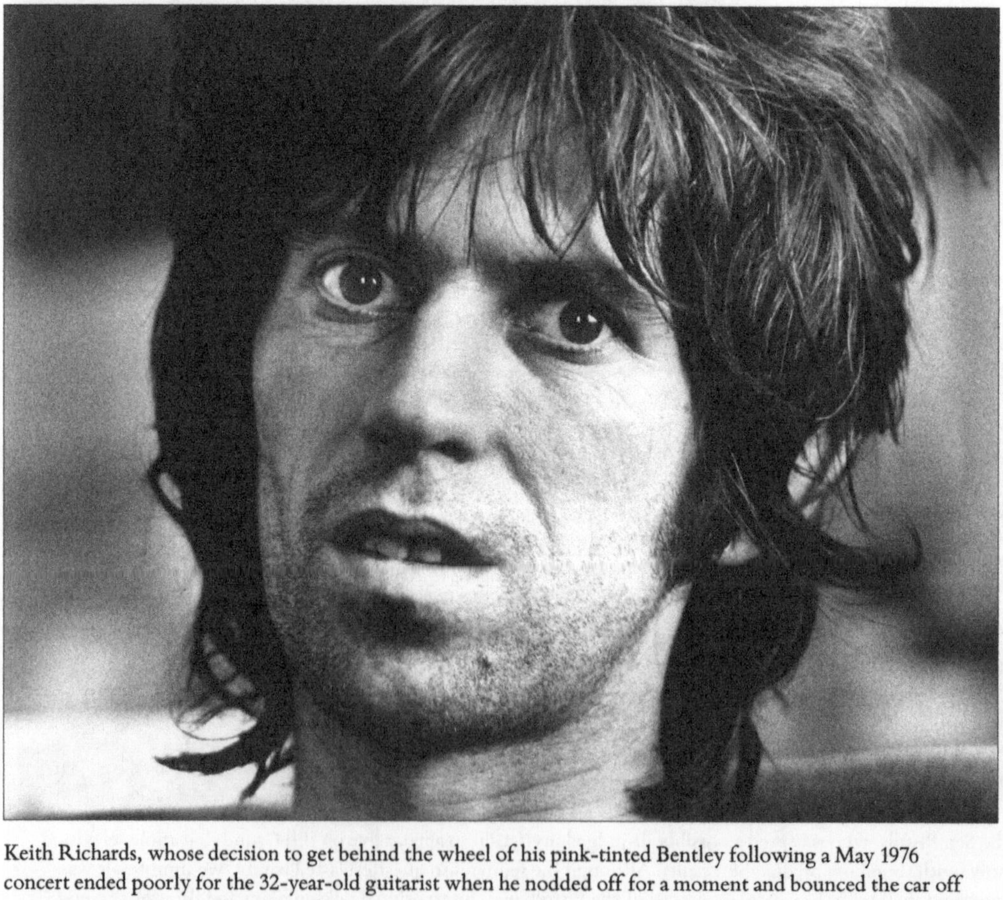

Keith Richards, whose decision to get behind the wheel of his pink-tinted Bentley following a May 1976 concert ended poorly for the 32-year-old guitarist when he nodded off for a moment and bounced the car off a motorway guardrail. When the police arrived on the scene at 4 a.m. they found the legendary 'Human Riff' wearing sunglasses and wandering up the side of the M1 with his infant son in tow. (Gijsbert Hanekroot/Alamy)

The serial killer Ted Bundy, a name now synonymous with evil, who confessed to twenty-eight murders but may have been responsible for dozens more. (State Archives of Florida, *Florida Memory*)

Bradford Bishop, another peculiarly American psychopath, who disappeared after bludgeoning his wife, mother and three young children to death one night in 1976. His whereabouts remain unknown today.

Dead man smiling: The president of Liberia, William Tolbert, shakes hands with US vice-president Nelson Rockefeller while visiting Washington in September 1976 as Rockefeller's cabinet colleague Earl Butz looks on. The African head of state might not have appreciated the racist joke Butz had made earlier that month; it would cost him his job a few days after this photo was taken. (Carl Albert Research and Studies Center, Congressional Collection/Wikimedia Commons)

The National Front on the march. (Tav Dulay/Wikimedia Commons)

IV

Autumn

THE COON DOG AND THE SKUNK

Some national political campaigns seem to drift serenely on, the electorate faced with a choice between inoffensive and sometimes even quite capable people who are quietly doing their jobs to the best of their abilities, content to debate the finer points of overseas earnings and domestic spending priorities. And then there are moments when a party leader or one of their surrogates goes so spectacularly off message as to render all the speeches and talking points, prepared for them by impeccably trained functionaries for whom sober recitation of policy detail is the rule and freewheeling spontaneity the exception, all but redundant in an instant.

Such a moment occurred on 24 August 1976, when President Ford's 67-year-old Secretary of Agriculture, Earl Butz, found himself sharing the first-class cabin of a flight from Kansas City to Los Angeles with the entertainers Pat Boone and Sonny Bono, and John Dean, the former White House counsel who had played a major role in Richard Nixon's downfall and been rewarded by being appointed a political correspondent for *Rolling Stone* as a result. All four men were returning from the recent Republican Party Convention. Butz himself was en route to an engagement later that afternoon to dedicate a screw-worm eradication plant located outside the town of You Bet, California. (Screw-worms, You Bet, Butz, Boone, Bono: the more you study the events of that day, the more you find its distinguishing characteristics – apart from the political fallout for the Ford administration – to have been the striking names of the parties involved.) On hardly any other occasion has a US Agriculture Secretary seized an opportunity to potentially change his nation's electoral history, but he did so now.

A gregarious man, who liked to exercise his earthy sense of humour, shortly after take-off Butz wandered down the aisle of the plane to engage his fellow VIP passengers in conversation. By way of an ice-breaker, the Cabinet official began by regaling them with a joke involving intercourse between a coon (hunting) dog and a skunk. All three members of his audience being men of deep religious faith, Butz did not perhaps enjoy the acclaim he might have wished for with this opening pleasantry. After some further stilted small talk, the discussion then turned to politics. Boone, a card-carrying evangelical Republican, asked Butz why the party of Abraham Lincoln was not able to attract more black people to its ranks, which gave the chortling secretary the opportunity to again work his unique brand of comedic magic on his listeners.

If Boone had thought that the man who then ranked fifth in the presidential line of succession might care to expound on the shared values and common aspirations of all US people, heedless of their race or ethnicity, he was mistaken. Butz chose a notably different approach for his response. 'I'll tell you what the coloureds want,' he began, in terms that possibly harked back to his days growing up on the family dairy farm in Indiana. 'It's three things. First, a tight pussy. Second, a loose pair of shoes. And third, a warm place to shit.'

After some hesitation, John Dean quoted the aphorism in full in *Rolling Stone*, attributing it to an unnamed Cabinet officer. It did not prove difficult to check the travel itineraries of all such officials to discover the name of the party guilty of the airborne gaffe, which broke on the front pages of the national newspapers which reached the White House at around 7 a.m. on Friday, 1 October. Four hours later, Butz found himself on the carpet in front of a splenetic Gerald Ford. The president told his soon-to-depart ministerial colleague that any attempt at being funny in front of the press, let alone an accredited correspondent of *Rolling Stone*, was doomed to failure. The hapless Butz formally tendered his resignation twenty-four hours later, although this was to do no more than formalise the arrangement the president had outlined at their Oval Office meeting.

That spectacular own-goal aside, Butz also deserves mention as the man who had used his department's subsidy programmes to aggressively push US farmers to increase their production of high-fructose corn syrup – like sugar, but cheaper – which still remains the go-to ingredient for a wide variety of processed foods and soft drinks, many of which were soon offered in bigger serving sizes than ever before. Not coincidentally, from 1971 to 1980, US obesity rates more than doubled from 13 per cent to 27 per cent of the adult population, before reaching a peak of around 42 per cent – compared to an even more striking 63 per cent in the UK – today. Butz himself later served a short jail term for tax evasion and died in 2008 at the age of 98.[1]

At the beginning of October, as the US presidential race shifted into high gear, polls still showed Jimmy Carter maintaining a razor-thin lead. In what proved a bumper week for the nation's cartoonists, the fallout from Carter's *Playboy* interview had now been offset by that of the Earl Butz affair. Ford had the home-court advantage of incumbency, with the wind of bicentennial-year patriotism at his back. Amidst other encouraging economic data, both inflation and strike action had been significantly reduced over the summer. A total of 490,000 US workers had walked off the job during the second half of 1975, while only 205,000 did so in the period from January–July 1976.

But set against that, Ford was to the Republican Party's conservative wing an accidental president who held the office only because Richard Nixon had been forced to resign. Those same conservatives favoured Ronald Reagan, and many of them preferred not to vote at all once their candidate had left the race. Reagan's own support for Ford was equivocal at best; the two men made exactly one campaign appearance together, in Beverly Hills, where the former actor sat stony-faced at the end of the platform, as the *Los Angeles Times* correspondent put it, 'looking as though his pet dog had just been run over'.

While an estimable human being and a quietly effective president in his way, Ford was also a plodding campaigner and only a mediocre public speaker. His speechwriters once tried to improve his delivery by writing the words 'WITH EMPHASIS' in the margin of his text. Ford, denouncing one of Carter's economic initiatives as 'nonsense', incorporated the notes into his speech and told the bemused audience, 'I say to you, this is nonsense with emphasis!'

All this led up to the moment on Wednesday, 6 October, during the second presidential debate held at the Palace of Fine Arts in San Francisco, when Ford made the gaffe that perhaps did as much as anything else to seal his fate in the election. Reading the transcript of the candidates' exchanges without seeing

---

1   Set against the alarming obesity statistics, Butz was later at pains to point out that by the year 2000, the average American family was spending 16 per cent of its net income on food, whereas fifty years earlier, the figure had been around 33–35 per cent, an improvement in part due, he insisted, to a combination of improved production techniques and the prevalence of the low-cost sweeteners he introduced during his time in office.

the spectacle on television, it might be difficult to understand what all the fuss was about. Over the course of ninety minutes, both men overstated their positions and misstated important facts, as they often did in their campaign speeches. Neither one had anything new or particularly startling to say. But the public sparring matches known as presidential debates have never been exercises in the in-depth exploration of the issues. What they are, of course, are personality contests that generally end indecisively, with a vague feeling of dissatisfaction all round, but just occasionally contain a 'gotcha' moment that provides the next morning's headline.

What Ford said in response to a question about his administration's relations with the Soviet Union was this:

In the case of the Helsinki Agreement, thirty-five nations signed a treaty – including the Secretary of State for the Vatican – I can't under any circumstances believe that the Pope would agree that by signing the agreement that those thirty-five nations had just turned over to the Warsaw Pact the domination of Eastern Europe. It just isn't true. And if Mr Carter alleges that His Holiness by signing that has done so, he is totally inaccurate … Now, what has been accomplished by the Helsinki accord?

Number one, we have an agreement with the Soviet Union that they notify us and we notify them of any military manoeuvres that are to be undertaken. They have already done it. In both cases where they've done so, there is no Soviet domination of Eastern Europe and there never will be under a Ford administration.

At that moment, one of the debate's panellists, Max Frankel of the *New York Times*, not bothering to conceal a note of amused incredulity, cut in. 'I'm sorry – did I understand you to say, sir, that the Russians are not using Eastern Europe as their own sphere of influence in occupying most of the countries there?'

Digging the hole still deeper, Ford replied:

I don't believe, Mr Frankel, the Yugoslavs consider themselves dominated by the Soviet Union. I don't believe that the Rumanians consider themselves dominated by the Soviet Union. I don't believe that the Poles consider themselves dominated by the Soviet Union. Each of those countries is fully independent and autonomous. It has its own territorial integrity, and the

United States does not concede that those countries are under the domination of the Soviet Union.

What Ford had meant to say was that the spirit of the Eastern European nations in question had not been crushed, despite Soviet occupation. But that was not the key takeaway message of the debate in the following day's press, which led with headlines of the 'PRES. DENIES REDS INFLUENCE IN EASTERN BLOC' variety, raising serious doubts about whether the leader of the free world was in fact fully alive to the nature of the post-war balance of power across the Atlantic.

Ford himself later admitted that his remarks in San Francisco had 'not come out quite right', a memorable understatement on his part, and for the remaining four weeks of the campaign, 'nothing else really mattered ... one had appeared not to be in control of events, and that is something the American public will never tolerate in their leader'.

The reality was that the Soviet Union was then at the apogee of its all-service military build-up initiated in 1966, a process carried out while the United States was preoccupied with successive waves of self-torment. Of the three countries specifically cited by Ford for their national integrity and avoidance of any undue Soviet interference in their affairs, the Socialist Federal State of Yugoslavia was then a one-party quasi-Marxist regime in the thirty-first year of dictatorship by Marshal Josip Tito; the Socialist Republic of Rumania similarly remained the fiefdom of Nicolae Ceauşescu and his wife Elena, who simultaneously espoused hardline communist rhetoric while personally leading lives of such opulence it approached squalor; and the People's Republic of Poland was then wracked by widespread food and fuel shortages, press censorship and anti-clerical measures under the iron rule of Edward Gierek, whose United Workers Party had recently reintroduced bread rationing for its 35 million citizens.

In the East German general election held in October 1976, meanwhile, the Soviet sock puppet Erich Honecker, General Secretary of the only officially sanctioned political party, was lucky enough to be returned to office by a 99.86 per cent vote in favour of his regime. Honecker and his like-minded colleagues continued to serve as custodians of 'the anti-fascist protection device' – or Berlin Wall, as others preferred to call it – on the front line of the Cold War, imposing a shoot-to-kill policy should any of their 18 million citizens inexplicably choose to explore their options in life on the other side.

An especially poignant reminder of the human toll of the Iron Curtain came on 5 August 1976, when a 38-year-old Italian long-distance lorry driver named Benito Corghi legally crossed into East Germany at a checkpoint near Hirschberg, south of Berlin. Realising he had left some of his personal possessions behind at his lodgings in the West, Corghi had parked his vehicle and started to walk back along what he apparently assumed to be an open footpath at the side of the road. Seeing this, a border guard, thinking he was making an illegal departure from the country, first shouted at him in German – a language Corghi did not speak – and then shot him dead. The next day, Honecker's government formally apologised for the 'tragic accident', the only time in East Germany's forty-one-year existence its leadership was ever moved to express regret for the closed-border policies responsible for the deaths of 753 individuals, quite apart from the misery inflicted on the tens of thousands of those forcibly separated from family and friends, or from any contact with the free world, as a result.

***

In Britain, the government had now taken significant steps to creating what it saw as a more egalitarian society, with a steadily accumulating range of provisions on pensions, health, education and housing. Under James Callaghan, the state continued to lubricate the wheels of daily life for millions of those who relied on public services, drew benefits or fell back on the National Health Service when taken ill. The legislation taken as a whole was not universally attractive to impatient or marginalised members of the community, as the lure of the Sex Pistols and others demonstrated. But the consensus in 1976 was that the state would always do a better job than the unfettered market, not just in fairly distributing goods and services, but in imposing a blueprint for social cohesion and general welfare.

The irony was that Callaghan himself, the figurehead of this seemingly unstoppable momentum for change, remained a paragon of sound traditional values. That October, in a speech at Oxford, he questioned the merits of the 'new informal methods of teaching' and called for a return to basic standards of 'numeracy, literacy and due respect for our island history' among the young.

A family man, contentedly married to his wife, Audrey, whom he had met when she was a Baptist Sunday school teacher, Britain's premier was, like Gerald Ford, in office only because of his predecessor's resignation. The two men bore similarities in their paths to power, but also in their dislike of the permissive society. To Callaghan, pornography was repellent, and drug use of whatever description a heinous crime. He was made uneasy by the very idea of homosexuality, remained ignorant of lesbianism until it was explained to him in his mid-twenties, liked to quote the lyrics of Victorian hymns to illustrate a point, staunchly supported the armed forces and positively revered the monarchy, once becoming rhapsodic when writing of a visit to the Royal Yacht:

> Her Majesty the Queen held an evening reception aboard *Britannia* and the Royal Marines beat the Retreat, marching and playing as only they can … I felt my spine tingle as dusk fell and the ceremony drew to an end with the tune 'Sunset' blowing softly on the bugles.

When surveying the horizon for good news in that season of sterling's continued fall against the dollar and the rise of feral youth gangs roaming the streets with their distressed bin-liner wardrobes and relentless, pneumatic-drill music, Callaghan could nominate only the Inter-City 125 rail service, which began operating between London and Bristol on 4 October. It was an immediate success with the travelling public, if less so with the trade unions, who had wanted no fewer than three drivers in each 125 cab. In the end, they compromised on two, to be seated side by side whenever the train exceeded speeds of 100 mph, and even that necessitated a last-minute design change in order to accommodate the wider front windscreen required, with a resulting loss in aerodynamic performance.

During a Cabinet meeting held largely to debate the consequences of drawing on the International Monetary Fund, 'whose terms of business could strain our relationship with the trade union movement to breaking point', the foreign secretary Anthony Crosland had cleared his throat to mention in passing that these were 'grave times in the area of international security', too. It was not just a question of mischief-making by the Soviet Union, who 'continue to interfere on an ideological basis in the internal affairs of countries where domestic factions are vying for power'. That, at least, was part of a recognisable pattern of behaviour, and statesmen could devise a response to it accordingly. 'It [was also] a period of profound, and to some extent unique, dislocation perpetrated by entities or individuals advancing an agenda by violent means,' Crosland noted. The animating spirit of many of these groups was 'distinctly unpleasant and restless'.

In some cases, the parties involved sought 'nothing less than to make their respective states ungovernable', Crosland continued, and thus bring about the state of anarchy they desired. All the established politicians could do was issue statements of condemnation after each fresh outrage and order their security forces to respond accordingly. Taken as a whole, such incidents served to further darken a 'deeply troubled' international landscape, Crosland added, and contributed to an already pervasive sense that 1976 was not going to be confused with one of those years that are primarily remembered for their air of carefree optimism or outpourings of universal peace and goodwill.

***

On the morning of 2 October, Argentina's President Jorge Videla narrowly escaped assassination when a timebomb exploded under the stand where he had been reviewing troops just minutes earlier at an army barracks outside Buenos Aires. This was effectively the start of a period in Argentinian history later characterised as the 'Dirty War', when, over a span of six years, the state's security forces killed or 'disappeared' some 30,000 dissidents thought to be a political or ideological threat to the ruling junta. It was neither the first nor last such attempt on Videla's life, although in the end, he survived long enough to be tried and convicted of human-rights abuses and to die of natural causes while in prison in 2013 at the age of 87.

On 4 October, a group of three ETA gunmen succeeded in killing Juan María de Araluce Villar, the state-appointed president of the local council in the Basque region of northern Spain. The terrorists' approach to their task that day was direct. They waited outside Araluce's San Sebastian home until he emerged after lunch with his family to be driven back to work, then drew their pistols and submachine guns and started firing. Three other individuals died in the attack and a fourth succumbed to his injuries later that evening. When he heard the noise from outside on the street, Araluce's young son rushed downstairs and managed to drag his mortally wounded father into a nearby car and drive him to hospital, where doctors were unable to save his life.

ETA claimed both a political and a moral component for their agenda. They wanted to raise the price of their remaining under 'the jackboot of the [Madrid] regime to intolerable levels'. But they also objected to certain symbols of cultural 'decadence' in Spanish life and were known to target cinemas, bars and clubs to advance their ideal of a spiritually pristine nation, 'untainted by the filth of Hollywood and the plutocrats of Wall Street'. There was a strong if not unconditional link between the Basque separatists and members of the Roman Catholic Church, who portrayed incidents such as Araluce's murder not so much as a criminal act but as something that was 'about saving souls'. In place of marriage, or of any other form of lifelong partnership, at least some local clergy devoted themselves to a cause that was prepared to kill in what they deemed to be the greater good.

On 6 October, all seventy-three passengers and crew on board Cubana de Aviación Flight 455 died when their DC8 jet exploded and fell into the sea off the coast of Barbados. The official report into the cause of the crash concluded simply, 'The detonation of a controlled device at the rear of the cabin initiated an uncontrollable fire producing toxic gasses resulting in eventual incapacitation of the pilots.'

This stark summary barely hinted at the actual horror experienced by the plane's occupants during the three minutes after the explosion had ripped a hole in the DC8's fuselage, while the crew of the stricken jet attempted to steer it back to its starting airport at Barbados. In the end it fell just 2 miles or a minute's flying time short. The noise and smoke would have been 'significant', a later CIA report into the affair put it delicately, with 'injuries including eardrum rupture, burns, fractured limbs and those parties directly in the blast zone pulverised in the initial energy release', as the plane itself then began its sharp but not at first vertical descent towards the ocean.

It was thought that the captain of the flight, realising at the last moment that a successful landing was no longer possible, deliberately turned his craft away from heavily populated beaches on the south of Barbados and back out to sea, potentially saving the lives of hundreds of civilians on the ground as a result.

Two Venezuelan nationals were subsequently arrested for aggravated homicide in the matter, and each given a twenty-year sentence. Both men claimed that they had been acting under the orders of one Luis Carriles, a CIA operative, apparently as part of an attempt to destabilise the Castro regime in Cuba, although this remained a matter of dispute up to and beyond Carriles' death in 2018. He gave his unpublished autobiography a preliminary title, *The Butcher of Havana*.

★★★

When surveying the map for further evidence of the 'profound and unique' dislocation that he had spoken of in Cabinet, Anthony Crosland would also have been painfully aware of the unquiet status quo across the Irish Sea. Two Royal Ulster Constabulary officers were killed in separate IRA gun attacks in

Derry on 8 October. The following week, an Ulster Volunteer Force (UVF) supporter was shot dead outside his home in County Armagh, and his teen-aged son, also wounded in the attack, later died in hospital.

On 15 October, two men were convicted of the July 1975 murders of three members of the popular Dublin-based Miami Showband and given thirty-five-year sentences. In a grimly familiar scenario, the killings took place after a UVF gang had ambushed the band's minibus on a lonely road outside Newry, just north of the border.

The musicians at first assumed it was a standard military checkpoint when they were flagged down. While the group members lined up in the dark, as instructed, dutifully giving their names and addresses, an explosion suddenly ripped through their bus. It was caused by a clumsily handled timebomb con-cealed in a briefcase, which was being planted by two of the UVF gang, both of whom were killed in the blast. The windows of the bus had been blown out, and bits of the dead men's bodies, covered in flames, were catapulted into the road. A ball of flame rose about 50ft into the sky, and even at night, the column of black smoke could be seen from across the border over 10 miles away. Following that, the would-be bombers' accomplices promptly opened fire. Some of their victims fell where they stood, while others managed to run for the cover of a nearby wood.

There long remained a suspicion that members of the British security forces had colluded in the massacre. One of the surviving musicians later speculated that they had been meant to unknowingly carry the timebomb with them until it exploded on their arrival in Newry, thus convincing the authorities that the band were Republican sympathisers smuggling explosives on behalf of the IRA – a scenario that would have seemed almost ludicrous but for the lives that were lost.

On the day after the 1976 verdicts against the two UVF members, a Garda policeman was killed in a boobytrap bomb attack in Mountmellick, 50 miles from Dublin. Meanwhile, across the border, three IRA volunteers in turn died when a bomb they were transporting to a Belfast gas-storage facility exploded prematurely. And so the individual acts of violence and inevitable retaliations continued in a ghastly game of tit-for-tat, during which men, women and children were bombed, shot and maimed on both sides of the Irish border and across mainland Britain. 'The Troubles' remained one of the deep patholo-gies of the era and did not end with the human bloodshed. On 17 October, the Irish Defence Minister, Paddy Donegan, not caring for the response of his own President Cearbhall Ó Dálaigh to recent terrorist events, referred to him as a 'thundering disgrace' (or possibly 'fucking disgrace') while visiting a Garda barracks in County Westmeath. This proved to be the last straw for Ó Dálaigh, who was then under pressure for his conciliatory approach to the IRA, causing him to resign from office 'to protect the dignity and independence of the presidency as an institution'. He died of a heart attack just two years later, at the age of 67.

★★★

In the meantime, there was also the matter of the pending IMF loan and Britain's parlous economic position generally. The pound had continued to fall against the dollar on the foreign exchange markets following Denis Healey's abrupt U-turn at Heathrow, and by 25 October, it stood at a new low for the year of $1.52. The Grunwick dispute had also recently taken a turn for the worse when the Union of Post Office Workers voted not to cross the picket lines at the company's gates, a significant blow for a business that processed roughly 95 per cent of its customers' orders by mail.

Other unions were also showing signs of chafing under the terms of the across-the-board 5 per cent pay increases negotiated between the TUC and the government. Appraising the industrial landscape, the journalist Auberon Waugh, with his gift for leavening serious news with comic flights of fancy, wrote in *Private Eye*:

> Just back from six days' recuperation in East Africa, I learn of the government's secret plans for bread rationing in December. Fortunately, I still have 500 metric tons of wheat in my driers. It is the coming shoe shortage which will bite hardest. I suppose we will all have to get used to wearing the same pair of shoes more than once. Still, I expect it will teach the lower classes to vote Conservative next time around – if there ever is another time.

Waugh would probably not have been among those investing their 45p to buy the Damned's 'New Rose', released in the chart that week and now widely recognised as the first commercially available punk-rock single. In a further sign of the desire of one generation to distinguish their tastes in popular music from the one before it, the song's B-side was a cover of the Beatles' 'Help!', played at roughly twice the speed of the original.

For their growing number of admirers, bands like the Damned were at the forefront of a revolution in pop: combative, driving, edgy, and, above all, their own. Some of the musicians were genuinely a bit out there, too, with their impressively threadbare attire offering asylum to a rich harvest of lice and fleas, communicating largely in belches and promiscuously swallowing handfuls of pills, often without knowing exactly what they were. Others seemed to have embarked on a more self-consciously bohemian process of reinvention from their middle-class selves, a metamorphosis which saw Marianne Elliott-Said abandon her Kentish roots for a life as the pioneering punk feminist Poly Styrene; Christopher Millar of leafy Kingston-upon-Thames trade as Rat Scabies; and the privately educated John Mellor emerge as his better-known alter ego, Joe Strummer of the Clash.

A key moment in the long if not untroubled marriage between the punk sensibility and the corporate machine came on 8 October 1976, when the Beatles' old label EMI signed the Sex Pistols for a £40,000 advance – an eye-watering £320,000 in today's money – on a two-year contract. Well before the stated expiry date, a certain coolness had come to taint the relations between the creative imperative of the one party and the hucksterish, often venal, ways of the other, although in this case, it would not always be entirely easy to say which side represented which set of values.

Acrimoniously parting with the company just three months later, the Pistols turned their sacking to good advantage with their gloriously incoherent song 'EMI', in which Johnny Rotten proceeded to express all the rage, pain, bile and frustration he harboured toward the label that had summarily dumped them. 'There's unlimited supply,' he sang. 'And there's no reason why/ I tell you it was all a frame/ They only did it 'cos of fame/ Who? / EMI!'

For all that, older music lovers in Britain, and for that matter around the world, might have experienced a pleasurable glow of recognition when entering their local high-street record shop or slipping into the warm jacuzzi that was the regular Thursday-night ritual of *Top of the Pops*. The singles chart that October was still largely the preserve of Barry Manilow, Peter Frampton, Elton John, Rod Stewart and his ubiquitous 'Tonight's the Night', and the even then middle-aged Engelbert Humperdinck, of the mutton-chop sideburns and porn-star moustache, whose career renaissance continued apace with his easy-listening smash 'After the Lovin''.

Back in the Record Plant studio in Los Angeles, the Eagles were meanwhile hard at work putting the finishing gloss on an album then called 'Mexican Reggae', which they released on the world on 8 December as *Hotel California*. It has since been certified platinum twenty-seven times over, on its way to 35 million global sales, and still with no end in sight. However, even these figures would be eclipsed over time by its equally cutting-edge contemporary, Fleetwood Mac's *Rumours*, which to date has shifted 5 million copies in Britain alone and roughly ten times that number around the world.

AMERICAN PSYCHOS

'Airline passenger safety is still in a deplorable state,' *The Times* announced in its report of the crash of Flight 455 into the sea off Barbados. It was true that new security measures had come into place in 1974, but even then there were gaps in a system that was enforced with greater or lesser degrees of consistency in different countries, or even in different cities, and often in the face of determined opposition by individual air carriers reluctant to endorse any measure that might inconvenience their customers. If you were queuing up before boarding an international flight at, say, Heathrow in October 1976, you might have been discreetly asked to step out of line into a private area where a bell-bottomed airport employee would listlessly sweep a U-shaped metal wand over your body – or equally, you might avoid this formality altogether.

There was still no requirement for a passenger to actually board the plane onto which he or she had previously checked their luggage. In those days, most US domestic flights were as informal as catching a bus. Airlines didn't limit the number of carry-ons, and you could take pretty much whatever you wanted with you into the cabin where, it seemed, half your fellow passengers spent the flight smoking. In certain cases, you could simply stroll onto the plane and pay the stewardess for your ticket once aloft, had you so wished.

Coincidentally or not, this was also the season of all-too-frequent air disasters of one sort or another. On 12 October, all ninety-five passengers aboard Indian Airlines Flight 171 were killed when their Caravelle jet caught fire shortly after take-off from Bombay. The next morning, ninety-one people died, eighty-eight of them on the ground, when a chartered Bolivian cargo plane crashed into a residential neighbourhood near the town of Santa Cruz. The following week, a further thirty-six individuals lost their lives when their DC-3 developed 'stability issues', apparently the result of an in-flight disturbance of some sort, causing it to plough into a field outside Yopal, in central Colombia.

There were, at least, no fatalities when a group of five hijackers took over a TWA flight en route from New York to Chicago, intending to draw attention to the repression of the Croat minority in Yugoslavia. Later that day, a bomb planted by one of the hijackers' colleagues exploded in a locker at New York's Grand Central Station, killing a policeman and injuring three members of the public.

In between these incidents, President Ford was obliged to apologise to the Emperor of Japan for the 'poor taste' shown at a rural Texas air show that had re-enacted the atomic bombing of Hiroshima, complete with a simulated mushroom cloud, with the pilot of the original 1945 *Enola Gay* at the controls of a restored B-29 Superfortress. Forty thousand spectators at the show had marked their appreciation by breaking into a lusty chant of 'USA! USA!' at the climactic moment of the explosion.

★★★

David Berkowitz, the so-called 'Son of Sam', continued his murderous spree when on 23 October he shot and wounded a young couple sitting in a parked car in a residential neighbourhood of New York. As we've seen, the seemingly unexceptional Berkowitz was in fact a sadistic psychopath, who sought out random victims at the behest of a demonic dog, taunted police with satanic references and claimed he was Beelzebub.

Late one warm Saturday night, a month later, two teenaged girls were standing on the porch of one of their homes in Floral Park, a neighbourhood about a dozen miles from Manhattan, after returning from a day out in the city, when they were approached by a stranger in his twenties dressed in army fatigues. The man started asking directions and then abruptly pulled out a handgun and fired five shots, hitting each of the young women once. One of the two recovered from her injury, while her friend was hit in the spine and ultimately rendered paraplegic. Berkowitz's latest victim had graduated from high school earlier that summer, lived at home with her parents a few blocks away from the scene of the crime and was looking for a job as a secretary so that she could save money for a place of her own, leading an entirely blameless and conventional life until it was shattered by a gunman's bullet, that otherwise quiet Thanksgiving weekend night.

Grotesque as it is to use the word 'prolific' in relation to serial killers, it might be fairly applied in the case of Ted Bundy. Another prominent example of the seemingly inexhaustible supply of cold-blooded psychopaths at large that year, he would go on to take an estimated thirty young women's lives in the period 1974–78, although the actual figure may be significantly higher. Bundy decapitated at least twelve of his victims and kept their severed heads as souvenirs in his refrigerator. This was by no means the most depraved of his post-mortem habits.

Beginning in the Pacific Northwest and cutting a homicidal swathe through the United States, Bundy specialised in preying on university communities, selecting young female students for abduction from campuses at night or crowded parks in daytime when their defences were lowered in familiar settings. Survivors remembered that he had used his boy-next-door looks and soft-spoken charm – often bandaging an arm to gain sympathy – to lure them away. Bundy usually throttled his victims and then sexually abused and mutilated them, sometimes performing penetrative acts on the corpses until decomposition made further such activity impractical.

Over the years, Bundy also acquired something of a reputation as an escapologist, although this was as much a result of lassitude on the authorities' part as any latent genius on his. This aspect of the story somehow only added to his appeal among certain members of the public not themselves directly affected by his rampage. In June 1976, Bundy was convicted of kidnapping and assault by a Utah court and later extradited to face similar charges in Aspen, Colorado. During a recess in his trial there, he jumped out of an open courthouse window and fell 25ft to the ground, injuring his ankle but managing to flee into the nearby wilderness, only to be recaptured a week later.

After digging a hole in the ceiling of his jail cell, Bundy was later able to escape a second time, on this occasion remaining at liberty for seven weeks and making it as far away as northern Florida, where he killed or maimed another six young women. In one such case, he broke into the bedroom of a 20-year-old college student and beat her unconscious, strangled her, bit off one of her nipples and then sexually violated her with a metal hairspray canister before stepping across the hallway to assault a sleeping 21-year-old in the next room by breaking her jaw and knocking out most of her teeth. A crowd of some 200 people broke into loud cheers at the gates of the Florida prison where Bundy was eventually put to death by electrocution in January 1989.

Separated by 4,000 miles but joined by their mutual taste for homosexual necrophilia, 16-year-old Jeffrey Dahmer and 30-year-old Dennis Nilsen rounded out the already overfull nightmare chapter in the era's book of deviant self-gratification. In 1976, Nilsen, a former army corporal, was a trainee police constable living in reduced circumstances in Cricklewood, north London, in a non-exclusive romantic arrangement with a man who ultimately survived the break-up of their relationship with nothing worse than a few cuts and bruises to show for it.

For his part, Dahmer, then a high-school student in suburban Akron, Ohio, largely confined his pathologies to storing a variety of freshly slaughtered household pets in bottles of formaldehyde he kept in his bedroom, prior to embarking on an extended homicidal spree in which his typical modus operandi was to lure vulnerable young men to the apartment where police would eventually find four severed heads, one of them in a cardboard box under the bed, and assorted other body parts. There were also more than 100 photographs of people taken at various stages of dismemberment, many of them so graphic that seasoned US homicide detectives could not look at them without feeling faint. Nilsen and Dahmer are now thought to have murdered at least twelve and seventeen young men respectively.

Following his attack on the pregnant Marcella Claxton as she relieved herself behind a bush in Roundhay Park, Leeds, Peter Sutcliffe had paused in his own homicidal rampage, before returning to murder an estimated eleven women over the following four years. The accumulating death toll and the failure to catch the man responsible created an air of fear and dismay throughout the area, and in time, provoked grim taunts of the investigating authorities at home Leeds United football matches, such as 'Ripper 10, Police Nil', as the number of victims mounted. Later classified while in custody as a psychopath, a diagnosis many non-professionals might well have already reached, Sutcliffe was sent to Broadmoor secure hospital in Berkshire, where he could sometimes be seen sitting in the dayroom still wearing the same double-breasted velvet suit in which he had liked to go out drinking in the old days.

***

At least for public consumption, Gerald Ford remained defiantly upbeat on the US presidential campaign trail. 'During the past thirty years, the United States has been the unquestioned leader in worldwide efforts to develop the benefits of nuclear power, as in so many other areas of human endeavour,' he declared in a speech given in Delaware, ostensibly dedicated to the nation's energy policy, which soon veered off topic into a more general paean to US exceptionalism. Ford continued, now sounding increasingly like an old-time revivalist minister:

I hope that those listening here tonight will maximise your efforts, and turn out for the biggest vote on November 2, a vote for America, a vote for America's future. We are on the march, we are on the way … There is a new faith, a new spirit. What you do between now and when the polls close next Tuesday will make a significant difference in the third century of America's God-blessed greatness. I know you won't let the United States down, and as your next president neither will I … Like our intrepid astronauts, let us aim for the stars.

Ford concluded, slightly awkwardly, throwing his hands up high above his head for emphasis, 'Our best days are yet to come. Thank you! Goodnight! God bless America!'

As campaign rhetoric, this was all fine and good as far as it went. But in late 1976, there were millions of Americans for whom life wasn't necessarily great or conspicuously God-blessed at all. The inhabitants of greater New York, for instance, found themselves living in a city that in certain parts resembled some nightmarish *Bladerunner*-like post-apocalyptical wasteland with pimps and prostitutes populating the streets, a decaying and verminous infrastructure, a pervasive economic crisis, and now with a psycho killer on the loose.

The specific menace of David Berkowitz aside, New York was not wholly unrepresentative of many of America's major cities. Denny Laine, a Birmingham-based musician then playing alongside Paul and Linda McCartney in Wings, would long remember the band's extensive coast-to-coast US tour that year, and like many before and after him, being simultaneously thrilled and appalled by the experience.

'You went up into your bloody great hotel room, turned on the telly, and the picture snapped on in colour right away, instead of warming up like it did back home,' Laine told me, again proving that what many people most register about a foreign country isn't so much its great socio-historical heritage as its fine detail. 'Everything seemed to be open all night, and the shops were piled to the ceiling with every luxury you could possibly want.' On the other hand, Laine continued, 'outside of the big cities a lot of people were very uptight if you had long hair or looked the least bit funny, and you still got called a "fag" in some towns when you walked down the street. What they said to black people was even worse.'

The discrepancy among the fortunes of different groups of Americans was even greater in the rural South. Despite the sea of happy children's faces that graced Gerald Ford's campaign commercials, poverty exploded in many Southern states in the mid-1970s, claiming children as its principal victims. By 1976, some 14 million young people in America lived below the breadline, more than when Lyndon Johnson had declared his 'war on poverty' a decade earlier. To drive through certain remote pockets of the South was to be transported back to a place of almost medieval squalor, where you saw children with hair cut close to the scalp to avoid lice and nits, with teeth uneven, broken or missing, wrapped in sack-like garments and, as often as not, reared in neighbourhoods where indoor plumbing was the exception and a wooden outhouse the rule, and where a dog of uncertain pedigree and the rusted carcass of a car stood sentinel in the front yard.

This was the 'real America' of 1976, just as much as the star-spangled nation of undoubted scientific and cultural excellence of the sort Ford extolled in his Delaware speech, or the one where, on 21 October, Saul Bellow won the Nobel Prize for Literature. His compatriot, Milton Friedman, took the award for Economics, and Americans also won the prizes for Physics, Chemistry and Medicine, failing only in the Peace category, which later went to Mairead Corrigan and Betty Williams, the co-founders of the organisation dedicated to promoting a non-violent solution to the Troubles in Northern Ireland.

Ford himself survived his third and final televised debate with Jimmy Carter, held on the evening after the Nobel announcement in Williamsburg, Virginia. The next morning, Gallup put the Republican incumbent at 45 per cent and his Democratic challenger at 47 per cent, while other polls showed the two candidates in a statistical dead heat. With just ten days to go, it was still anyone's race to win.

***

In Britain, the key point of dispute that autumn wasn't so much which political party might be more congenial to God or the electorate, but whether the country was effectively governable at all. If you read the *Daily Mail*, you might have concluded that the most powerful man in the UK just then wasn't James Callaghan, but a 63-year-old bespectacled trade union organiser named Jack Jones.

Much of the government's employment-protection legislation of the era was formulated at Jones's behest, and in his capacity as General Secretary of the 2.2 million-strong Transport and General Workers' Union, he made little pretence about what he saw as his role in the smooth administrative function of the state, which, in his view, was one far removed from the mere whims of some transient Cabinet minister. 'Much better they [ministers] should talk to me first before they make speeches which are often far from reality,' Jones informed one TV interviewer. Speaking of the much-vaunted social contract between the government and the trade union movement, he announced, 'We have worked out a TUC policy on pay. We shall now apply it … I think that's the priority, and not some here-today, gone-tomorrow official's attempt to re-write something that is a matter for others.'

As the *Daily Mail* explained to its readers, Jack Jones was in some ways more powerful than the nation's Chancellor 'and effectively second in command only to the prime minister', although Jones himself might have questioned what made Callaghan superior. He was strongly in favour of abolishing the House of Lords and of higher taxes for 'the landed gentry, who don't contribute anything to society', and equally firmly against Britain's continued membership of the Common Market. Jones always insisted that he wanted a fairer, gentler society in which employers and employees treated each other with mutual respect, as opposed to a Soviet-style oligarchy dressed up as a workers' paradise. It was really all about dignity, he once told the *New York Times*. 'Unions should be pressing not just for more money for their members, but for a civilised life [for] the working-man … with a home, time for the wife and kids, leisure, fun.'

A veteran of the Spanish Civil War, the austere, tea-drinking Jones seemed personally incorruptible, although allegations of his being a Soviet dupe were later made by Oleg Gordievsky, a KGB colonel who also worked as a double agent for MI5. Gordievsky said that the two men had met together several times, and he had given his contact the codename 'Dream' in his reports back to Moscow. Jones had apparently been 'very helpful' in passing on the names of his fellow union organisers who might make good recruits for the Russian security services. 'For this I paid him £200,' Gordievsky added.

On 5 November, the International Monetary Fund negotiators arrived in London to discuss their terms for the loan required to keep Britain afloat for a further six months. When one hears terms like 'Assessment of Balance of Payment Discrepancies' and 'Possible Drawing Rights on Freely Usable Currencies', one somehow thinks of an orderly process involving meetings between serious-minded men in business suits being driven around in official cars, with an appropriately reassuring word for the expectant public about the paramount importance of balancing the nation's vital social services with an equally essential measure of fiscal probity. But the events of that month were not always quite like that.

In scenes more reminiscent of *Mission: Impossible*, the six IMF men checked into London's discreet Brown's Hotel – over the years, a favourite haunt of visiting European royalty – using assumed names. Nothing much happened during the party's first week in residence except for a midnight appearance made through one of the hotel's back doors by the Chancellor, Denis Healey, who told them that the charts of detailed economic data they required for their deliberations were not yet ready. To while away their time, the IMF men and their staff went out to lunch, tea and dinner each day, and took a box for the opening of the ballet *Adagio Hammerklavier* at the Royal Opera House in Covent Garden.

On 8 November, Callaghan's government narrowly survived two contentious votes in the House of Commons. Three of the four by-elections held that month were won by the Conservatives, reducing Labour's effective majority in the Commons to one. These were the 'highly singular' circumstances, as Callaghan put it, in which the IMF team began their meetings in earnest two days later. The prime minister told a *Guardian* journalist on 10 November, with a presentiment that proved correct, 'This may prove to be the most trying period of a political career not wholly untouched by shadow.'

Later that evening, three of the IMF delegation met for detailed discussions with Treasury officials, while the remaining three passed through a little-used garden door into 10 Downing Street for more free-ranging talks over the brandy decanter with Callaghan and Healey. The essential position was that the IMF wanted their hosts to cut state spending by £3 billion in the fiscal year 1977–78 and by £4 billion in 1978–79, a reduction of roughly 6 and 8 per cent respectively. Callaghan and Healey countered that the best that they could manage was just half that total.

To add a further note of urgency to the proceedings, the British needed the new IMF funds to be in place by no later than Christmas, just six weeks away, if only so that they could repay the interest due on the existing loans taken out from the central banks of other Western countries earlier in the summer. To some of its critics, it almost seemed as if the entire UK government was embroiled in a massive Ponzi scheme, designed to maintain the illusion of a sustainable business model by persuading new investors to contribute fresh funds while fending off existing creditors just long enough to avoid total ruin. Meanwhile, sterling plunged by another five points against the dollar on the single day of 11 November. The following morning, it hit a new low of $1.51, down roughly 30 per cent on the year to date.

***

It hardly qualified as high finance in the traditional sense of the term, but the events that ended in a guilty verdict at the Old Bailey that week still exercised a morbid fascination among those who admire the ingenuity of an especially daring and apparently victimless institutional robbery. While people hate muggers who pull knives on their victims or thieves who break into the homes of the elderly, carrying out a spectacular multimillion-pound jewel or bullion heist will always win the grudging admiration of a public who, even in 1976, were widely disillusioned with banks and bankers as the nation's guardians of corporate or private wealth. The press headlines that described the meticulous planning and brazen *chutzpah* behind the job in question had all the appearance of the celebration of a major pools win.

The tale began at the European headquarters of the Bank of America at Davies Street in Mayfair, central London, an international repository some-what incongruously set between a transport café and a newsagent's shop, with garish 1970s-style back-slanted lettering above the glass front door. Sometime earlier, the bank's manager and his young secretary, who constituted the building's personnel department, saw fit to engage a freelance south London electrician named Stuart Buckley.

In those largely analogue days, they had no immediate way of knowing that their new hire had just completed a nine-month stretch in Wormwood Scrubs for handling stolen goods, nor that he was cunning, vindictive and above all, contemptuous of those individuals or institutions he deemed to represent the unacceptable face of capitalism that was responsible for his own lowly status in life – a broad category. After only a day or two on the job, Buckley was handed the keys to the building and told that he was free to continue the extensive rewiring work required on the premises whenever was convenient to him, just as long as he remembered to first set the burglar alarm and lock the door to the street on his way out.

This turn of affairs led him to telephone an old criminal acquaintance from the Scrubs, an elaborately coiffured, medallion-wearing individual known to the police as 'Fingers' Frank Maple, with an incredible story. He, Buckley, literally had the keys to a major international financial institution in his pos-session, and all that now stood between them and a truly spectacular payday was the six-digit combination to the bank's downstairs vault where the cash and valuables lay.

In the end, the code in question did not prove unduly difficult for Buckley to acquire. He did so by the expedient of positioning himself in a room directly above the vault and then peering through a gap in the floorboards until the manager appeared one morning to obligingly tap in the missing numbers. In the meantime, Frank Maple had engaged the services of a six-man crew of accomplices and, dressed for the occasion in their best formal suits, they used Buckley's key to let themselves in to the front door of the bank, shortly after the close of business on a spring Thursday evening. When they left the premises again, roughly forty minutes later, they were carrying £9 million (the equivalent of £70 million today) in cash, jewellery and other valuables stuffed into a variety of innocuous-looking briefcases, making it the biggest single bank job in Britain to date.

The relative efficiency of the snatch itself was not, however, matched by the unfailing ingenuity of the subsequent arrangements. The robbers' designated fence, a used-car dealer known to police as Sam the Snail and described as somewhat dim but affable when he was sober, was duly dispatched to a north London pub one evening to discuss matters with a criminal contact. That was the first mistake the gang made. '"Sam" was definitely three sheets to the wind,' the later police report put it.

The individual Sam met in the pub that night introduced himself as a friend of the expected contact, who was said to be indisposed. In fact, the party who discussed terms with Sam over a steadily mounting number of pints was one of those members of the Flying Squad who, at the time, often convincingly carried themselves off in the same manner as the villains they pursued. It later transpired that the police had had the flamboyant Frank Maple under surveillance for some time and had known in advance about the rendezvous in the pub.

After that, it was a relatively straightforward matter to detain the electrician Stuart Buckley, who had dutifully reported for work on the Friday morning following the disappearance of the bank's valuables, even as the police were inside the building dusting it for prints. Buckley soon found that he was willing to cooperate with the law in exchange for a reduced sentence, and six of the seven gang members still at large were swiftly rounded up as a result.

Passing judgement on them, Justice King-Hamilton said that he was determined the thieves should not enjoy the fruits of their haul, only £500,000 of which had been recovered. 'What has been concealed will remain salted away from your clutches for a very long time,' the judge announced, before passing sentences on the gang of between three and twenty-five years apiece. It remains a matter of opinion whether they were in fact criminal masterminds or displayed something closer to the sort of comic ineptitude of a Woody Allen heist caper. The archetypal chancer, Frank Maple eluded the police dragnet at the last moment and apparently made his way to Morocco, a country without an extradition treaty with the UK, and has not been publicly seen since.

In the same week that Judge King-Hamilton brought down his gavel with such emphasis at the Old Bailey, the Scottish police opened their investigation into what became the United Kingdom's longest-running missing persons case. It began on the wintry Friday afternoon of 12 November 1976, when 36-year-old Renee MacRae and her two young sons got in the family's blue BMW to leave their detached house in the affluent Cradlehall neighbourhood of Inverness. Mrs MacRae dropped her older child at her estranged husband's nearby home, where he was to spend the weekend, before turning south with 3-year-old Andrew in the back seat, apparently intending to visit her sister, 100 miles away in Perth. Neither mother nor son was ever seen again.

Late that evening, MacRae's burnt-out BMW was found abandoned in a layby beside a remote stretch of the road in Dalmagarry, about a dozen miles from Inverness. It was a desolate spot, and to make matters worse for investigators, it proved to be a particularly wet and wild weekend, which meant that much of the physical evidence had been washed away by the time police came to properly examine the car the following Monday. MacRae's estranged husband Gordon was questioned and found to have an airtight alibi. He told police that Renee was a kind-hearted woman, who was fond of children and animals, and without a known enemy in the world.

The evidence eventually accumulated in the case suggests something rather different and more complicated.

At intervals over the next forty-six years, the investigation into the MacRaes' disappearance stopped and started again in response to the changing state of available forensic technology. In the initial phase, 200 volunteers armed only with lanterns and sticks helped the Northern Constabulary search an area covering 100 square miles. In due course, an RAF Canberra spy plane was deployed to sweep the surrounding hills with an infrared camera capable of detecting the disturbed earth of a hastily dug grave, although still without result.

The following summer, cadaver dogs were brought in, and officers agreed to once again go out on the moors with a Swiss clairvoyant, who assured them she knew what had happened to the two missing parties. Again, nothing.

In 2014, forensic archaeologists were engaged to sift forlornly through the soil and debris of a local quarry thought to be a possible resting place for the bodies, with what police called 'some interesting developments', but still no result. Blood samples taken from Renee MacRae's car were finally available to be tested for DNA but again proved inconclusive.

In 2018, the police drained a second quarry of 3 million gallons of water, while removing 100,000 tons of earth, silt and other material and uprooting 800 trees. No fewer than thirty-two abandoned vehicles or parts of vehicles were found submerged on the site, but no human remains.

'The police find themselves brought up against a dead end of seemingly impenetrable negatives,' *The Scotsman* reported in 2019, adding that the case had all the ingredients of an especially ghoulish Sherlock Holmes mystery, with its cast of the missing woman and her young son, the burnt-out car left by the side of the lonely Highlands field, the enigmatic quarry and the fact that it all took place in one of the most austerely beautiful – or, if you prefer, bleak – locations in the United Kingdom.

It was only at this point that an elderly man named Dennis Tyronney, apparently suffering a fit of remorse, wrote to the police with a startling revelation. Back in 1976, fresh from serving a prison term for housebreaking, he had worked at the same building firm as a William MacDowell, who, it turned out, had been having an affair with Renee MacRae and was the biological father of young Andrew. In his letter to the authorities, Tyronney claimed that MacDowell had asked him one day if he would kill someone, and in reply, 'I said I would not stoop that low, not even for a million pounds', although the fee mentioned at the time had been significantly lower, at just £300. 'He wanted me to douse the bodies in acid,' Tyronney added. 'I refused point blank. He said it was the wife and bairn. I might be a lot of things, but I'm not a killer,' his letter concluded.

In September 2022, nearly half a century since their disappearance, 80-year-old William MacDowell was found guilty of the murders of Renee MacRae and her young son, Andrew. He had denied the charges and instead suggested that the police investigate the missing woman's estranged husband. The judge sentenced MacDowell to a minimum of thirty years in prison, but he died while in custody just five months later. During the trial, jurors were told that there had been 123 reported sightings of Mrs MacRae and her son, who by then would have been 82 and 49 years old respectively, but all had been eliminated.

The most plausible theory is that MacDowell killed his two victims following a violent argument with Renee, and buried their bodies in a shallow grave that he knew would shortly be covered over by a new extension to the A9. A contemporary artist's sketch of how young Andrew MacRae might have looked at the moment of his death was published in the popular tabloid *Reveille*. This was widely considered low, even by the media standards of 1976, and condemned by readers who wrote in to protest at the paper's lapse in good taste.

'LET'S DO IT'

Jimmy Carter duly won the presidential race in the United States. As predicted, it was close. In the end, Carter took 297 of the all-important electoral college votes to Gerald Ford's 240, while the incumbent won twenty-seven individual states to his challenger's twenty-three. Ford took public responsibility for the loss, while privately blaming it on two Republican colleagues: Richard Nixon, whose peremptory pardoning for any Watergate-era crimes had cost Ford dearly among the sizeable number of Americans who apparently wanted to see their disgraced former president thrown in jail; and Ronald Reagan, whose support for his party's official nominee had been, at best, lukewarm. During his long retirement years, when asked about his greatest regret in life, Ford said that it was having had too little time to play on the 1930s University of Michigan football team. Only after being reminded did he mention losing the 1976 election.

Carter inherited a country distinguished by its dualism, if not by a case of full-blown collective schizophrenia. In late 1976, the United States was home to a remarkable number of pioneering scientists and engineers: the sort of men and women who dominated the year's Nobel prizes, started companies with slightly improbable names like Apple and Microsoft, and led the world in space technology. That same autumn, NASA rolled out its first reusable orbital shuttle, named *Enterprise* in a ceremony appropriately witnessed by the *Star Trek* creator Gene Roddenberry and most of the cast of his show. The world's only continuous-use spacecraft at the time, it was launched like a rocket, manoeuvred around the earth like a satellite and landed again like an aeroplane.

Enterprise was a remarkable technical achievement, far beyond the scope of America's space-race competitors, and just one of the advances we take for granted today, including GPS devices, personal computers and smartphones, that lie downstream of products that were invented or commercialised in the United States of the mid-1970s. Carter was right to point that autumn to America's starring role in 'revolution[ising] the conduct as well as the content of the world's business, [so much] of which can now be accomplished by the touch of a button'.

One of Carter's first priorities in November 1976 was to contact Russ Theisen, head of the American Federation of Information Societies, the umbrella group of the nation's tech entrepreneurs, and ask him to replace the tens of thousands of typewriters and mimeograph machines used in all branches of the federal government with the first large-scale email software connected to a network of IBM 5100 portable computers. Whatever you made of his politics, Carter was an articulate and forceful figurehead of a culture that was not afraid to try new ways of doing business to succeed faster.

Set against this there was America's sclerotic political class as a whole, whose denizens could seemingly be prised out of office only by dynamite and whose senators would probably have worn togas if they felt they could get away with it. The whole tottering edifice was sustained by an army of bureaucrats and regulators with little apparent purpose in life but to obstruct brash young start-ups like Apple, whose Steve Jobs would remember the 'halo of idiocy, and often of corruption' that hung over the heads of those 'who put barriers in the way of the real innovators'.

It wasn't just the tragicomic humbling of Richard Nixon and much of his staff in the wake of the Watergate scandal. It seemed that US politicians of all stripes were at it. The nation's legislative branch in 1976 still largely lay in the hands of stalwarts of the Franklin Roosevelt era like 67-year-old Wilbur Mills of Arkansas, chairman of the House of Representatives' all-powerful Ways and Means Committee, until he was stopped by police while driving erratically around Washington DC in the early hours of the morning with a lightly clad stripper named Fanne Foxe seated on his lap, or Wayne Hays, 66, a Democratic representative from Ohio, who took an overdose of sleeping pills but failed to kill himself after it was revealed that he was paying a young woman $14,000 each year to serve solely as his mistress.

Or, for that matter, John Hastings, a Republican from New York, who persuaded three of his congressional staff members to kick back parts of their salaries so that he could buy cars, snowmobiles and boats for himself and pay the college expenses of his children. Convicted of mail fraud and filing false payroll information, Hastings served fourteen months in prison before deciding to leave politics and live under an assumed name in Florida.

In the same vein, there was John Dowdy, a Democrat from Waco, Texas, convicted of accepting a $25,000 bribe to interfere in a federal investigation into a local construction company, and Frank Clark, his party colleague from Pennsylvania, who was found guilty of paying the salary of a young woman officially described as his private secretary. The woman's employment conditions were not very demanding. She 'had no skills', a jury later heard. 'She couldn't type.' The woman's sole function had been to accompany the congressman on his overnight hotel trips.

There may well have been public-spirited and incorruptible elected officials within the US political system of late 1976, quietly going about their sworn duty to uphold the constitution and serve the interests of their constituents and the nation as a whole, but it was also an era characterised by politicians of every affiliation behaving badly and, on occasion, criminally, which goes some way to help explain the arrival in the White House of a born-again Baptist Missionary figure who was at least able to claim with conviction, on leaving office four years later, 'I told the truth. I obeyed the law. I kept the peace.' He was also democratically elected.

In Cuba, by contrast, which also went to the polls on 2 November, Fidel Castro's ruling Communist Party was fortunate enough to scrape home by winning all 489 seats in the National Assembly. In Mexico, the incumbent President Luis Echeverría was succeeded that month by his childhood friend and Institutional Revolutionary Party (IRP) colleague, José Portillo, marking the IRP's forty-seventh consecutive year of uninterrupted power.

There were political upheavals even in France, where Jacques Chirac abruptly resigned as prime minister to serve as Mayor of Paris, a role in which he was later convicted of embezzlement and misuse of public funds and given a suspended two-year sentence. Elsewhere in Paris, a bomb ripped apart the flat of the National Front leader Jean-Marie Le Pen. The late-night blast tore off the roof and opened a hole in the wall of the building where the far-right politician's three young children were sleeping, including 8-year-old Marine, the future French Deputy and perennial presidential candidate.

In sport, the Cincinnati Reds swept the New York Yankees by four games to nil in US baseball's so-called World Series, the Reds' feisty sparkplug of a hitter Pete Rose doing much of the damage. Rose's boundless competitive zeal helped make him one of the most triumphant and tragic figures in US sports history, rising to the top of baseball's career hits list but subsequently earning a lifetime ban for betting on – and against – his own team.

Aged 34, Muhammad Ali officially remained the world heavyweight boxing champion, now taking punches that five years earlier he would have avoided and narrowly earning points decisions against younger opponents. Perhaps the old magic was gone, but at least the humour remained. The Belgian Jean-Pierre Coopman drank champagne in his dressing room to calm his fear of facing the champion in a bout held in Puerto Rico. After four rounds, Ali leant over the ropes to the ringside TV producer and remarked, 'I hope you've finished with your commercials, because I can't hold this bum up much longer.' Richard Dunn, from Halifax in West Yorkshire, made £75,000 for his title fight with Ali in Munich in 1976. As they were introduced, Dunn, to intimidate his opponent, told Ali he was a former paratrooper. 'Ah, so you know how to fall,' said the champion. Ali was at his best that night, constantly changing his tactics in the ring – boxing's equivalent of improvised jazz. Dunn lost in five.

Wales's Ray Reardon did better, winning snooker's world championship and narrowly failing in the final of the match-play tournament that followed in Melbourne, Australia. A former miner, Reardon enjoyed a drink, drove a second-hand Ford Prefect he labelled the 'Gutless Wonder' and sometimes emerged from his dressing-room wearing a striking, red-lined cape, top hat and smoking jacket ensemble that he rented from his high-street tailor, earning him the inevitable nickname of Dracula.

None of these individuals or events, however well attended, came close to rivalling the box-office power of a teenaged Egyptian pharaoh who had died over 3,000 years earlier. When the travelling 'King Tut' Exhibition opened at Washington DC's National Gallery on Wednesday, 17 November 1976, the line of would-be customers wrapped around the three-block-long building. Some 900,000 people, more than the entire population of Washington at the time, paid to see the boy king's funeral artefacts, which eventually attracted 11 million visitors on a tour of seven major US cities over the next two years.

That same Wednesday was also the date set for the first execution to be carried out in the United States since June 1967. The condemned man in the case was 35-year-old Gary Gilmore, who had been swiftly tried and convicted for the murder of Ben Bushnell, a young hotel night-clerk in Provo, Utah, who left behind a pregnant widow and their first child. It was about as simple, and as brutal, an example of gratuitous homicide as can ever have been brought before a US court.

Late one evening the previous summer, Gilmore had walked in to the City Center Motel and demanded that Bushnell, a recent business graduate of the nearby Brigham Young University, hand him the petty cash box he kept under the front counter. There had been no argument on the matter. Bushnell, who lived on the premises with his family, promptly complied. Gilmore then ordered the young man to lie down on the floor and shot him twice through the head with his pistol. Hearing the noise, the victim's wife had rushed in from the next room to cradle her dying husband in her arms as the killer calmly made off into the night.

'I don't know why I did it,' Gilmore later told a jury. 'I felt there was no way what happened could have been avoided. There was no other choice or chance for Mr Bushnell. It was something that couldn't be stopped.'

It is hard to say why 1976 should have proved to be such a bumper year for American criminal psychopaths. Perhaps it was something to do with the sheer sweep and size of the country that provided a playground for their malignity, allowing them to travel at will down the dark miles of highway between the enticing points of neon signifying the location of their next potential victim. Or perhaps, in Gilmore's case, it was simpler than that, and no more than another example of the fact that when a materially and emotionally stunted childhood like his gives way to a half-baked adolescent grasp of nihilistic literature, and factors such as a penchant for cheap drugs and petty theft and the ready availability of handguns are added to the mix, normal standards of self-restraint can be relaxed to the point where tragic results ensue. Gilmore later admitted that on the night before he killed Ben Bushnell he had walked into a local filling station and shot dead the young clerk on duty, Max Jensen, in identical fashion. He was charged with the Jensen slaying but in the end was never tried for it.

What distinguished Gilmore from the scores of other homicidal maniacs who come before the American courts was that, once tried and convicted, he actively lobbied for his own execution. Not that this prevented the decadent lunacy of the US criminal justice system and its many interested parties from petitioning for clemency on the prisoner's behalf. At one stage that autumn, an excommunicated Mormon preacher named Douglas Wallace secured a hearing in front of the nation's supreme court to halt Gilmore's execution because, he claimed, it was part of 'a paganistic ritual' supported by the Mormon-dominated Utah state legislature. The court dismissed his motion. Two further efforts to spare Gilmore's life were successively launched by the American Civil Liberties Union (ACLU) and Amnesty International, before being joined in turn by an attorney representing other death-row inmates who was fearful, in his pointed words, that 'Mr Gilmore's demise might create an atmosphere injurious to my clients' interests'. This motion, too, was denied. The lawyer in question may have had grounds for concern, because there have been approximately 1,650 judicial executions in the United States in the intervening years, a rate of one every ten days.

In another peculiarly American development, highlights of Gilmore's life story then appeared in the supermarket tabloid, the *National Enquirer*, in which he claimed his jailers had repeatedly tied him down and injected him with mood-altering drugs, before going on to share his thoughts about life and death and including letters he had sent to his sometime girlfriend, who was herself hospitalised at the time after having recently joined her lover in an unsuccessful suicide pact. On sleepless nights in prison, Gilmore said, he had been haunted by ghosts. 'They're slippery, sneaky and get tangled in your hair like bats ... Demons with dirty, furry bodies whispering vile things ... creeping, crawling, red-eyed soulless beasts.' In between these nocturnal visitations, Gilmore sat in his condemned cell, guarded around the clock, frequently writing to the press and answering his voluminous fan mail from his largely female admirers. Many of the latter included photos of themselves which he deemed 'Playboy hot'.

By contrast, Gilmore was not pleased at the would-be intervention of the ACLU and others to prevent his execution. 'They always want to get in on the act,' he informed one of the numerous interviewers summoned to his cell in the final weeks of 1976. 'I would like them all – including the reverends and rabbis from the big city – to butt out. This is my life and this is my death. It's been sanctioned by the courts that I die and I accept that.'

In early December, following a hunger strike by Gilmore, a state review board decided that his wish to meet his maker could move forward. Asked by a judge whether he had anything more to say, the condemned man's only request was that he be shot, rather than hanged, and he not be hooded during the execution.

Gilmore finally got his way shortly after dawn on 17 January 1977, when he was led into an old cannery known as the Slaughterhouse on the grounds of the Utah State Prison at Draper. The occasion combined solemnity with a touch of the haphazard. Wearing a black shirt and white trousers, Gilmore was strapped into an old mahogany office chair with half a dozen pillows and mattresses rather randomly piled behind it. Twenty feet away hung a sailcloth partition with five slits torn into it. Hidden behind the curtain stood five volunteer executioners, each armed with a .30 calibre Winchester deer rifle. Four of the rifles were loaded with a steel-jacketed shell, and the fifth with a blank.

Gilmore was administered the last rites. A paper target was pinned over his heart, and he was hooded, despite his earlier request. His final words, spoken in a level voice, were, 'Let's do it'. All four of the live rounds hit their mark.

Ten years later, an Oregon advertising executive named Dan Wieden tailored the condemned man's parting line to provide a marketing slogan for the Nike company that still resonates with millions of people around the world, most of them unfamiliar with the Gilmore story. In time, it became a rallying cry of personal achievement and perseverance – surely a defining example of the American gift for adapting even the most macabre source material into something that can be profitably retailed as an exercise in cheery self-empowerment.[2]

★★★

In the week Gary Gilmore began his final hunger strike in rural Utah, Americans might have seen the first public reference to *Star Wars*, six months before its screen debut, in the form of an undemanding illustrated paperback co-authored by the film's creator, George Lucas. The next day, Jimmy Carter's Baptist church in Plains, Georgia, narrowly voted to allow 'coloured' worshippers to attend their services, after Carter himself had remarked that their current whites-only policy was 'out of step with our times ... and not sustainable'.

An 18-year-old named Harry De La Roche, on leave from his military academy in Charleston, South Carolina, let himself in to his family's New Jersey home that same evening, fixed himself a snack in the kitchen and then walked upstairs and shot dead his parents and his two younger brothers while they were sleeping. He later said that he had been bullied, both at home and during his time at the academy, which caused him 'to snap'. Unlike Gary Gilmore, once convicted of murder, De La Roche made numerous attempts to be released on parole, eventually succeeding forty-seven years later in June 2023.

A tense moment ensued in the Atlantic alliance that week, when the British government ordered the expulsion of both Mark Horsenball, an American journalist working for the *London Evening Standard*, and the former CIA officer Philip Agee. The former was a standard-issue investigative reporter – or muckraker, as they were then called – who had published details of Britain's signals-intelligence headquarters in Cheltenham, while, as we've seen, Agee was one of those cases of the intelligence operative who undergoes an ideological U-turn and comes to aggressively denounce the same organisation he once served.

In his 1976 book *Inside The Company*, Agee wrote of visiting the CIA station in Uruguay and hearing a man being tortured while he spoke with his unconcerned chiefs in the next room, and of personally arranging for death squads to be trained in Panama. He added that he had even once put his family Labrador in a coma to test a nerve drug he would later use to subdue guard dogs in a

---

2   'Just Do It'.

foreign embassy. In a subsequent news conference, Agee not only provided the names of his one-time fellow CIA spies but also disclosed their home addresses and phone numbers. Finding his presence more sparingly required in the UK and several other Western European countries, he eventually settled in Cuba, having been offered a pension and free lifetime healthcare by a grateful Fidel Castro. He died there due to ulcer surgery complications at the age of 72.

★★★

The British government now had only a month left in which to repay the first instalment of the loan it had secured from the European central banks during the summer, or else face the institutional equivalent of the sort of reprisal routinely meted out in a Martin Scorsese film in which the defaulting party finds his head being clamped in a table vice. In James Callaghan's measured words at the Cabinet meeting of 23 November:

> We now face a very serious question: do we think that we could and should afford to pay the price the International Monetary Fund are asking for a further capital infusion, and, if not, what might be the consequences? If we fail to reach agreement with the IMF, we face the risk of the exchange rate falling out of control, with reserves totally inadequate for the purposes of intervention, and with severe implications for prices and unemployment which could test the partnership between HM government and the unions.

'On the other hand,' Callaghan allowed, displaying his gift for understatement:

> ... if an agreement is reached on the lines at present envisaged by the IMF, this too could strain our relationship with the trade unions to breaking point, and put the social contract beyond repair ... The situation is not made easier by the need to take very early decisions.

To this bleak overview, Denis Healey could add only:

> The situation is very difficult, but it would be more so if the current negotiations were to break down ... It is a matter of some real urgency, and [I] remind colleagues that if the present discussions with the IMF fail there would be no hope of obtaining further bilateral aid from other countries. That is the choice now before us.

All this set the scene for the somewhat surreal events surrounding the arrival in London that week of the broad-shouldered, pipe-smoking William E. Simon, Healey's counterpart at the US Treasury. Simon landed at Heathrow on his 49th birthday wearing a wide-lapelled sports jacket with tartan golfing trousers and insisting to reporters that he was there solely to do some early Christmas shopping with his wife, although the press noted that he came accompanied by a forty-two-strong entourage, including his immediate family, three secretaries, his personal doctor and several Secret Service agents and drivers, a retinue that contained roughly forty-one more personnel than Healey took with him on his travels.

Later that same Saturday afternoon, a convoy of black limousines pulled up at the front door of Wells of Mayfair, a bespoke gentleman's tailor that had occupied the same oak-fronted premises since the reign of King George IV. In time, William Simon emerged from one of the cars, still wearing his golf trousers, and announced to the sales clerk who opened the door for him that he would like to buy two of his best dark pinstriped business suits. But before completing the transaction, the distinguished American visitor had an unusual request. Might he make use of the shop's small back fitting room to 'discuss matters' with some colleagues for half an hour?

In scenes again reminiscent of *Mission: Impossible*, a smaller number of cars in turn pulled up in a narrow alley at the rear of the building and several middle-aged men carrying briefcases briskly entered the kitchen of the adjacent Chinese restaurant and passed through its connecting passage to the tailor's premises to join Simon and his associates in the shop's back room, where two burly US Secret Service agents now stood on guard at the door.

There is no formal record of what took place inside the room over the next few minutes, but Simon himself left a clue when he later remarked that both he and his principal assistant, Edwin Yeo, 'met the British Treasury team at Wells. Then we went off and talked to the IMF guys for a few hours, and also saw all the senior British government officials.' Four days later, the IMF negotiators in turn met Callaghan and Healey for further talks over drinks in the prime minister's private flat above the shop at No. 10. Again, no minutes were taken of the after-hours talks, but Callaghan pulled no punches when he went on to summarise the state of play in the following morning's cabinet.

'A go-it-alone policy [is] simply not viable,' he reminded ministers, 'since the country would be unable to finance the needs of our basic industries ... It is agreed that although the morale of the [Labour] party is very low, it should still hold together sufficiently to see through these proposals.' The Cabinet

Secretary noted that, set against this, 'the view was taken by others present that it was too much to ask the government's supporters to stomach another loan package, including cuts in the social security field and other services.' There had been 'some division of opinion' about this in the meeting. 'It is now necessary to decide which of the courses before us is the least disagreeable,' Callaghan himself concluded, with some emphasis.

According to the IMF historian, Callaghan and Healey had, by this point, 'finally agreed to support a reduction in public spending', which, 'while not as large as that proposed by our staff was, nonetheless, substantial'. The protracted UK Cabinet debate on the matter occupied most of the remaining time until the Christmas parliamentary recess.

Tony Benn, the firebrand Energy Secretary, wanted nothing to do with 'any IMF or US Treasury bullies dictating terms' to their hosts' government, and took the opportunity to pass around the Cabinet table a copy of the famous 1940 cartoon showing a British soldier after Dunkirk waving a defiant fist aloft over the slogan, 'Very well, alone'. To Benn, the whole matter was about more than just balancing the books or stabilising the pound. It was a point of principle that touched on the fundamental issue of who truly governed Britain: an elected government led by James Callaghan, or a cabal of wealthy overseas nations and foreign bankers of the type Callaghan's predecessor in office had stigmatised as the 'gnomes of Zurich'?

Denis Healey later remembered that those last weeks in the countdown to Christmas had been the worst of his twelve years in government, or for that matter, nearly half a century in politics. 'Three hours of sleep a night, old boy,' he recalled with some warmth, 'and I got a nasty dose of shingles into the bargain.'

***

The Britain that William Simon and the IMF negotiators were variously concerned with saving as a sovereign nation was in some ways – not least its perennial boom and bust economic cycle – eerily similar to the country today. But in other aspects, it had a planetary remoteness about it. As we've seen, something as basic as going to the local shop was often to be exposed to certain parties who actively advertised their dislike of the customer, not so much in the spirit of some quaintly comic *Fawlty Towers* routine as simply part of the everyday fabric of the retail experience.

The daily business of life in 1976 is worth lingering over for the diminished expectations it reveals. The food writer Carol Block founded the influential

Les Dames d'Escoffier Society that November with the aim not only of help-ing women to break through what she called the 'Pyrex ceiling' of the culinary industry, but improving the variety and quality of the typical household meal. The fruits of her initiative remained limited at first. Meat and two veg was still the staple fare on most dinner tables, although the popular frozen Vesta curries and chow mein provided the first taste for many Britons of 'foreign grub'.

If, in 1976, you were driving around the country and weren't previously famil-iar with your destination, you might have scribbled down directions for yourself along the lines of 'Third to the left past the vandalised scout-hut at the back of the pub', rather than those of today's personal-navigation industry. When the time came to correspond with someone about a business matter, you generally did so by writing them a letter, putting it in an envelope, affixing a stamp, taking it to the nearest post box and awaiting developments. People still spoke of 'BBC English' without the phrase necessarily being tainted by irony or satire.

It was perfectly acceptable to say that you were staying in because you were expecting a phone call or that you didn't want to miss an episode of a TV show such as *I, Claudius* or *Porridge*. Most editions of Saturday night's *Match of the Day* concluded with an interview of a gloriously inarticulate footballer, all kipper tie and sideburns, his wardrobe typically a mishmash of primary colours and chunky jewellery, such as might have been flaunted by Sammy Davis Jr in his 'Ring-a-Ding' phase. If you happened to treat yourself to a new TV or hi-fi, or just about any other electrical appliance, however expensive, it still came without a plug.

Many of the conversations you heard in pubs or in private homes, as opposed to on the BBC, were about race, with approval of that November's legislation exempting turbaned Sikhs from the need to wear motorcycle helmets being far from universal. Cigarette smoking remained a social ice-breaker ('Fag?', 'No, thanks.', 'Mind if I do?') People quite often spat lustily in the street when they were out walking. The ambient smell in many public places was that of stale tobacco, among other, less immediately identifiable aromas.

Although there were many honourable exceptions, the average British adult in 1976 tended not to overdo it in terms of their personal hygiene, a nationwide House Conditions Survey that autumn revealing that some 35 per cent of the public restricted themselves to a once- or twice-weekly 'bath night'. In some ways, Britain still looked and felt like it was dealing with the dregs of the wartime blockade, an existence characterised by carefully rationed hot water, communal or 'party' phone lines and a diet rich in toad in the hole and Spam fritters.

All this was the backdrop into which the Sex Pistols lobbed the grenade of their debut single, 'Anarchy in the UK' on 26 November 1976. The group's manager Malcolm McLaren once remarked that the pivotal release day, filled as it was by the many pressing calls on his time, had gone by 'in a flash'. It must have seemed like a mushroom cloud for much of the record-buying public, and in the boom and smoke of it McLaren would have taken satisfaction that this part of his masterplan for the band's global domination had worked spectacularly well. With an opening snarl of 'Right now!', followed by the memorable rhyme, 'I am an Antichrist/ I am an anarchist', the song gave immediate notice that this was not the work of a McCartney-style suburban everyman.

The number's first live performance, from the stage of Tony Wilson's Granada TV pop-anthology show *So It Goes*, was arguably the big-bang moment of the whole punk phenomenon. Johnny Rotten, his hair dyed an untamed red for the occasion, an impressive number of military-looking badges and crosses hanging off his shredded pink blazer, writhed around the stage, sounding much like an animal with its foot caught in a trap. His colleague, Glen Matlock, realising that his own mike didn't work, booted it from his presence, while a young woman with an enormous beehive hairdo and a military blouse with a stencil-sprayed Nazi armband, pogoed around the floor, all further evidence that this was not your standard-issue young person's teatime variety hour.

Written in the band's suitably threadbare rehearsal room in London's Denmark Street, like all great songs 'Anarchy' both paid homage to its roots while pointing the way to the future. Glen Matlock once said of it:

> Steve [Jones] was supposed to come up with something, and the lazy sod didn't do anything so I had a pop at him. I said, 'I feel like I do all the work.' He said, 'If you're so bleeding clever, what you got, then?' Not much, was the answer. I had a couple of ideas in the back of my head I was farting around with on acoustic guitar, and one of them was a ripoff of the theme tune by the Royal Ballet Sinfonia of *Sunday Night at the Palladium*. That was the riff that became 'Anarchy'.[3]

In a departure from the Sinfonia's own working practice, Malcolm McLaren's only requirement for the recording of 'Anarchy' was that it be done as loud as

---

3   *Sunday Night at the Palladium* (1955–69, with later revivals): a much-loved weekly British TV ritual, with a bill of fare consisting of choice, family oriented acts, from Nureyev and Fontaine to Sooty & Sweep, with a few concessions to youth culture as the years passed.

possible and, in particular, that Paul Cook's drums 'sound like dustbins being kicked downstairs'. That had concluded the technical input. It might have amused McLaren, who died in 2010, to see the song later included prominently in the Rock and Roll Hall of Fame's list of '500 Songs That Shaped Popular Music'.

In another sign that the old ways of doing business might now be under review, Glen Matlock later said of the Pistols' regimen in late 1976:

> It was fun, but it was also boring because we were cooped up all the time and we had to keep going to places and playing in front of the local mayor and his dignitaries at the soundcheck, him approving it. It was stupid because we would go and do a tame version in the afternoon, and then go back at night and do it our way. It just seemed like there were really two Britains at the time, and we saw both of them.

Five days after the release of 'Anarchy' came the epic confrontation pitting the casual disdain of one side against the affronted impotence of the other in a generational clash for the ages.

THE PISTOLS ARE LOADED

Much of the Western world was meanwhile flocking to the first screenings of *Rocky*, Sylvester Stallone's timeless saga about realising your potential, taking your best shot, and sticking by your girl – and also, perhaps, about the United States still being a land of opportunity. Well made and undoubtedly inspirational as it was, *Rocky*'s greatest quality lay in its good timing. Like Jimmy Carter in that month's election, the film about the little guy who seizes his chance seemed to offer the promise that the United States remained a place where a rank outsider armed with the right stuff could go all the way to the top. Many of the film's audiences started out merely clapping and cheering, before the dominant noise gradually changed from one of sustained applause to one of frenzied shrieking. 'It resonates' was the consensus.

Overall, it seems unlikely that many Americans would have decided to drive out to their nearest multiplex cinema to see *Rocky*, or for that matter any other film, because of its supposed allegorical insights into their culture. But it would be fair to say that Stallone's pugilistic morality tale, with its central theme of perseverance against the odds, struck a chord. With its initial

$40 million at the domestic box office, *Rocky* would prove to be the highest-grossing film in North America in 1976 and the second highest in 1977, behind only *Star Wars*.

★★★

A generally poor year for commercial air travel continued with two more major accidents. On 23 November, all forty-six passengers and four crew of a domestic Olympic Airways flight died when their prop plane struck a mountain at Servia, 200 miles north of Athens, after the pilot became disoriented in fog. Five days later, an Aeroflot Tupolev 104 narrow-bodied jet crashed in broadly similar conditions shortly after take-off from Moscow, en route to Leningrad, with the loss of all seventy-three occupants.

It was an especially bad year for the Soviet Union's national air carrier, with no fewer than thirty-nine reported accidents, the equivalent of one roughly every nine days. In September, two Aeroflot flights even managed to collide with one another in the sky over the Black Sea, apparently due to error by air traffic controllers, with the loss of all seventy souls on both planes. Some Western observers believed that the total number of Soviet air disasters for the year was significantly higher than that given by the government, particularly when an incident took place over Russian territory and there were no foreign casualties to report.

Aeroflot's futuristic, dart-shaped Tu-144 had actually beaten Concorde into the air as the world's first supersonic passenger airliner, only to crash on its subsequent appearance at the Paris Air Show, with the loss of all six of its crew and eight people on the ground. Putting this setback behind them, the plane's designers had a modified Tu-144 ready for commercial operation in December 1976, although, as noted by the aviation author Howard Moon, even then teething issues remained. 'Passengers complained that the loud onrushing sound of wind made conversation impossible, and communicated with each other by passing notes,' Moon wrote in his book, *Soviet SST*. 'The cabin also had shortcomings,' Moon continued:

> Several ceiling panels were usually ajar, service trays stuck, and window shades dropped without being pulled. The five-abreast seating was criticised as cramped. Not all the toilets worked. On-board speakers continually played the 'Theme from *Love Story*', 'Gloomy Sunday' and 'Raindrops Keep Falling on my Head', but perhaps mercifully few aboard could hear them ... The dominant impression was not speed but noise.

All these accumulating Soviet air losses, however distressing, paled in comparison to the single catastrophic shock of the earthquake on 24 November at Çaldiran, in eastern Turkey. Lasting just six seconds, the 7.3 magnitude event took a reported 5,200 lives. It was said that 95 per cent of the houses in Çaldiran itself were destroyed outright, and this was in large part due to their scrap masonry and mud construction.

The government of President Fahri Korutürk took some pains to categorise and record the aftermath of the tragedy, if not in its possible prevention. Photographers and statisticians crowded into the devastated area over the days and weeks that followed, leaving an immense documentary portrait of human misery. Great jumbled groups of charred and gutted cars and trucks were blackened by fire, their frames rent and twisted by falling masonry. Piles of rubble were often stacked 30 or 40ft high, with civilian volunteers, many visibly distressed, forlornly sifting through the debris for potential survivors. In profusion were the pictures of the dead. In long rows and in heaps, stretched out and tranquil, or huddled in agony, contorted and mangled, sometimes it was plain that they had been killed by blunt force. Others, as the captions primly assert, had died because of 'lack of proper ventilation' while lying trapped beneath the ruins of their homes.

The pictures released to the Western press were seemingly specially selected for their graphic content. In sorting through this wealth of assembled material, the apparent sense of Turkish exultation in bloodshed and destruction is palpable. Horrific as the event was, Korutürk's government almost seemed to be at pains to make it even more pitiful than its reality.

★★★

William Simon, the pipe-smoking US Finance Minister, had flown home to Washington on the afternoon of 30 November, now sporting one of his dapper new Wells of Mayfair suits and assuring the press how much he had enjoyed his 'excellent' talks with British officials. As the more astute reporters noted, the representative of the US government did not, however, definitely state for the record that his hosts had consented to any specific degree of national austerity in exchange for the desired IMF loan. He was right not to do so, because the UK Cabinet once again took up the issue in a spirited meeting held at Downing Street at ten o'clock the following morning. In the formal tones of the minutes, 'the Secretary of State for Energy [Tony Benn] reminded his colleagues that this was a political decision as grave as any in our history'.

'The country is in the depths of a slump which can only deepen,' Benn himself continued, characteristically avoiding the lure of the understatement:

255

With one-and-a-quarter million unemployed, the government must go for reflation in order to move towards our target of reducing this figure to 700,000 by 1979. We must expand the manufacturing base; and we must safeguard social security benefits … I see no prospect for the survival of the government if we were to allow unemployment to increase to meet the demands of unelected international financiers.

Following this presentation, the Environment Secretary Peter Shore, a more pragmatic-minded left-winger, offered the voice of compromise:

If the chancellor is seriously proposing a reduction of £1 billion in public expenditure in 1977–78, to be followed by a further cut of £1 billion in 1978–79, this would be a political time bomb for the government. In response to such measures, the IMF would issue the loan in tranches to enable them to effectively police the United Kingdom's economic behaviour … This is wholly unacceptable to the Labour movement … In my view it should be possible to adopt import controls, and to persuade other countries that it is sensible for us to do so. This would lead to a surplus of £4 billion on our current account in 1978.

Admittedly, there remains the short-term problem of obtaining the necessary fiscal assistance, but it should be possible to bridge this gap, perhaps by introducing import deposits. The IMF could surely not afford to refuse help to a major democracy engaged in an initiative of this kind, but if this should happen one alternative possibility would be to seek to roll forward to a later date the settlement of the short-term standby credit due for repayment later this month.

Winding up the debate, Denis Healey, sleep-deprived and now plagued with shingles, was blunt in his assessment of the prospects for the nation's finances, if not for its continued survival as a sovereign state:

The country's public borrowing has to be cut, simply because it is impossible to finance it at the present high level save by printing money or maintaining excessive interest rates. Without the IMF loan our external debt could not be financed, there would be no safety net for the sterling balances, no acquiescence by other countries in a scheme of import deposits and no bilateral lending. In my view, failure to reach agreement with the IMF would cause unemployment to rise very rapidly … The alternative steps proposed here today would involve all the short-term disadvantages to our finances without any of the longer-term prospects of improvement ... Any [other] course of action to the one [I] propose would be contrary to the maintenance of the mixed economy and of the basic exercise of government authority to which we are committed.

Healey concluded by reminding his colleagues that they now had exactly a week in which to start repaying the earlier loan they had taken out in the summer, and any attempt to do so without first extracting more capital from the IMF would be 'utterly ruinous'.

Perhaps what was really on show that rainy Wednesday morning in Downing Street was not so much the specifics of the Cabinet's competing monetary theories as it was the three essential faces of the hybrid that constituted the mid-1970s Labour Party. There was the pristine ideological certainty of Tony Benn and his followers that capitalism was inherently dysfunctional and socialism was both morally and economically superior. The Peter Shore school, by contrast, believed that the answer to Britain's problems lay neither in isolationism nor in surrendering to the hard-hearted men from Washington. Gradual improvements in the terms of trade could be obtained, instead, by creative and incremental steps such as placing temporary restrictions on imports and other technical procedures to protect the economy.

And finally, there was Denis Healey, the man required to manage the nation's books, typically blunt in pointing out that he and his colleagues could debate the nuances of public spending parameters or import controls until the proverbial cows came home, but the stark fact remained that Britain had a looming debt to service and inadequate funds without the IMF's intervention with which to do so. The overwhelming threat to the maintenance of democratic government was not so much that of the pressure exerted by rapacious Washington bankers, Healey added, but of the spectre of utter national ruin that confronted ministers, were they not to address the facts he had put before them.

At the end of the meeting of 1 December, the minutes note, 'The prime minister went around the table one by one, inviting the opinion of every member of the Cabinet.' The IMF terms were accepted in principle by eighteen out of twenty-three of those present. Tony Benn, Peter Shore and the Foreign Secretary Anthony Crosland were the most prominent dissidents, although none of them felt compelled to resign as a result.

The vote did not necessarily signify the government's collective agreement to the fine detail of the IMF package, however, as Healey discovered when he went on to hold a further meeting with the Washington delegation just two days later. Informed that his visitors were now proposing even deeper spending cuts than before, as well as enquiring into the future ownership of British Petroleum, 'the Chancellor', in the careful words of the minutes, 'expressed a note of concern at these developments'.

This was a significant euphemism. 'I told the IMF to take a running jump,' Healey himself later wrote of the meeting. 'They smiled and said, "We seem to have reached an impasse".'

James Callaghan later recalled of that same Friday evening, during which he was packing for a weekend away at Chequers:

> [Healey] and I sat for some time in my bedroom at Downing Street, talking over the various drastic policy changes that would be needed if a loan was not forthcoming. On that night anything seemed possible. The next morning, I was handed a message ... the IMF negotiators had reported back [to] Washington and had shortly afterwards telephoned No. 10, suggesting a renewal of contact.

***

Of course, most Britons would have been blissfully unaware of the political drama being brought to a climax that first week of December. But very nearly all of them would have heard something of the events taking place on the weekday *Today* television show being filmed at the Thames TV studio on Euston Road, central London. This was the iconic teatime encounter between the Sex Pistols and the show's presenter, 53-year-old Bill Grundy, a University of Manchester geology graduate known for his blunt interviewing technique and also, it was widely believed, his fondness for a drink. Although the segment in question lasted barely two minutes, it was enough to spell both the overnight arrival of the Pistols as an international talking point and the effective end of Grundy's career.

The whole affair very nearly didn't happen. Grundy had been led to expect that he would be interviewing the members of Queen, but at the last moment the band's frontman Freddie Mercury had decided he had to urgently visit his dentist for the first time in twenty years. At that stage, a desperate publicist at Queen's record company, EMI, which by sheer chance also part-owned the

Thames TV franchise, called the *Today* studio to offer the exciting new prospect on the label's books as an alternative.

The Pistols themselves were not thrilled to be roused from the Tottenham
Court Road pub in which they had installed themselves that afternoon and
told to instead report post-haste to an only locally available, early evening
show typically featuring a line-up of an elderly visiting Hollywood actor
or two alongside the occasional mild concession to youth like Cliff Richard.
They relented only when Malcolm McLaren threatened to withhold their
wages for the week if they failed to comply. 'After that we were all in the car
like a shot,' Glen Matlock recalls.

Twenty minutes later, the Pistols and their travelling entourage, including
both their friend Siouxsie Sioux and the young woman with the stencil-
sprayed SS uniform, were ensconced in the Thames green room. This being
1976, it was liberally stocked with half a dozen bottles of sickly sweet Blue
Nun white wine, a barrel-shaped tin of Watneys Party Seven and several plastic bowls of assorted crisps. In due course, a nervous handler arrived to usher
the band onto the studio floor to meet Grundy, who was not pleased to forsake
what might otherwise have been a pleasant mutual dip in the PR jacuzzi with
the artists behind the likes of 'Bohemian Rhapsody' for the mixed charms of
the feral-looking group of youths glaring back at him from the other side of
a small Formica table, one of whom, it did not go unnoticed, was wearing a
T-shirt screen-printed with a close-up image of a pair of breasts.

A patronising introduction when the cameras rolled further failed to
ingratiate him to the four musicians, who in turn variously responded by vig-
orously scratching themselves, belching and mimicking their host by reading
off the studio autocue. By now visibly irritated, Grundy turned to camera to
remark, 'I am told that this group have received £40,000 from a record company. Now,' he enquired, 'doesn't that seem, er, to be slightly opposed to an
anti-materialistic view of life?'

'No, the more the merrier', Glen Matlock volunteered.

'Really?'

'Oh, yeah.'

'Well, tell me more, then.'

'We've fuckin' spent it, ain't we?' interjected Steve Jones. 'Down the
boozer,' he elaborated, lest anyone assume they might have invested the funds
in government-backed gilts.

Grundy afterwards said that he had recognised that remark and its choice
intensifier 'as the signal for trouble starting', particularly as the programme

was being broadcast live, with no technical means to prevent profanity or other undesirable material from making it to air. Composing himself, the presenter then seemed to glean the comic potential in engaging two of the band members in an exchange of views about the respective merits of their music as opposed to that of earlier composers.

Grundy: Beethoven, Mozart, Bach and Brahms have all died.
Rotten: They're all heroes of ours, ain't they?
Grundy: Really ... What? What were you saying, sir?
Rotten: They're wonderful people.
Grundy: Are they?
Rotten: Oh yes! They really turn us on.
Jones: But they're dead!
Grundy: Well, suppose they turn other people on?
Rotten [sotto voce]: That's just their tough shit.
Grundy: It's what?
Rotten: Nothing. A rude word. Next question.
Grundy: No, no, what was the rude word?
Rotten: Shit.

It was only at this point, as Grundy engaged in some ill-advised banter with the band's female entourage, that the pre-transmission Blue Nun and Party Seven seems to have well and truly asserted itself:

Jones: You dirty sod. You dirty old man!
Grundy: Well, keep going, chief, keep going. Go on, you've got another five seconds. Say something outrageous.
Jones: You dirty bastard!
Grundy: Go on, again.
Jones: You dirty fucker! [Titters from the group.]
Grundy: What a clever boy!
Jones: What a fucking rotter.
Grundy [hurriedly]: Well, that's it for now. I'll be seeing you soon. I hope I'm not seeing you [the band] again. From me, though, goodnight.

Even then, the whole ghastly ordeal for *Today*'s presenter and his staff wasn't quite over. At the end of the transmission, the Sex Pistols were once again ushered into the studio's hospitality room to await their transport back to the

Tottenham Court Road pub. By the time the Pistols were safely backstage, the show's flustered production team were already being bombarded by the first of what proved to be over 200 complaints from irate viewers protesting at the barrage of smut that had just been beamed into their homes. There was so much incoming traffic that the studio switchboard jammed and some of the calls were accordingly diverted to a row of phones in the green room, only to be answered by the Pistols themselves, who then treated the aggrieved parties to yet more abuse.

For its part, Fleet Street was not slow to whip up the whole episode into one of those end-of-days moral panics that distinguished the tabloid press of the era. The *Daily Mirror*'s 'The Filth and the Fury' was only the most indelible of the many indignant headlines.

Taken as a whole, the nearly continual front-page coverage 'wasn't bad for business', as Malcolm McLaren coyly allowed years later, even if it brought with it an immediate backlash in the form of the council watch committees in several of the towns where the Pistols were scheduled to play later that month. By now the band were a formidable live act, even after all the local code of conduct restrictions had been dutifully read out to them by some town-hall clerk who came backstage before every show.

In Caerphilly, for instance, 'lewd or suggestive material', whether appearing in spoken or musical form, was out. As if to reinforce the injunction, a crowd including several carol singers and a luxuriantly bearded Pentecostal minister took the opportunity to stage an alternative entertainment outside the front door of the Castle Cinema where the Pistols were appearing.

The authorities at Leeds similarly made it clear that no member of the group was to 'remove any item of attire' during their performance there, nor to 'engage in any activity that might cause or be likely to cause distress' to the public. The civic watchdogs in Derby, Bristol and Newcastle avoided the need to narrowly circumscribe the band's appearance in their communities by the expedient of banning them altogether.

In those areas where the Sex Pistols did perform, local shopkeepers often took the opportunity to pre-emptively board up their doors and windows, as if in preparation for a natural disaster. During most of the ensuing concerts, a man in a suit stood to the side of the stage holding a clipboard. Sometimes, the man would make note of a particularly provocative remark or gesture from one or more of the band members, and a day or two later, Malcolm McLaren would receive notice of a fine or some other penalty for the transgression, with yet more press headlines as a result.

Things seemed only to develop for the Pistols from there – up to the moment when they boarded an early morning flight at Heathrow en route to perform at the Paradiso Club in Amsterdam, the London *Evening News* reporting that the four musicians had 'vomited and spat their way' even on the short walk from the departure lounge to their plane. This was apparently too great an illustration of their role as situationist provocateurs for EMI, leaving the burden of their employment to be taken up by A&M briefly, and then by Richard Branson's Virgin Records. Glen Matlock had meanwhile left the group by mutual consent, to be replaced by Sid Vicious, a performer whose technical aptitude for the bass guitar fell some way short of real proficiency.

The Sex Pistols effectively disbanded at the end of a suitably chaotic US tour in January 1978, although they continue to make periodic revivals from behind their marble slab, most recently without their original lead singer, who resides in southern California and has commented enthusiastically on Donald Trump. It remains a matter of opinion whether the Pistols in their prime were gifted social critics whose music was a powerful clarion-call for change, or followed more in a peculiarly English tradition of knock-kneed turns who end up in panto, straightening their toupees and shedding a tear for the death of Variety. Perhaps it was part of their appeal that they were all these things at once.

Bill Grundy always insisted that he had been doing nothing more in his infamous *Today* interview than seeking to provoke his guests to reveal themselves as the 'yobbos and cretins' he believed them to be, and that he had succeeded brilliantly well in doing so. Suspended for two weeks because of what the head of programming at Thames termed 'a gross error of judgement', Grundy ended up fronting a Sunday-morning book-review programme, alongside various regional assignments largely around his native Manchester. He died of a heart attack in February 1993, aged 69.

THE END OF THE AFFAIR

By late 1976, the Cold War had generated a grey area of superpower conflict beyond the confines of formal diplomacy or military action. A worldwide network of terrorists, guerrilla forces and even rogue state operatives, often subsidised if not openly directed by Washington or Moscow, posed a continual threat to the established order. Whether it was the Americans tapping into Soviet satellite technology to eavesdrop on the Kremlin's conversations or the Soviet Union, in turn, infiltrating groups such as the Ku Klux Klan and the Black Liberation Army in order to exploit racial tensions in US cities, the struggle for global supremacy, in both the great undertakings of state policy and in more targeted acts of sabotage or subversion, remained a constant fact of life. On hearing of any major incident affecting a nation's armed defences in 1976, the immediate assumption was that this was the result of shadowy and inherently hostile covert activity on the part of one ideological bloc to undermine the strategic resources or public morale of another.

Sometimes, however, those same destructive acts had another explanation altogether, as in the strange case of the fire that December, which destroyed or damaged beyond repair twelve of the thirteen of the Australian Navy's fleet of medium-range Grumman S-2 Tracker aircraft while they were parked inside a military hangar near Sydney. It soon transpired that the blaze was started not by balaclava-clad foreign operatives but a troubled 19-year-old Australian sailor named John Trent, who later told a court that he had simply opened the fuel tanks of two of the planes, then 'got a piece of paper, made an aeroplane, set it alight and threw it', before adding, 'I can't really say why I did it. I don't know what came over me. Whatever it was, it left as soon as it had come.' The Australian taxpayer was left an estimated $50 million out of pocket as a result of the seaman's passing whim, which also effectively crippled his nation's ability to monitor nearby Soviet submarine activity until sixteen second-hand Grummans could be ordered from the Pentagon the following summer. John Trent was found guilty at his court martial but declared insane at the time of his crime. Ten other Australian Navy personnel were disciplined for their failure to properly ensure the safety of their nation's front-line aerial surveillance assets.

Another in the long series of 1976's more materially minded crimes followed a week later, when three masked men broke into the Louvre in Paris in the pre-dawn hours and removed a nineteenth-century royal coronation sword belonging to Charles X from its showcase. The gang members climbed up scaffolding erected by workers cleaning the façade of the building and smashed an unbarred window on the second floor. After grabbing the jewel-encrusted sword from a display featuring the Bourbon king, the gang made their way down the hallway, subduing two guards who confronted them, before leaving the same way they came. According to French press reports, there could be 'no room for doubt' that the thieves had had help from someone inside the museum. Neither the royal sword nor its 1,500 inlaid diamonds have ever been recovered.

★★★

Any rock star's greatest potential is for disaster, and perhaps never more so than in the drug-fuelled days of the mid-1970s. On top of their youth and personal volatility, often a toxic combination, there's the proximity of mood-altering substances and other inducements, not to mention the Punch-and-Judy bickering that seems to distinguish the internal chemistry of groups as far removed from one another on the pop evolutionary ladder as the Beatles and the Sex Pistols.

On 3 December 1976, the highly regarded US guitarist, Tommy Bolin, late of Deep Purple, gave an ecstatically received show in Miami Beach, following which he sat down in the dressing room for an interview with the local newspaper. The reporter's final words to his subject were to implore him to look after himself, to which Bolin replied, 'Don't worry about me. I'm going to be around for a long time.'

Following that, Bolin returned to his hotel, where he drank far into the night with other members of his band, retiring to his room at about 2 a.m. By all accounts, it was a representative 1970s rock-and-roll scene, with drink, drugs and various spandex-clad young women of, as the jargon of the day had it, easy virtue. An hour later, Bolin was in the midst of an animated phone conversation with a business colleague about their possible investment in a Los Angeles limousine-rental firm, when he abruptly lost consciousness. At that point, the head of his security detail – later recalling that this sort of thing had happened before – carried him to his bed. At around 5 a.m., the same employee returned to check on Bolin and found him semi-conscious, kneeling in his bathtub with the water running. The guitarist's minder couldn't immediately decide on whether to seek medical assistance to deal with the evolving situation, but in the end, he lifted him out of the tub and put him back in bed with his oblivious-seeming girlfriend. Four hours later, the young woman awoke to find Bolin lying beside her, blue-faced and unresponsive. He was just 25 at the time of his death.

Later that month, the Texas-born guitarist Freddie King, a mentor of Eric Clapton, died at the age of 42. He had lived hard, drinking copiously, smoking like a laboratory beagle and always downing a couple of industrial-sized Bloody Marys before stepping on stage because, as he told a reporter, 'they've got food in them'. Playing a club in New Orleans on 18 December, King blacked out in the middle of a solo. Following that, he cancelled a Christmas show scheduled for his native Dallas and instead checked into a local hospital, where he died the following day, riddled with ulcers and suffering from pancreatitis. The coroner who performed his autopsy believed him to be a 65-year-old man.

In between these two losses, the veteran stage and screen actor Jack Cassidy, father of the teen heartthrob David Cassidy, also succumbed to what could be called the rock-and-roll lifestyle when he died in a fire that swept through his West Hollywood apartment. The blaze had been touched off by a cigarette left burning in his mouth when he passed out on a plastic couch. Cassidy's behaviour in the preceding weeks had given friends and family some cause for alarm, and just a few days earlier, his recently divorced second wife, the actress Shirley Jones, had gone to the apartment to get him ready to do a show, only to find him sitting nude in the middle of the floor. When she asked him if he was all right, Cassidy had looked up at her and announced calmly, 'Yes. I know now that I am Christ.' He was 49 at the time of his death.

In a contrasting example of man's higher potential, there was Saul Bellow's Nobel acceptance speech that same week in December. 'Writers are greatly respected,' the new Laureate told the white-tie audience assembled in Stockholm's Grand Hall, notwithstanding the note of grievance that had often characterised his dealings with publishers, critics and the book-buying public over the years:

> The intelligent reader is wonderfully patient with them, enduring disappointment after disappointment while waiting to hear from art what he or she do not hear from theology, philosophy, social theory or politics, and what they cannot hear from pure science ... Out of the struggle at the centre has come an immense, painful longing for a broader, more flexible, fuller, more coherent, more comprehensive account of what we human beings are, who we are, and what this life is for.

A confirmed Anglophile, Bellow had a particular word to say about contemporary life in Britain:

> Everywhere, we see disorder or near-panic. In families, confusion. In civic behaviour, further confusion. And with this private disorder goes public bewilderment. In the papers we read what used to amuse us in science-fiction – the *New York Times* speaks of death rays and of Russian and American satellites at war in space. In *Encounter*, so sober and responsible an economist as my colleague, Milton Friedman, declares that the United Kingdom by its public spending will soon go the way of poor countries like Chile. He is appalled by his own forecast. What – the source of that noble tradition of freedom and democratic rights that began with Magna Carta ending in

dictatorship? 'It is almost impossible for anyone brought up in that tradition to utter the word that Britain is in danger of losing freedom and democracy,' Friedman writes. 'And yet it is a fact!'

It is with these facts that knock us to the ground that we try to live. If I were debating with Professor Friedman I might ask him to take into account the resistance of institutions, the cultural differences between Great Britain and Chile, differences in national character and traditions, but my purpose is not to get into debates I can't win but to direct your attention to the terrible predictions we live with today, the background of disorder, the visions of ruin, even in the United Kingdom and around the world.

***

Politics in mid-1970s Britain, then, whatever their patina of high-minded debate, were primarily a matter of the struggle for national survival. At a meeting in Downing Street on 9 December, the Cabinet discussed such pressing business as the second reading of the Water Charges Equalisation Bill and the relocation of certain London-based civil servants to the provinces, before turning to the outstanding matter of the IMF loan. As James Callaghan reminded his colleagues:

> Timing is now of utmost importance ... It is essential to preserve secrecy about the final package, in order to offset any market uncertainty due to the fact that we are required to repay the stand-by credit at the same time. It should be made known simply that the cabinet has agreed that the chancellor of the exchequer will make a full statement on Wednesday, 15 December.

The final terms provided for a loan of $3.9 billion, or about £2.45 billion taking an average of the fluid exchange rate of the day, in return for which the Chancellor committed to cutting £2.5 billion in public spending over two years. The department of employment lost an immediate £320 million, defence, £300 million, and the environment, £280 million. In the Commons division a week later, thirty-seven Labour MPs voted against the deal, but in the end the Conservatives abstained and the government duly carried the day – a case of MPs voting 'in the paramount national interest', Callaghan believed, if not of their desire to get away to their constituencies for Christmas.

At that point, the six IMF negotiators themselves left the suites at Brown's Hotel, where they had been in near-continuous residence for the past seven weeks, leaving their bill for the attention of HM Treasury. 'Like having to pay the bailiffs who come to turf you out of your home,' Tony Benn, one of the thirty-seven dissenters, later remarked with some asperity.

For his part, Denis Healey was not pleased to learn in later months that he had been put in the position of negotiating with the IMF based on 'ludicrously inaccurate' figures, supplied to him by his own officials. The Treasury had predicted that the UK Budget shortfall for 1976–77 would be between £10.7–10.8 billion, and for 1977–78, around £10.5 billion. In fact, the deficits turned out to be £8.3 billion and £5.6 billion respectively.

In his memoirs, Healey described an economist as 'someone who, when you ask him for a telephone number, gives you an estimate'. His private assessment of the advice given him in 1976 was considerably more caustic. Coming to assess the matter thirty years later, Healey called the whole IMF exercise 'totally unnecessary ... I would never have gone cap in hand to Washington if one had had anything like the true figures'. In the months ahead, the pound steadily gained ground against the dollar, so much so that it began to raise fears of hindering British exports and thus contributing to a recession. 'If anything, I did my job too bloody well,' Healey was left to remark sardonically.

Healey's Cabinet colleague Roy Mason was unable to vote on at least some of the IMF proposals under discussion, being detained at his desk in Belfast. By late 1976, the reigning state of affairs in Ireland broadly resembled that in Germany: the central governing authority acknowledged the presence of a small but highly insistent number of nationalists agitating for the reunification of the country but were quietly content to see the matter postponed *sine die*. Where Mason parted company from his predecessor, Merlyn Rees, was in his tolerance, or lack of it, for the intransigent gunmen on all sides of the sectarian divide. Northern Ireland, he told the Labour Conference shortly after his appointment in September 1976, 'had had enough of [political] initiatives, White Papers and legislation', and henceforth, 'republican terrorism [would be] treated as a security problem and nothing else'.

To add to Mason's challenge in confronting the men of violence, the IRA itself was no longer a single entity. It fragmented first into the Officials and Provisionals, which, in turn, mutated into the Soviet-themed Irish Republican Socialist Party (IRSP) and the Irish National Liberation Army (INLA), which, as its name implies, took a more narrowly martial stance to the issues of the day. Opposing them on the loyalist side were the Democratic Unionist Party (DUP), under its fire-breathing leader, Ian Paisley, with, as we've seen, its own paramilitary offshoots, the Ulster Defence Association (UDA) and the Ulster

Volunteer Force (UVF). Both of these spawned several transient or regional sub-groups, such as the Ulster Defence Force (UDF), Ulster Freedom Fighters (UFF) and the Red Hand Commando (RHC), which emerged from the successive schisms that distinguished both the republican and loyalist camps of the mid-1970s. In this forest of acronyms, the one constant factor was violence.

One name to cross Roy Mason's desk in late 1976 was that of 28-year-old Ronnie Bunting, once of the Official IRA and latterly a founder member of the INLA. Bunting had an unusual background for a gun-toting Republican fanatic. He was the son of a senior British Army officer, and had grown up in Malaysia, Germany, Cyprus and England, where he excelled at school, winning a place at university and working as a history teacher before becoming involved with the more militant wing of the struggle for a united Ireland. Perhaps inspired by his academic studies, Bunting saw himself in the classic mould of a revolutionary freedom-fighter, sporting a bushy Zapata moustache and speaking admiringly of Josef Stalin's purges. 'Kill the kulaks!' he was fond of repeating as a catchphrase.

On 25 November 1976, members of Bunting's INLA ambushed and killed a young private serving with the Royal Welsh Fusiliers when he responded to a report of a robbery in progress at a post office in a small town close to the border between the two Irelands. Indignant that the soldier's murder was at first attributed to the Provisional IRA, Bunting personally called the BBC, using an agreed code name, to take credit for the crime. In fact, he went further. It was his 'fixed resolve' not to rest until every last one of the British forces occupying his country had been removed 'by any means necessary, including direct attack'.

This was by no means the INLA man's only transgression of the law in 1976. Like his role-model Stalin in his youth, Bunting was also known to rob banks to help purchase the weapons with which he and his colleagues would take the armed struggle to the British. One such heist relieved a Brinks-Mat security van travelling between pick-ups in County Limerick of the significant sum of £462,000, or £3.6 million at today's prices.

Bunting frequently remarked that he went in greater fear of attack from his former IRA comrades than from the hated security forces, with at least five serious attempts on his life in the years 1975–77. There remains a suspicion that he and his confederates were responsible for the car bomb that killed the Conservatives' Northern Ireland Spokesman and Colditz escaper Airey Neave, as he drove away from the House of Commons in March 1979. The next edition of the INLA periodical, *The Starry Plough*, reported:

The retired terrorist [*sic*] Neave got a taste of his own medicine when a unit pulled off the operation of the decade and blew him to bits inside the 'impregnable' Palace of Westminster. The nauseous Margaret Thatcher snivelled on television that he was an 'incalculable loss', and so he was – to the British ruling class.

Bunting himself died in the early hours of 15 October 1980, when masked gunmen broke into his family home in Belfast, shooting both him and his wife while their three young children were sleeping in the next room. There would be persistent claims that the state security forces were involved, although the paramilitary UDA were always more than happy to take sole responsibility.

On 22 December 1976, meanwhile, a young UDA member named Thomas Easton was found beaten to death in a deserted churchyard in west Belfast. It was thought Easton's murder, blamed on the evocatively named group the Shankhill Butchers, was a consequence of the strained relations of the various factions vying for supremacy under the loyalist umbrella. He was the 308th known victim of Irish sectarian violence during the year.

★★★

The atmosphere of menace and extremism surrounding extra-parliamentary political cells was by no means a peculiarly Irish problem in 1976. On 13 December, Argentinian security forces summarily executed twenty-two members of the far-left Montonéros faction in the latest twist in the country's continuing 'dirty war', and two days later, the Montonéros responded by detonating a bomb in the nation's Defence Ministry headquarters in Buenos Aires, killing eleven soldiers and civilians and injuring twenty-three others.

Later that day, an explosion at Baghdad International Airport killed four and left 235 requiring hospital treatment, many of them for shattered or severed limbs. The blast occurred in the baggage claim area of the airport's main terminal and was thought to have been caused by a time bomb intended to destroy an incoming Egyptian flight from Damascus, which had landed forty minutes ahead of schedule.

Later that week, 6,000 miles away in Baltimore, Maryland, a Piper Cherokee light aircraft dived into the upper stands of a downtown stadium where 61,000 people were watching a football game between the home team Colts and the Pittsburgh Steelers. For once, there were no fatalities, although several stewards were trampled in the ensuing panic. It transpired that the plane's 33-year-old pilot had a personal grievance against one of the Baltimore team's players, from whose restaurant he had been ejected for using abusive language. It further emerged that he had previously used his plane to drop several toilet rolls on the roof of the player's home. The pilot survived his own intentional crash and later served three months of a two-year sentence for reckless damage on condition that he undergo psychiatric counselling on release.

The worst peacetime year of the twentieth century for air travel concluded when an Aeroflot flight crashed while attempting to land in poor visibility at Kiev Airport, killing forty-eight of its fifty-five passengers and crew. It was followed by the loss on Christmas Day of an EgyptAir 707, which came down 5 miles short of the runway at Bangkok, killing all fifty-two of those on board. The plane's landing gear struck a factory roof and nineteen workers inside were killed. Pilot error was blamed.

The whole concept of premature or violent death while engaged in some form of mass transportation was a sadly familiar feature of life in 1976. It's not in any way to diminish the individual stories of suffering and loss to say that it sometimes seems almost surprising to learn that anyone walked safely away from a plane or a ship that year. In just eleven days that December, an Italian freighter caught fire and exploded while docked in the harbour at Los Angeles; an Egyptian passenger liner sank in the Red Sea after fire broke out in her engine room; and a Taiwanese oil tanker foundered in heavy seas off the coast of Nova Scotia, with the collective loss of 187 lives, and scores of others left injured or traumatised.

***

In May 1976, a commission led by the Belgian Prime Minister Leo Tindemans sought to define exactly what was meant by the term 'European Community' and what direction an entity of that name might take in the future. Among other things, the Tindemans Report called for the creation of a central policy-making body to regulate its member states' foreign affairs and for a similar coordination of economic, environmental, social and educational strategy.

Tindemans himself died in 2014, with his vision of a fully harmonised and socially egalitarian 'people's Europe' still a work in progress, but not entirely without something to show for his efforts. By late 1976, the budgets of all nine members of the European Community (EC) had a distinctly redistributive quality to them, transferring resources from wealthy members like West Germany and France to relatively indigent ones such as the UK, Ireland and

Italy, and contributing to a steady, if never fully achievable, reduction in the aggregate gap between rich and poor.

Even at the time, the illusion that the sort of benign social engineering the Tindemans group advocated might lead to a post-national or post-state utopia of universal harmony and communal prosperity does not seem to have been embraced by all its intended beneficiaries. In a series of surveys conducted that December, the number of European citizens claiming to be 'very satisfied' with the EC ranged from 61 per cent in Belgium to 38 per cent in the UK, with most respondents in the other seven states divided roughly 50–50 on the issue. The polls also revealed that the Spanish and Irish were the most likely to be 'very proud' of their individual countries, with the citizens of West Germany and the UK at the foot of the list.

None of the groups questioned exhibited anything near the patriotic fervour of that expressed in the United States on the eve of Jimmy Carter's inauguration in January 1977, although even then the presidential honeymoon proved to be short-lived. Wearing a cardigan, Carter's first televised address to the nation served to warn Americans that they faced an energy crisis he likened to 'the moral equivalent of war', before going on to conclude that 'a malaise' and a 'crisis of confidence' lay at the heart of US life:

> It is a crisis that strikes at the very soul of our country's will. We can see this crisis in the growing doubt of the meaning of our own lives, and in our loss of unity and purpose as a people. The erosion of confidence in the future is threatening to destroy the social and political fabric of our nation.

Looking around for evidence of this existential cancer, the president pointed to such matters as the apparent miscarriage of justice suffered by his near-namesake, the middleweight boxer Rubin 'Hurricane' Carter. In 1966, Carter and a co-defendant, both black, had been arrested for allegedly gunning down three victims, all of whom were white, following a late-night confrontation in a New Jersey bar. A similarly all-white jury found the two men guilty, and each received a life sentence. In time, some of the witnesses who had come forward to identify the men recanted their testimony, only for some of them, in turn, to recant their recantations. The once world-title contending Carter became a cause célèbre, publicly championed by Muhammad Ali and the subject of a popular Bob Dylan protest anthem. In March 1976, the New Jersey Supreme Court overturned his conviction, noting that the prosecution at the original trial had withheld critical evidence.

In the event, Carter was at liberty for just nine months before being tried for the crime a second time. His case was not helped by the fact that, even as jurors were considering their verdict, the front pages of many US newspapers displayed a prominent photograph of a petite court-appointed bondswoman lying in a hospital bed, claiming that the defendant had beaten her up following a disagreement about his bail provisions.

A further nine years passed before an appeals court ruled that the original case against Carter was 'predicated upon the basis of race rather than reason, and of concealment rather than disclosure'. The defendant was released after eighteen years' incarceration and joined a commune in Toronto, where he died in 2014 at the age of 76 – either one of those hoodlum-boxers with an unfortunate tendency to display their professional skills outside the ring, or a victim of prosecutorial misconduct which proceeds not so much on the basis of the available evidence in a case as on the colour of the defendant's skin.

★★★

In the West, 1976 sometimes felt like an era of perpetual catastrophe. On top of the successive economic woes affecting even the free world's most prosperous states, there was to be a litany of political and social problems, class and racial conflict, natural and man-made disasters, human-rights abuses, revolutions, riots, terrorist outrages and a whole series of high-profile crimes whose gory details held a firm grip on the public's imagination. But at least in those countries there were also elections, the rights of assembly and protest, and the presence of a robust and often contrarian press.

No such fripperies existed under the administrative and repressive apparatus on which the Soviet Union and its satellite states depended for their survival. By December 1976, the USSR was embarking on the thirteenth successive year of the regime headed by Stalin's one-time protégé, Leonid Brezhnev. As we've seen, Brezhnev, now aged 70, was in rapidly declining health, suffering from cardiac failure, gout, leukaemia, obesity, alcoholism, depression, chronic bronchitis, memory loss and advanced emphysema after six decades of chain smoking. By this stage, his doctors needed three to four weeks to prepare him for any sort of major state event, and even then things would go wrong.

Josip Tito later remembered meeting Brezhnev at the White Palace in Belgrade that November with some distaste, particularly recalling his guest's 'grizzled fat cheek [into] which my nose sank as if into a half-inflated balloon as I was drawn into his unexpected and clammy embrace'. On his return home, the Soviet supremo felt well enough to attend a reception in his honour held at the Auezov Theatre in Alma-Ata, 2,000 miles east of Moscow on the border of the socialist republics of Kazakhstan and Kyrgyzstan. More than 1,000 invited guests had gathered, and after they were seated the Kazakh republic's First Secretary had proposed a fulsome toast to their supreme leader. However, as soon as the audience raised their glasses, Brezhnev unexpectedly stood up and headed towards the exit, prompting his entire entourage to hurriedly follow suit. The Kazakh chief was later to conclude sadly that their distinguished visitor had evidently forgotten the purpose of his trip, which was nonetheless portrayed as a 'wonderful triumph of fraternal unity and oratorical dynamism' in the following day's *Pravda*.

Brezhnev went on to modestly promote himself to the rank of Marshal of the Soviet Union in December 1976, an appointment that brushed aside any technical cavil about his lack of any prior battlefield experience, and to promptly summon a meeting of senior Red Army chiefs. It was remembered that he dressed for the occasion in a long leather tunic bedecked with medals, and bellowed, 'Attention, your commander is coming!' as he entered the room. Even following Brezhnev's death, autocratic Soviet power was not so much dismantled as effectively downsized during the nine years until the Soviet Union ceased to exist in December 1991.

Based purely on GDP, the United States unsurprisingly led the list of the world's richest nations in 1976, followed by Japan, West Germany, Canada and France. The United Kingdom followed in mid-table, alongside the likes of the Netherlands, Spain, Sweden, Mexico and China, the last of which remained wracked by the turmoil that followed the deaths of its two guiding political figures within eight months of each other. Largely agrarian, insular and long in thrall to a culture that combined socialist utopianism with merciless uniformity, China was not naturally constructed to be an industrialised superpower; her present economic miracle would take decades more to mature.

That life in the Western democracies was often imperfect and sometimes approaching chaotic that year the preceding pages have, perhaps, shown. But by and large the citizens of those countries still enjoyed the benefits of a more or less stable mixed economy, a sophisticated and disciplined military and a degree of latitude for their citizens' personal behaviour that a previous generation could only have dreamt of. By contrast, 1976 marked a low tide in the affairs of the world's two major communist superpowers.

In Britain, the year ended with an animated discussion by the Cabinet on the future not of the Anglo-US alliance, or the sclerotic but still ominously bellicose Soviet or Chinese regimes, but the fortunes of the Meriden Motorcycle Cooperative of suburban Solihull. Summing up the debate on the company's fate, and more specifically its application for an £8 million grant of public funds, James Callaghan remarked:

> While there are differing views, the balance of opinion around the table is that it would not represent a good use of available resources to make the large-scale investment requested, [even if] this should have unfortunate consequences for some of those 700 men and women currently employed on the premises.

Perhaps, in its small way, the premier's statement marked the true twilight of a climacteric of history – the election of an interventionist Labour government that had emerged from the rubble of war in 1945.

Sources and
Chapter Notes

This brief section shows at least the formal interviews, published works and/ or primary archive material used in the preparation of the book. As well as those listed, I also spoke to several people who prefer not to be named. Where sources asked for anonymity, usually citing a healthy respect for the UK's famously plaintiff-friendly libel laws, I've used terms such as 'a friend' or 'a colleague', as appropriate, and on one occasion, I have resorted to the use of an alias. (The reader should be assured that every fact stated in the book has nonetheless been sourced, and for obvious reasons corroborated, to the very fullest extent possible before publication.) No acknowledgement thus appears of the help, encouragement and kindness I received from several quarters, some of them, as they say, household names.

INTRODUCTION

I'm grateful for the help of the UK National Archives, and more particularly, their collection of Cabinet Papers dealing with everything from international relations in war and peace to the perennial matter of the UK's balance of payments deficit, which proved to be a sustaining source for the book. The specific quote beginning, 'Harold was sitting in his chair, obviously in a shattered state' appears in Barbara Castle, *The Castle Diaries 1964–76*, as cited in the bibliography, pp.345–46.

The description of Foreign Secretary Anthony Crosland's 'articulate petulance – combined with a languid, offhand manner' is from Henry Kissinger's *Years of Renewal*, also as cited in the bibliography, p.926.

Several other shorter quotes or descriptions in this section are taken from the likes of *The Times*, the *Daily Telegraph*, the *Daily Express* and the *Daily Mirror*, and can be found by subscribing to the British Newspaper Archive, essentially the successor (and now fee-requiring) organisation to the much-missed British Library Newspaper repository in Colindale, north London.

I was lucky enough to interview the late Bernard Nossiter of the *Washington Post* at Cambridge University in June 1977.

Background material on the IRA and its historic difference of opinion with the Westminster government can usefully be read in the pages of The IRA Nominal Rolls and other material held by The Military Archives, Dublin, located at: www.militaryarchives.ie. I took the opportunity to revisit Balcombe Street.

I. WINTER

I should particularly thank the late Kingsley Amis, the late Tony Benn, the late Louis Kirby of the *London Evening News*, the late Tom Wolfe, and the still-with-us Sir Geoffrey Boycott, Bill Payne and Roman Polanski, all of whom I had the pleasure of interviewing, as well as the trustees and staff of the Gerald R. Ford Museum in Grand Rapids, Michigan, and the Jimmy Carter Museum and Library of Atlanta, Georgia, for their input. Without them, there would have been a very different Chapter I, or no chapter at all.

The quote beginning, 'The widespread impression was that there are serious and acrimonious differences' can be found in the Minutes of the Cabinet meeting of 15 January 1976, contained in the Cabinet Papers of the UK National Archives, Reference No. CAB 128/58/1. The quote beginning, 'The dispute over fishing limits with Iceland' is from the same source.

The direct quotation beginning, 'News began to drift out of No. 10 of recurrent stomach upsets' is from Ben Pimlott's *Harold Wilson*, as cited in the bibliography, pp.674–75.

The quote by Peter Wright beginning, 'Because for ten years, he collected a large group of advisers and friends' is from the transcript of Wright's interview on the BBC's *Panorama Special* programme of 13 October 1988. I was lucky enough to be one of a small party of Cambridge undergraduates to be introduced to Henry Kissinger in April 1976, at which time, Kissinger commented on the hard reality of negotiating with the Soviet Union, with the specific request that we not quote him on the subject during his lifetime.

The quote beginning, 'The rot gets worse every year – the rotting away of simple courtesy, I mean' is taken from the Anthony Burgess interview published in *The Guardian* under the title 'The Author of *A Clockwork Orange* finds middle age does not mellow him', as reprinted on 14 December 2012.

The quote beginning, 'The house is one of those neat little joints between the King's Road and the Chelsea Embankment' is from Kingsley Amis, *Memoirs* (London: Hutchinson, 1991).

The figures for UK public expenditure quoted in this chapter were taken from *The Public Expenditure General Review*, published as a White Paper on 19 February 1976 and found in the Cabinet Papers of the UK National Archives, Reference No. CAB 129/18/76.

The quote beginning, 'one of the rebels used demotic language to cast aspersions on my paternity' is from Denis Healey, *The Time of My Life*, as cited in the bibliography, p.455.

The music and lyrics of the immortal 'Love Machine' (Griffin-Moore) are the copyright of Sony/ATV Music Publishing LLC/Warner Chappell Music.

The quote beginning, 'I believe the House will share the Government's deep regret that the opportunity provided by the recent' is in the *Hansard Reports* of 5 March 1976. The quote by the UK Chancellor Denis Healey beginning, 'It is true that the Retail Price Index rose' is similarly from *Hansard*, 4 March 1976.

The quote beginning, 'I can tell you that, in spite of the possible outcry here, we will not accept' is from Henry Kissinger, *Years of Renewal*, as cited, p.913.

The quote by Shirley Williams beginning, 'Harold took me into the Cabinet chamber' is from Andy Beckett, *When the Lights Went Out*, as cited in the bibliography, p.166.

The quote beginning, 'It wasn't corrupt but it was a bad mistake' is from Ben Pimlott, *Harold Wilson*, as cited, pp.689–90.

The quote beginning, 'The Secretary of State for Defence said that our garrison in the Falklands' is from the Minutes of the Cabinet meeting of 18 March 1976, held by the UK National Archives, Reference No. CAB 128/58/11.

The letter by Henry Kissinger beginning, 'Dear Harold, The announcement of your decision to retire' is in the file 'Messages to and from Prime Minister, March 1976', held by the UK National Archives, Reference No. PREM 16/1072. The message from Idi Amin is from the same source.

II. SPRING

I was lucky enough to have exchanged messages with Peter Hain, Steve Wozniak and the late Jeremy Thorpe, and would like to take the opportunity to thank them for their contributions. I also at one time lurked on the outer fringes of what could be called the Rolling Stones set, and I'm similarly grateful to Patricia 'P.P.' Arnold, the late Hal Ashby, Stanley Booth, Bebe Buell, Allan Clarke, Lol Creme, Janice Crotch, Micky Dolenz, the late Adam Faith, Chris Farlowe, Jeff Griffin, Bob Harris, Peter Holland, the late Joe and Eva Jagger, the late Tom Keylock, Nick Lowe, Dave Mason, May Pang, Wayne Perkins, the late Harold Pinter, Chris Spedding, the late Mary Wilson and, if he'll pardon me, my friend Bill Wyman, among others, who put their recollections of that group and what then seemed like their Late Period of 1976 at my disposal. I'm grateful, too, for the help of the late Tony Benn, Rob Boddie and Sussex CCC, John Bond, Tony Gill, the late Tony Greig, the late John Murray, Neil Robinson and his colleagues at the MCC Library, and the late Alan Yentob. I visited David Bowie's old home in Berlin.

The quote beginning, 'If Harold Wilson had friends in the Labour party [after his resignation] they kept their heads' is from Ben Pimlott, *Harold Wilson*, as previously cited, p.689.

The quote beginning, 'Unless action is taken swiftly there will be either a continuation' is from the paper, 'State of Play', prepared by the Cabinet Secretary Sir John Hunt for the Prime Minister on 5 April 1976, held in the UK National Archives, Reference No. PREM/16/908.

The quote beginning, 'I began to wonder if divorce is now a *rite de passage*' is from Gail Sheehy, *Passages* (New York: E.P. Dutton, 1976), p.208.

The quote beginning, 'The Minister of Agriculture, Fisheries and Food said that the previous evening' is from the Minutes of the Cabinet meeting of 13 April 1976, held by the UK National Archives, Reference No. CAB 128/59/1.

The quote beginning, 'Mankind's recent history unfortunately indicates that we are not adapting' is from Thomas L. Burrus and Herbert J. Spiegel, *Earth in Crisis* (St Louis: C.V. Mosby Company, 1976).

The quote beginning, 'The main reason for the present weakness of sterling, apart from the uncertainty over a further agreement on pay' is from the Minutes of the Cabinet meeting of 29 April 1976, held by the UK National Archives, Reference No. CAB 128/59/2.

James Callaghan's quote about the hoped-for 'amelioration' of man's existence on the planet was given on a private visit to my late godfather John Riley, who in turn passed it on.

The figures in *New Society* reporting on average monthly disposable income in the UK in the years 1974–76 are quoted in Andy Beckett, *When the Lights Went Out*, as cited, p.176.

The quote beginning, 'What they were doing was wrong ... It's the way I was raised' is from an article entitled 'Monday's Act Heroic after Thirty Years' by Ben Platt, published by the Chicago Cubs organisation on 25 April 2006. In the same baseball context, I had the rare pleasure of visiting Detroit in the summer of 1976 and am grateful to Fred and Cindy Smith for the experience.

James Callaghan's quote beginning, 'The Conservatives [are] likely to run into trouble' is from the Minutes of the Cabinet meeting of 24 June 1976, held by the UK National Archives, Reference No. CAB 128/59/11.

The off-the-record conversation between Callaghan and Margaret Thatcher of 14 June is summarised in a 'Confidential Note of Meeting Between the Prime Minister and Leader of the Opposition', held by the UK National Archives, Reference No. PREM 16/1035.

It was a distinct pleasure to have known the Soviet Cosmonaut Alexei Leonov (1934–2019), the first man to walk in space, among other achievements, to whom I'm grateful for his observations on the workings of the Moscow politburo of 1976.

III. SUMMER

I'm especially grateful to the late Tony Greig, whom I first met as a starstruck cricket fan in 1967 and who kindly put some of his thoughts and recollections of the 1976 England–West Indies Test Series at my disposal. It's a pleasure to pay tribute here to a much-misunderstood character, whose notorious 'Grovel' remarks, while perhaps ill-judged, were never intended in the more racially inflammatory sense in which some chose to take them.

On another front, several sources I interviewed at the time of writing two slim books on the John F. Kennedy administration kindly put their subsequent thoughts on Kennedy's successor presidents at my disposal. I should again thank, personally, the late Dan Evans, peerless Governor of Washington State from 1965–77 and, institutionally, the staff of the UK National Archives, the US Department of State Archives, the British Newspaper Archive, Companies House, London, and the University of Cambridge Library, where I spent significantly longer researching this book than, alas, I did in three years as a Cambridge undergraduate.

The quote by the UK Minister for Planning John Silkin, regretting that 'the present law gave no authority to prohibit non-essential and even ostentatious uses of water' is from the Minutes of the Cabinet meeting of 1 July 1976, held by the UK National Archives, Reference No. CAB 128/59/12.

The quote beginning, 'We were getting little benefit from North Sea Oil' is from Denis Healey, *The Time of My Life*, as cited.

The quote beginning, 'The Chancellor ... said that it was essential to keep both the economy and the contract' is from the Minutes of the Cabinet meeting of 6 July 1976, held by the UK National Archives, Reference No. CAB 128/59/13.

I'm particularly grateful to Bill Wyman for his remarks to me about the Rolling Stones as configured in mid-1976, and the state of the pop music industry generally.

The quote beginning, 'All their lives they had been exploited by unscrupulous dealers' is from Tom Keating, *The Fake's Progress* (London: Hutchinson, 1977).

The exchange between Henry Kissinger and his colleagues concerning the incident on the border of North and South Korea in August 1976 can be found in the paper 'Minutes of Special Actions Group Meeting: Eyes Only!' [emphasis in the original], held by the Office of the Historian, US Department of State.

The quote beginning, 'He was neither a strategist nor a geopolitician, and he knew it' is from Henry Kissinger, *Years of Renewal*, as cited, p.609.

The list of UK ministerial options beginning, 'To consider new ways of funding our short term overseas debt' is from the Minutes of the Cabinet meeting of 3 August 1976, held by the UK National Archives, Reference No. CAB 128/59/22.

The quote beginning, 'At [that] time we lived in one of the 2-bedroom flats' is from an online article by Dr Patricia Daley entitled 'Recalling 1970s London', posted on 19 August 2011.

The quote by the Foreign Secretary Anthony Crosland beginning, 'The death of Chairman Mao' is from the Minutes of the Cabinet meeting of 9 September 1976, held by the UK National Archives, Reference No. CAB 128/60/1.

The late Shirley Williams was kind enough to give me her views on the mainstream teaching standards of the day, as quoted.

The great Saul Bellow's quote beginning, 'As a onetime anthropologist, I know a taboo when I see one' is from James Atlas, *Bellow* (New York: Random House, 2000), p.575. Bellow himself was kind enough to respond when, in December 1999, I impertinently sent him a list of questions about some of his experiences. I also had the pleasure at around that same time of interviewing Mick Jagger's parents, Joe and Eva, then living in retirement in Margate, Kent.

IV. AUTUMN

I should again thank Kate Armstrong, the Collections of the Chicago Public Library, the Manuscripts Room of the Cambridge University Library, the late Tony Greig, Steve and Jo Hackett, Peter Hain, the late Alexei Leonov, the late Selwyn Lloyd, Bill Payne and the late Tom Wolfe, all of whom provided interviews or other direct input to this chapter, as well as the staff of both the collections of the Rare Books Room of the British Library and the Margaret Herrick Library in Los Angeles. Every effort has been made to comply with the copyright provisions involved.

For all the challenges of successfully mining the material, the FBI Freedom of Information Division holds important files on the political, commercial and criminal backdrop to the United States of 1976, as do the archives of the US State Department and Treasury Department. I'm grateful for the help of all the individuals and groups.

The statistics regarding obesity rates in the years from 1971 can be found in the paper 'Obesity Profile: A Short Summary', published on the UK Government website on 8 May 2024.

For a complete transcript of the critical Gerald Ford–Jimmy Carter debate of 6 October 1976, including Ford's faux pas on the matter of Soviet influence in eastern Europe, see 'Report of Presidential Debate at the Palace of Fine Arts, San Francisco', available on the Commission on US Presidential Debates website.

For the remarks by Oleg Gordievsky insisting that the KGB had paid Jack Jones a stipend for information about British trade union activity, see the *Daily Telegraph* of 22 April 2009.

The quote beginning, 'The Government now faces a very serious question: do we think that we could and should afford' is from the Minutes of the Cabinet meeting of 23 November 1976, held by the UK National Archives, Reference No. CAB 128/60/11.

The deathless Sex Pistols song 'Anarchy in the UK' was written by Glen Matlock, John Lydon, Paul Thomas Cook and Stephen Philip Jones and is under copyright to BMG Rights Management/Universal Music Publishing Group/Warner Chappell Music, Inc., thus cleverly skirting the very corporate control the Pistols themselves so memorably railed against.

The description of conditions on board the Soviet supersonic airliner is from Howard Moon, *Soviet SST: The Techno-Politics of the Tupolev-144* (New York: Crown Publishing Group, 1989).

The quote beginning, 'This is a political decision as grave as any in our history' is from the Minutes of the Cabinet meeting of 1 December 1976, held by the UK National Archives, Reference No. CAB 128/60/13.

Saul Bellow's remarks beginning, 'Everywhere today, we see disorder or near-panic' form part of his Nobel Prize Lecture, delivered in Stockholm on 12 December 1976; see the website NobelPrize.org, among other sources, for full details.

The quote beginning, 'In order to offset any market uncertainty due to the fact' is from the Minutes of the Cabinet meeting of 9 December 1976, held by the UK National Archives, Reference No. CAB 128/60/18. Roy Mason's remarks insisting that he had 'had enough of [political] initiatives, White Papers and legislation', in response to the continuing Troubles in Northern Ireland, formed part of his platform speech at the Labour Party Conference, given on 27 September 1976.

James Callaghan's quote beginning, 'While there are differing views, the balance of opinion [in the government] is that it would not be a good use of resources' is from the Minutes of the Cabinet meeting of 22 December 1976, held by the UK National Archives, Reference No. CAB 128/60/21.

Select Bibliography

Adams, Gerry, *Before the Dawn: An Autobiography* (London: Heinemann, 1996).

Alter, Jonathan, *His Very Best: Jimmy Carter, A Life* (New York: Simon & Schuster, 2021).

Beaton, Cecil, *The Unexpurgated Beaton* (London: Weidenfeld & Nicolson, 2002).

Beckett, Andy, *When the Lights Went Out: What Really Happened to Britain in the Seventies* (London: Faber and Faber, 2009).

Bellow, Saul, *To Jerusalem and Back* (New York: The Viking Press, 1976).

Benn, Tony, *Against the Tide: Diaries 1973–77* (London: Hutchinson, 1989).

Booker, Christopher, *The Necrophiliacs* (London: Pimlico, 1992).

Buckley, William F., *Stained Glass* (New York: Doubleday, 1978).

Cannadine, David, *Class in Britain* (New Haven: Yale University Press, 1998).

Castle, Barbara, *The Castle Diaries 1964–76* (London: Weidenfeld & Nicolson, 1980).

Cherry, Gordon E., *Town Planning in Britain Since 1900* (Oxford: Blackwell, 1996).

Cronkite, Walter, *A Reporter's Life* (New York: Knopf, 1996).

Crosland, Anthony, *The Future of Socialism* (London: Jonathan Cape, 1956).

Crosland, Susan, *Tony Crosland* (London: Jonathan Cape, 1982).

Dallek, Robert, *Flawed Giant: Lyndon Johnson and His Times* (New York: Oxford University Press, 1998).

Davenport-Hines, Richard, *The Macmillans* (London: William Heinemann, 1992).

Donoughue, Bernard, *Prime Minister: The Conduct of Policy under Harold Wilson and James Callaghan* (London: Jonathan Cape, 1987).

Frum, David, *How We Got Here: The 70s* (New York: Basic Books, 2000).

Gaddis, John Lewis, *The Cold War* (New York: Penguin, 2005).

Gelman, Harry, *The Brezhnev Politburo and the Decline of Détente* (Ithaca, NY: Cornell University Press, 1984).

Haslam, Dave, *Not Abba: The Real Story of the 1970s* (London: HarperCollins, 2005).

Healey, Denis, *The Time of My Life* (London: Michael Joseph, 1989).

Heath, Edward, *The Course of My Life* (London: Hodder & Stoughton, 1998).

Hirsh, Arthur, *The New French Left* (Boston: South End Press, 1981).

Horne, Alistair, *Macmillan 1957–1986: Volume II of the Official Biography* (London: Macmillan, 1989).

Judt, Tony, *Postwar: A History of Europe Since 1945* (London: Penguin Books, 2005).

Kissinger, Henry, *Years of Renewal* (New York: Simon & Schuster, 1999).

Mason, Roy, *Paying the Price* (London: Robert Hale, 1999).

Oldham, Andrew, *Stoned* (London: Secker & Warburg, 2000).

Pimlott, Ben, *Harold Wilson* (London: HarperCollins, 1992).

Sadat, Anwar, *In Search of Identity* (New York: Harper and Row, 1977).

Sandbrook, Dominic, *White Heat* (London: Little, Brown, 2006).

Sandford, Christopher, *Roman Polanski* (New York: St. Martin's Press, 2008).

Sassoon, Donald, *One Hundred Years of Socialism: The West European Left in the Twentieth Century* (New York: The New Press, 1996).

Savage, Jon, *England's Dreaming* (London: Faber and Faber, 1992).

Shapiro, Harry, *Waiting for the Man: The Story of Drugs and Popular Music* (London: Mandarin, 1988).

Shellard, Dominic, *British Theatre Since the War* (New Haven: Yale University Press, 1999).

Smith, Richard Norton, *An Ordinary Man: The Surprising Life and Historic Presidency of Gerald R. Ford* (New York: Harper, 2023).

Snow, C.P., *Off the Rails: An Autobiography* (London: Weidenfeld & Nicolson, 1978).

Taylor, Peter, *Brits: The War Against the IRA* (London: Bloomsbury, 2001).

Thatcher, Margaret, *The Path to Power* (London: HarperCollins, 1995).

Walker, Martin, *The National Front* (London: Fontana, 1977).

Wheen, Francis, *Tom Driberg: His Life and Indiscretions* (London: Chatto, 1990).

Wright, Joanne, *Terrorist Propaganda: The Red Army Faction and the Provisional IRA, 1968–1986* (New York: Palgrave, 1991).

Wright, Peter, *Spycatcher* (New York: Viking, 1987).

Index

Index